THREE TRAGEDIES
WILLIAM SHAKESPEARE

HAMLET
MACBETH
KING LEAR

THREE TRAGEDIES
WILLIAM SHAKESPEARE

HAMLET

MACBETH

KING LEAR

SCHOLASTIC INC.
New York Toronto London Auckland Sydney

ISBN 0-590-08784-3

Copyright © 1956, 1957, 1958 by Penguin Books, Inc. Special contents copyright © 1970 by Scholastic Books, Inc. This edition is published by Scholastic Inc., by arrangement with Penguin Books, Inc.

31 30 29 28 27 26 25   8 9/9 0 1/0

Printed in the U.S.A.   01

CONTENTS

A Word to the Reader

HAMLET

Of all Shakespeare's plays, *Hamlet* seems the most modern. In the twentieth century, we have adopted it for our own. Literary critics have showered the play with attention. There have been at least three "historic" stage interpretations — Laurence Olivier's, John Gielgud's, Richard Burton's — and two important motion pictures. The question is, why are we so fascinated with *Hamlet?* Why does this play strike so close to home?

The answer, I think, lies in Hamlet's vision of the world. For Hamlet, as for contemporary man, the world assumes the shape of a question mark. He asks more — and more varied — questions than any other character in Shakespeare. There are questions about his own predicament — Why, for instance, can't he bring himself to avenge his father's murder?

> I do not know
> Why yet I live to say, "This thing's to do,"
> Sith I have cause, and will, and strength, and means
> To do't.

And there are questions that extend beyond his immediate personal dilemma to the universal human search for life's meaning, for answers to the problems of good and evil:

"What a piece of work is man! And yet to me what is this quintessence of dust?"

"To be or not to be, that is the question."

"I am myself indifferent honest, but yet I could accuse myself of such things that it were better my mother had not borne me. What should such fellows as I do crawling between earth and heaven?"

Always Hamlet is baffled, tentative, groping. He has learned that truth is elusive, that appearances deceive. His "seeming-virtuous" mother is an adulteress; his doting uncle is his father's murderer. "O most pernicious woman!" he cries at these revelations of the ghost.

O villain, villain, smiling, damned villain!
My tables — meet it is I set it down
That one may smile, and smile, and be a villain.
At least I am sure it may be so in Denmark.

But this sort of doubt, once established, spreads everywhere, even to the ghost itself. For if appearances deceive, can the ghost be trusted? "The devil hath power to assume a pleasing shape." According to Elizabethan folklore, spirits from the dead might be sent to abuse a person in Hamlet's vulnerable state of mind. Suppose it is no honest ghost, but a demon sent to lure him into murder and so to damn him? In his acute awareness of ambiguity, in his perplexity about where to begin looking for the truth, Hamlet seems very much a contemporary man.

The second "modern" aspect of Hamlet's world is its ugliness. There are beautiful gardens in Shakespeare where lovers meet under soft starlight, but they are not in this play. To Hamlet the world:

is an unweeded garden
That grows to seed. Things rank and gross in nature
Possess it merely.

With his mother's hasty and incestuous marriage, he has caught his first glimpse of corruption, and his imagination preys upon it. He sees, in sharp focus, whatever is tainted or impure. Hamlet comes upon Ophelia, kneeling at her prayers, the very image of innocent devotion. Yet he sees no fresh-faced virgin, but a painted whore. "I have heard of your paintings, well enough," he tells her abusively. "God hath given you one face, and you make yourself another. You jig, you amble, you lisp. Go to, I'll no more on't; it hath made me mad."

As Hamlet prowls about Elsinore, his mind runs to images of degeneration and decay. For him the clear air has turned to "a foul and pestilent congregation of vapors"; "something is rotten in the state of Denmark." At first we suspect the source of the foul odor is Claudius, the satyr, the bat, the king of reechy kisses. But the problem goes deeper than that. What is troubling Hamlet is the smell of human mortality. This "too, too sullied flesh" has properties to turn a delicate stomach, particularly when it is decomposing in the earth. In the graveyard scene, holding the skull of Yorick, his father's court jester, Hamlet asks his friend, Horatio, "Dost thou think Alexander looked o' this fashion i' th'earth? And smelt so?"

A Shakespearean scholar, G. Wilson Knight, has said of Hamlet: "He has seen through humanity. He has seen the truth, not alone of Denmark, but of the universe, and the truth is evil." It is a measure of our own disorders how much at home we are in this dark, disrupted world of Hamlet's.

MACBETH

Macbeth is a man pressed by his own ambition to commit murder, even though he can foresee the tragic consequences of his action. At first when he contemplates killing Duncan and seizing the crown of Scotland, he tries to persuade himself that he can murder and evade the consequences:

If it were done when 'tis done, then 'twere well
It were done quickly. If th'assassination
Could trammel up the consequence and catch
With his surcease success, that but this blow
Might be the be-all and the end-all.

Macbeth is wishing that Duncan's murder might be a deed removed from time, finished *with* when finished. He imagines that he might catch and trap the consequences of murder, enclose his action and its results, like fish ensnared in a net. But his reason tells him that the act of murder will boomerang against him, causing his own destruction:

> But in these cases
> We still have judgment here, that we but teach
> Bloody instructions, which, being taught, return
> To plague the inventor. This even-handed justice
> Commends th' ingredience of our poisoned chalice
> To our own lips.

Once Macbeth acts, the consequences are like ripples caused by a pebble thrown in a pool. They move outward in uncontrollable, everwidening circles until they finally blend imperceptibly in the general stream of time.

Unlike Hamlet, Macbeth is not concerned with the mental anguish that precedes action. Though Macbeth hesitates before killing Duncan ("We will proceed no further in this business," he tells his wife), he has pretty much made up his mind to the murder before the play opens. Macbeth starts guiltily when the Weird Sisters hail him as "king hereafter" because he has mentally been trying on the crown. For Macbeth there is no great struggle of conscience, only the inexorable aftermath of evil, the long train of horrors that the murder of Duncan brings in its wake. With the remorseless march of logic, they close in on Macbeth.

In the first place Macbeth finds he cannot stop with one murder. He must kill the guards outside Duncan's chamber if they are not to wake and protest their innocence. He must kill Banquo if Banquo's descendants are not to reign in Scotland. Blood, Macbeth finds, is not a substance that can be dabbled in. Once it starts to flow, it becomes a river. Macbeth, wading in the stuff, finds he cannot turn back. He "is in blood

9

stepped in so far, returning were as tedious as to go o'er."

A second penalty of murder is sleeplessness. Sleep in Shakespeare is the reward of purity and innocence. With the murder of the sleeping king, Macbeth creates for himself a lifetime of insomnia.

> Methought I heard a voice cry, "Sleep no more!
> Macbeth does murder sleep. . . .
> Glamis hath murdered sleep, and therefore Cawdor
> Shall sleep no more, Macbeth shall sleep no more."

Nor is it only Macbeth whose eyes have lost the art of closing. Lady Macbeth, who acted impetuously and never considered the consequences when she goaded Macbeth to murder, who boasted of her iron nerves, walks at night when she should lie quiet. She mutters of the murders that trouble her conscience. "The Thane of Fife had a wife. Where is she now?" "Who would have thought the old man to have had so much blood in him?" The result in the play is a soul-crushing weariness. Bad enough is "the affliction of terrible dreams" that shake Macbeth nightly. Worse is the fatigue that goes beyond desire and beyond fear. "The time has been my senses would have cooled to hear a night-shriek," says Macbeth, hearing the cry of the women who mourn his wife, but

> I have supped full of horrors.
> Direness, familiar to my slaughterous thoughts,
> Cannot once start me.

Macbeth is so drained he cannot find the emotional energy to respond to his wife's death.

Finally Macbeth has destroyed, with Duncan, the things which should have graced his time of life. When the King's body is discovered, Macbeth mourns with more truth than irony:

> Had I but died an hour before this chance,
> I had lived a blessed time; for from this instant
> There's nothing serious in mortality:

All is but toys. Renown and grace is dead,
The wind of life is drawn, and the mere lees
Is left this vault to brag of.

For Macbeth, as for Hamlet, the time is out of joint.
Only Macbeth has not inherited the situation, he has
brought it on himself. At the heart of this play is the
image of men ripening like grain in the fullness of
time. "If you can look into the seeds of time/And say
which grains will grow and which will not,/Speak
then to me," Banquo cries to the Weird Sisters.
The Shakespearean world was never far from the Bible,
and behind Banquo's words we can hear the echo of
Ecclesiastes. "To everything there is a season and a
time to every purpose under heaven: A time to be born,
and a time to die; a time to plant, and a time to
pluck up that which is planted." Macbeth's untimely
seizure of the crown disrupts this natural course of
things. Instead of "growing," in Banquo's sense of the
word, he descends prematurely into "the sear, the
yellow leaf." Time loses its meaning and becomes for
him an empty succession of days.

Tomorrow, and tomorrow, and tomorrow
Creeps in this petty pace from day to day
To the last syllable of recorded time.

For Macbeth Shakespeare has arranged a kind of
poetic justice. He who spills blood wades in it. He who
murders the sleeping guest goes without sleep. He who
hurries the future sees it stretch before him, an endless
expanse of dusty tomorrows.

KING LEAR

At the opening of the play, we find King Lear on
his throne, dividing his kingdom among his daughters.
In payment, he demands a declaration of love. To

11

his older daughters, Goneril and Regan, Lear gives generous estates, as they pledge their undying devotion. To his youngest, Cordelia, who can find no words to express her deep love, Lear gives nothing. Instead, he disowns her.

Here I disclaim all my paternal care,
Propinquity and property of blood,
And as a stranger to my heart and me
Hold thee from this for ever.

At this point in the play, most readers will identify with Cordelia. Like her, most of us have faced the parental demand to express our love and, like Cordelia, we have resented it. We cheer her on as she stands up to Lear and gives him some of the back talk he so richly deserves.

But Lear also merits the reader's sympathy. True, he is dogmatic and proud, but there are occupational hazards in being a king. Is it not true, as he charges, that no one has ever denied him before, but answered "yea and nay" to all he said? The things he demands from his children — respect and love — are good things. That he should find them in his daughters seems to him a part of the universal law. In Lear's view — as opposed to Edmund's — such things are *natural*.

The question that runs through *King Lear* — as relevant today as in Shakespeare's time — is "What is a natural child?" Lear thinks it natural for his daughters to love him. He has staked his life on it, turning over his kingdom to Goneril and Regan on the proviso that they shelter him and his train of one hundred knights. When Goneril goes back on her part of the bargain, refusing to house Lear's retinue, the king no longer recognizes her as his own. "Are you our daughter?" he demands. And a moment later, "Your name, fair gentlewoman?" To Lear it seems monstrous that a child would turn against its own flesh and blood. The only comparable image he can find is the human body tearing itself in two. "Filial ingratitude," he cries.

12

"Is it not as this mouth should tear this hand/ For lifting food to't."

For Edmund, Gloucester's illegitimate son, just the reverse is true. He believes that only the force of convention ties father to son; and he detests convention, which has cost him his share of Gloucester's estate. He thinks it natural for a son to turn on a father if there is any profit in it. "Thou, Nature, art my goddess," Edmund says, committing himself solely to his own service:

> to thy law
> My services are bound. Wherefore should I
> Stand in the plague of custom, and permit
> The curiosity of nations to deprive me,
> For that I am some twelve or fourteen moonshines
> Lag of a brother?

With that, he sets a plot in motion to discredit and destroy his half-brother Edgar, Gloucester's legitimate heir, so that he himself may possess his father's estate.

There are two Natures in *King Lear*: one — personified by Cordelia — is gentle, humane, affectionate, sweetened by gracious custom; the other is fierce and mechanistic, the brute force of instinct and greed. Reading the play, we may wonder about our society today. Is it natural, as we have been told in recent years, to break with home entirely, to feel no sense of obligation toward our parents, to "do our own thing" no matter who is hurt? Or is it natural to need the security of home, to love our parents and respect their wishes, to maintain the old ties?

There is a vision in *Lear* of a kind of shelter that is provided by love between parent and child. When this vanishes, man is suddenly in a world without roof or refuge. Scorned by his daughters, Lear wanders homeless in the storm. He returns to Nature — Edmund's Nature — with a vengeance.

> Return to her [Goneril], and fifty men dismissed?
> No, rather I abjure all roofs, and choose

To wage against the enmity o' th' air,
To be a comrade with the wolf and owl,
Necessity's sharp pinch.

King Lear reminds us of an old truth — that a man
destitute of love is naked in the universe. The storms
rage and the winds howl, and he has nowhere to lay
his head.

Sara Sheldon

The Tragedy of
HAMLET
Prince of Denmark

William Shakespeare
Edited by Willard Farnham

Note on the text: This edition is based on the quarto of 1604-05 (thought to be printed from the prompt-book of Shakespeare's acting company), as edited for the Pelican Shakespeare series in 1957. Footnotes are from the Pelican Shakespeare edition.

Names of the Actors

Claudius, King of Denmark

Hamlet, son to the late, and nephew to the present, King

Polonius, Lord Chamberlain

Horatio, friend to Hamlet

Laertes, son to Polonius

Voltemand
Cornelius
Rosencrantz
Guildenstern   courtiers
Osric
A Gentleman

A Priest

Marcellus
Bernardo   officers

Francisco, a soldier

Reynaldo, servant to Polonius

Players

Two Clowns, gravediggers

Fortinbras, Prince of Norway

A Norwegian Captain

English Ambassadors

Gertrude, Queen of Denmark, mother to Hamlet

Ophelia, daughter to Polonius

Ghost of Hamlet's Father

Lords, Ladies, Officers, Soldiers, Sailors, Messengers, Attendants

Scene
Elsinore

ACT I, SCENE I

Enter Bernardo and Francisco, two sentinels.

Bernardo. Who's there?
Francisco. Nay, answer me. Stand and unfold yourself.
Bernardo. Long live the king!
Francisco. Bernardo?
Bernardo. He.   5
Francisco. You come most carefully upon your hour.
Bernardo. 'Tis now struck twelve. Get thee to bed,
    Francisco.
Francisco. For this relief much thanks. 'Tis bitter cold,
  And I am sick at heart.
Bernardo. Have you had quiet guard?
Francisco.   Not a mouse stirring.   10
Bernardo. Well, good night.
  If you do meet Horatio and Marcellus,
  The rivals of my watch, bid them make haste.

Enter Horatio and Marcellus.

Francisco. I think I hear them. Stand, ho! Who is
  there?
Horatio. Friends to this ground.
Marcellus.   And liegemen to the Dane.   15

I, i, 13 *rivals* sharers

17

Francisco. Give you good night.

Marcellus.   O, farewell, honest soldier.
Who hath relieved you?

Francisco.   Bernardo hath my place.
Give you good night.   *Exit Francisco.*

Marcellus.   Holla, Bernardo!

Bernardo.   Say —
What, is Horatio there?

Horatio.   A piece of him.

Bernardo. Welcome, Horatio. Welcome, good Mar-
20   cellus.

Horatio. What, has this thing appeared again tonight?

Bernardo. I have seen nothing.

Marcellus. Horatio says 'tis but our fantasy,
And will not let belief take hold of him
25   Touching this dreaded sight twice seen of us.
Therefore I have entreated him along
With us to watch the minutes of this night,
That, if again this apparition come,
He may approve our eyes and speak to it.

Horatio. Tush, tush, 'twill not appear.

30 *Bernardo.*   Sit down awhile.
And let us once again assail your ears,
That are so fortified against our story,
What we two nights have seen.

Horatio.   Well, sit we down,
And let us hear Bernardo speak of this.

35 *Bernardo.* Last night of all,
When yond same star that's westward from the pole
Had made his course t' illume that part of heaven
Where now it burns, Marcellus and myself,
The bell then beating one —

Enter Ghost.

Marcellus. Peace, break thee off. Look where it comes
40   again.

15 *Dane* King of Denmark   29 *approve* confirm   36 *pole* polestar

Bernardo. In the same figure like the king that's dead.

Marcellus. Thou art a scholar; speak to it, Horatio.

Bernardo. Looks 'a not like the king? Mark it, Horatio.

Horatio. Most like. It harrows me with fear and wonder.

Bernardo. It would be spoke to.

Marcellus.   Speak to it, Horatio.   45

Horatio. What art thou that usurp'st this time of night
Together with that fair and warlike form
In which the majesty of buried Denmark
Did sometimes march? By heaven I charge thee,
speak.

Marcellus. It is offended.   50

Bernardo.   See, it stalks away.

Horatio. Stay. Speak, speak. I charge thee, speak.

                                                Exit Ghost.

Marcellus. 'Tis gone and will not answer.

Bernardo. How now, Horatio? You tremble and look
pale.
Is not this something more than fantasy?   55
What think you on't?

Horatio. Before my God, I might not this believe
Without the sensible and true avouch
Of mine own eyes.

Marcellus.   Is it not like the king?

Horatio. As thou art to thyself.   60
Such was the very armor he had on
When he th' ambitious Norway combated.
So frowned he once when, in an angry parle,
He smote the sledded Polacks on the ice.
'Tis strange.   65

Marcellus. Thus twice before, and jump at this dead
hour,
With martial stalk hath he gone by our watch.

---

48 *buried Denmark* the buried King of Denmark 49 *sometimes*
formerly 62 *Norway* King of Norway 63 *parle* parley 66 *jump*
just, exactly

Horatio. In what particular thought to work I know
      not;
    But, in the gross and scope of my opinion,
70   This bodes some strange eruption to our state.
Marcellus. Good now, sit down, and tell me he that
      knows,
    Why this same strict and most observant watch
    So nightly toils the subject of the land,
    And why such daily cast of brazen cannon
75   And foreign mart for implements of war,
    Why such impress of shipwrights, whose sore task
    Does not divide the Sunday from the week.
    What might be toward that this sweaty haste
    Doth make the night joint-laborer with the day?
    Who is't that can inform me?
80 *Horatio.*   That can I.
    At least the whisper goes so. Our last king,
    Whose image even but now appeared to us,
    Was as you know by Fortinbras of Norway,
    Thereto prickèd on by a most emulate pride,
85   Dared to the combat; in which our valiant Hamlet
    (For so this side of our known world esteemed him)
    Did slay this Fortinbras; who, by a sealed compact
    Well ratified by law and heraldry,
    Did forfeit, with his life, all those his lands
90   Which he stood seized of to the conqueror;
    Against the which a moiety competent
    Was gagèd by our king, which had returned
    To the inheritance of Fortinbras
    Had he been vanquisher, as, by the same comart

---

69 *gross and scope* gross scope, general view   73 *toils* makes toil
subject subjects   75 *mart* trading   76 *impress* conscription   78 *toward*
in preparation   84 *emulate* jealously rivaling   88 *law and heraldry*
law of heralds regulating combat   90 *seizèd* possessed   91 *moiety com-*
petent sufficient portion   92 *gagèd* engaged, staked   94 *comart* joint
bargain

And carriage of the article designed,   95
His fell to Hamlet. Now, sir, young Fortinbras,
Of unimprovèd mettle hot and full,
Hath in the skirts of Norway here and there
Sharked up a list of lawless resolutes
For food and diet to some enterprise   100
That hath a stomach in't; which is no other,
As it doth well appear unto our state,
But to recover of us by strong hand
And terms compulsatory those foresaid lands
So by his father lost; and this, I take it,
Is the main motive of our preparations,   105
The source of this our watch, and the chief head
Of this posthaste and romage in the land.

Bernardo. I think it be no other but e'en so.
Well may it sort that this portentous figure
Comes armèd through our watch so like the king   110
That was and is the question of these wars.

Horatio. A mote it is to trouble the mind's eye.
In the most high and palmy state of Rome,
A little ere the mightiest Julius fell,
The graves stood tenantless and the sheeted dead   11:
Did squeak and gibber in the Roman streets;
As stars with trains of fire and dews of blood,
Disasters in the sun; and the moist star
Upon whose influence Neptune's empire stands
Was sick almost to doomsday with eclipse.   :
And even the like precurse of feared events,
As harbingers preceding still the fates
And prologue to the omen coming on,
Have heaven and earth together demonstrated
Unto our climatures and countrymen.   :

---

95 *carriage* purport   97 *unimprovèd* unused   99 *Sharked* snatched in-
discriminately as the shark takes prey   *resolutes* desperadoes   101
stomach show of venturesomeness   106 *head* fountainhead, source
107 *romage* intense activity   109 *sort* suit   112 *mote* speck of dust
115 *sheeted* in shrouds   118 *Disasters* ominous signs   *moist star* moon
121 *precurse* foreshadowing   122 *harbingers* forerunners   *still* constantly   123 *omen* calamity   125 *climatures* regions

Enter Ghost.

But soft, behold, lo where it comes again!
I'll cross it, though it blast me. — Stay, illusion.
                     He spreads his arms.
If thou hast any sound or use of voice,
Speak to me.
130   If there be any good thing to be done
That may to thee do ease and grace to me,
Speak to me.
If thou art privy to thy country's fate,
Which happily foreknowing may avoid,
135   O, speak!
Or if thou hast uphoarded in thy life
Extorted treasure in the womb of earth,
For which, they say, you spirits oft walk in death,
                     The cock crows.
Speak of it. Stay and speak. Stop it, Marcellus.
140 *Marcellus.* Shall I strike at it with my partisan?
Horatio. Do, if it will not stand.
Bernardo.   'Tis here.
Horatio.   'Tis here.
Marcellus. 'Tis gone.   *Exit Ghost.*
We do it wrong, being so majestical,
To offer it the show of violence,
145   For it is as the air invulnerable,
And our vain blows malicious mockery.
Bernardo. It was about to speak when the cock crew.
Horatio. And then it started, like a guilty thing
Upon a fearful summons. I have heard
150   The cock, that is the trumpet to the morn,
Doth with his lofty and shrill-sounding throat
Awake the god of day, and at his warning,
Whether in sea or fire, in earth or air,
Th' extravagant and erring spirit hies

---

127 *cross it* cross its path   134 *happily* haply, perchance   140 *partisan*
pike   154 *extravagant* wandering beyond bounds *erring* wandering

To his confine; and of the truth herein   155
This present object made probation.

Marcellus. It faded on the crowing of the cock.
Some say that ever 'gainst that season comes
Wherein our Saviour's birth is celebrated,
This bird of dawning singeth all night long,   160
And then, they say, no spirit dare stir abroad,
The nights are wholesome, then no planets strike,
No fairy takes, nor witch hath power to charm.
So hallowed and so gracious is that time.

Horatio. So have I heard and do in part believe it.   165
But look, the morn in russet mantle clad
Walks o'er the dew of yon high eastward hill.
Break we our watch up, and by my advice
Let us impart what we have seen tonight
Unto young Hamlet, for upon my life   170
This spirit, dumb to us, will speak to him.
Do you consent we shall acquaint him with it,
As needful in our loves, fitting our duty?

Marcellus. Let's do't, I pray, and I this morning
   know
Where we shall find him most conveniently.   *Exit.* 175

※

ACT I, SCENE II

Flourish. Enter Claudius, King of Denmark, Ger-
trude the Queen, Councillors, Polonius and his
son Laertes, Hamlet, cum aliis (including
Voltemand and Cornelius).

King. Though yet of Hamlet our dear brother's death
The memory be green, and that it us befitted

---

156 *probation* proof   158 *'gainst* just before   162 *strike* work evil by
influence   163 *takes* bewitches   I, ii, s.p. *cum aliis* with others

To bear our hearts in grief, and our whole kingdom
To be contracted in one brow of woe,
5   Yet so far hath discretion fought with nature
That we with wisest sorrow think on him
Together with remembrance of ourselves.
Therefore our sometime sister, now our queen,
Th' imperial jointress to this warlike state,
10   Have we, as 'twere with a defeated joy,
With an auspicious and a dropping eye,
With mirth in funeral and with dirge in marriage,
In equal scale weighing delight and dole,
Taken to wife. Nor have we herein barred
15   Your better wisdoms, which have freely gone
With this affair along. For all, our thanks.
Now follows, that you know, young Fortinbras,
Holding a weak supposal of our worth,
Or thinking by our late dear brother's death
20   Our state to be disjoint and out of frame,
Colleaguèd with this dream of his advantage,
He hath not failed to pester us with message
Importing the surrender of those lands
Lost by his father, with all bands of law,
25   To our most valiant brother. So much for him.
Now for ourself and for this time of meeting.
Thus much the business is: we have here writ
To Norway, uncle of young Fortinbras —
Who, impotent and bedrid, scarcely hears
30   Of this his nephew's purpose — to suppress
His further gait herein, in that the levies,
The lists, and full proportions are all made
Out of his subject; and we here dispatch
You, good Cornelius, and you, Voltemand,
35   For bearers of this greeting to old Norway,
Giving to you no further personal power

9 *jointress* a woman who has a jointure, or joint tenancy of an estate
14 *barred* excluded 21 *Colleaguèd* united 31 *gait* going 32 *proportions* amounts of forces and supplies

To business with the king, more than the scope
Of these delated articles allow.
Farewell, and let your haste commend your duty..
Cornelius, Voltemand. In that, and all things, will we
 show our duty.   40
King. We doubt it nothing. Heartily farewell.
      Exit Voltemand and Cornelius.
And now, Laertes, what's the news with you?
You told us of some suit. What is't, Laertes?
You cannot speak of reason to the Dane
And lose your voice. What wouldst thou beg,
 Laertes,   45
That shall not be my offer, not thy asking?
The head is not more native to the heart,
The hand more instrumental to the mouth,
Than is the throne of Denmark to thy father.
What wouldst thou have, Laertes?
Laertes.   My dread lord, 50
Your leave and favor to return to France,
From whence though willingly I came to Denmark
To show my duty in your coronation,
Yet now I must confess, that duty done,
My thoughts and wishes bend again toward France 55
And bow them to your gracious leave and pardon.
King. Have you your father's leave? What says Polo
 nius?
Polonius. He hath, my lord, wrung from me my slow
 leave
By laborsome petition, and at last
Upon his will I sealed my hard consent.   60
I do beseech you give him leave to go.
King. Take thy fair hour, Laertes. Time be thine,
And thy best graces spend it at thy will.
But now, my cousin Hamlet, and my son —

---

38 *delated* detailed 45 *lose your voice* speak in vain 47 *native* joined
by nature 48 *instrumental* serviceable 64 *cousin* kinsman more distant than parent, child, brother, or sister

Hamlet. (*aside*) A little more than kin, and less than
kind!

King. How is it that the clouds still hang on you?

Hamlet. Not so, my lord. I am too much in the sun.

Queen. Good Hamlet, cast thy nighted color off,
And let thine eye look like a friend on Denmark.
Do not forever with thy vailèd lids
Seek for thy noble father in the dust.
Thou know'st 'tis common. All that lives must die,
Passing through nature to eternity.

Hamlet. Ay, madam, it is common.

Queen.   If it be,
Why seems it so particular with thee?

Hamlet. Seems, madam? Nay, it is. I know not
"seems."
'Tis not alone my inky cloak, good mother,
Nor customary suits of solemn black,
Nor windy suspiration of forced breath,
No, nor the fruitful river in the eye,
Nor the dejected havior of the visage,
Together with all forms, moods, shapes of grief,
That can denote me truly. These indeed seem,
For they are actions that a man might play,
But I have that within which passeth show —
These but the trappings and the suits of woe.

King. 'Tis sweet and commendable in your nature,
Hamlet,
To give these mourning duties to your father,
But you must know your father lost a father,
That father lost, lost his, and the survivor bound
In filial obligation for some term
To do obsequious sorrow. But to persever
In obstinate condolement is a course

---

65 *kin* related as nephew   *kind* kindly in feeling, as by kind, or nature,
a son would be to his father   67 *sun* sunshine of the king's undesired
favor (with the punning additional meaning of "place of a son")   70
vailèd downcast   92 *obsequious* proper to obsequies or funerals   *persever* persevere (accented on the second syllable, as always in Shakespeare)

Of impious stubbornness. 'Tis unmanly grief.
It shows a will most incorrect to heaven,   95
A heart unfortified, a mind impatient,
An understanding simple and unschooled.
For what we know must be and is as common
As any the most vulgar thing to sense,
Why should we in our peevish opposition   100
Take it to heart? Fie, 'tis a fault to heaven,
A fault against the dead, a fault to nature,
To reason most absurd, whose common theme
Is death of fathers, and who still hath cried,
From the first corse till he that died today,   105
"This must be so." We pray you throw to earth
This unprevailing woe, and think of us
As of a father, for let the world take note
You are the most immediate to our throne,
And with no less nobility of love   110
Than that which dearest father bears his son
Do I impart toward you. For your intent
In going back to school in Wittenberg,
It is most retrograde to our desire,
And we beseech you, bend you to remain   115
Here in the cheer and comfort of our eye,
Our chiefest courtier, cousin, and our son.
Queen. Let not thy mother lose her prayers, Hamlet.
I pray thee stay with us, go not to Wittenberg.
Hamlet. I shall in all my best obey you, madam.   120
King. Why, 'tis a loving and a fair reply.
Be as ourself in Denmark. Madam, come.
This gentle and unforced accord of Hamlet
Sits smiling to my heart, in grace whereof
No jocund health that Denmark drinks today   125
But the great cannon to the clouds shall tell,
And the king's rouse the heaven shall bruit again,
Respeaking earthly thunder. Come away.
                    Flourish. Exit all but Hamlet.

114 *retrograde* contrary   127 *rouse* toast drunk in wine   *bruit* echo

Hamlet. O that this too too sullied flesh would melt,
130   Thaw, and resolve itself into a dew,
       Or that the Everlasting had not fixed
       His canon 'gainst self-slaughter. O God, God,
       How weary, stale, flat, and unprofitable
       Seem to me all the uses of this world!
135   Fie on't, ah, fie, 'tis an unweeded garden
       That grows to seed. Things rank and gross in nature
       Possess it merely. That it should come to this,
       But two months dead, nay, not so much, not two,
       So excellent a king, that was to this
140   Hyperion to a satyr, so loving to my mother
       That he might not beteem the winds of heaven
       Visit her face too roughly. Heaven and earth,
       Must I remember? Why, she would hang on him
       As if increase of appetite had grown
145   By what it fed on, and yet within a month —
       Let me not think on't; frailty, thy name is
          woman —
       A little month, or ere those shoes were old
       With which she followed my poor father's body
       Like Niobe, all tears, why she, even she —
150   O God, a beast that wants discourse of reason
       Would have mourned longer — married with my
          uncle,
       My father's brother, but no more like my father
       Than I to Hercules. Within a month,
       Ere yet the salt of most unrighteous tears
155   Had left the flushing in her gallèd eyes,
       She married. O, most wicked speed, to post
       With such dexterity to incestuous sheets!
       It is not, nor it cannot come to good.
       But break my heart, for I must hold my tongue.

132 *canon* law 137 *merely* completely 140 *Hyperion* the sun god
141 *beteem* allow 149 *Niobe* the proud mother who boasted of having
more children than Leto and was punished when they were slain by
Apollo and Artemis, children of Leto; the grieving Niobe was changed
by Zeus into a stone, which continually dropped tears 150 *discourse*
logical power or process 155 *gallèd* irritated

Enter Horatio, Marcellus, and Bernardo.

Horatio. Hail to your lordship!
Hamlet.   I am glad to see you well.   160
   Horatio — or I do forget myself.
Horatio. The same, my lord, and your poor servant
   ever.
Hamlet. Sir, my good friend, I'll change that name
   with you.
   And what make you from Wittenberg, Horatio?
   Marcellus?
Marcellus. My good lord!   165
Hamlet. I am very glad to see you. *(to Bernardo)*
   Good even, sir.
   But what, in faith, make you from Wittenberg?
Horatio. A truant disposition, good my lord.
Hamlet. I would not hear your enemy say so,
   Nor shall you do my ear that violence   170
   To make it truster of your own report
   Against yourself. I know you are no truant.
   But what is your affair in Elsinore?
   We'll teach you to drink deep ere you depart.
Horatio. My lord, I came to see your father's funeral.   175
Hamlet. I prithee do not mock me, fellow student.
   I think it was to see my mother's wedding.
Horatio. Indeed, my lord, it followed hard upon.
Hamlet. Thrift, thrift, Horatio. The funeral baked
   meats
   Did coldly furnish forth the marriage tables.   180
   Would I had met my dearest foe in heaven
   Or ever I had seen that day, Horatio!
   My father — methinks I see my father.
Horatio. Where, my lord?
Hamlet.   In my mind's eye, Horatio.
Horatio. I saw him once. 'A was a goodly king.   185

163 *change* exchange   164 *make* do   181 *dearest* direst, bitterest

Hamlet. 'A was a man, take him for all in all,
 I shall not look upon his like again.

Horatio. My lord, I think I saw him yesternight.

Hamlet. Saw? Who?

Horatio. My lord, the king your father.

190 *Hamlet.*   The king my father?

Horatio. Season your admiration for a while
 With an attent ear till I may deliver
 Upon the witness of these gentlemen
 This marvel to you.

Hamlet.   For God's love let me hear!

195 *Horatio.* Two nights together had these gentlemen,
 Marcellus and Bernardo, on their watch
 In the dead waste and middle of the night
 Been thus encountered. A figure like your father,
 Armèd at point exactly, cap-a-pe,

200 Appears before them and with solemn march
 Goes slow and stately by them. Thrice he walked
 By their oppressed and fear-surprisèd eyes
 Within his truncheon's length, whilst they, dis-
      tilled
 Almost to jelly with the act of fear,

205 Stand dumb and speak not to him. This to me
 In dreadful secrecy impart they did,
 And I with them the third night kept the watch,
 Where, as they had delivered, both in time,
 Form of the thing, each word made true and good,

210 The apparition comes. I knew your father.
 These hands are not more like.

Hamlet.   But where was this?

Marcellus. My lord, upon the platform where we
      watched.

Hamlet. Did you not speak to it?

Horatio.   My lord, I did,
 But answer made it none. Yet once methought

---

191 *Season your admiration* control your wonder   199 *at point* completely   *cap-a-pe* from head to foot   203 *truncheon* military command-
er's baton

It lifted up it head and did address   215
  Itself to motion like as it would speak.
  But even then the morning cock crew loud,
  And at the sound it shrunk in haste away
  And vanished from our sight.

Hamlet.   'Tis very strange.

Horatio. As I do live, my honored lord, 'tis true,   220
  And we did think it writ down in our duty
  To let you know of it.

Hamlet. Indeed, indeed, sirs, but this troubles me.
  Hold you the watch tonight?

All.   We do, my lord.

Hamlet. Armed, say you?   225

All. Armed, my lord.

Hamlet. From top to toe?

All.   My lord, from head to foot.

Hamlet. Then saw you not his face?

Horatio. O, yes, my lord. He wore his beaver up.

Hamlet. What, looked he frowningly?   230

Horatio. A countenance more in sorrow than in
  anger.

Hamlet. Pale or red?

Horatio. Nay, very pale.

Hamlet.   And fixed his eyes upon you?

Horatio. Most constantly.

Hamlet.   I would I had been there.

Horatio. It would have much amazed you.   235

Hamlet. Very like, very like. Stayed it long?

Horatio. While one with moderate haste might tell a
  hundred.

Both. Longer, longer.

Horatio. Not when I saw't.

Hamlet.   His beard was grizzled, no?

Horatio. It was as I have seen it in his life,   240
  A sable silvered.

---

215 *it* its   229 *beaver* visor or movable faceguard of the helmet   237
tell count   239 *grizzled* gray   241 *sable silvered* black mixed with white

Hamlet.   I will watch tonight.
  Perchance 'twill walk again.
Horatio.   I warr'nt it will.
Hamlet. If it assume my noble father's person,
  I'll speak to it though hell itself should gape
245 And bid me hold my peace. I pray you all,
  If you have hitherto concealed this sight,
  Let it be tenable in your silence still,
  And whatsomever else shall hap tonight,
  Give it an understanding but no tongue.
250 I will requite your loves. So fare you well.
  Upon the platform, 'twixt eleven and twelve
  I'll visit you.
All.   Our duty to your honor.
Hamlet. Your loves, as mine to you. Farewell.
                                    Exit all but Hamlet.
  My father's spirit — in arms? All is not well.
  I doubt some foul play. Would the night were
255   come!
  Till then sit still, my soul. Foul deeds will rise,
  Though all the earth o'erwhelm them, to men's
    eyes.
                                          Exit.

ACT I, SCENE III

Enter Laertes and Ophelia, his sister.

Laertes. My necessaries are embarked. Farewell.
  And, sister, as the winds give benefit
  And convoy is assistant, do not sleep,
  But let me hear from you.

247 *tenable* held firmly   255 *doubt* suspect, fear   I, iii, 3 *convoy* means
of transport

Ophelia.   Do you doubt that?
Laertes. For Hamlet, and the trifling of his favor,   5
  Hold it a fashion and a toy in blood,
  A violet in the youth of primy nature,
  Forward, not permanent, sweet, not lasting,
  The perfume and suppliance of a minute,
  No more.
Ophelia.   No more but so?
Laertes.   Think it no more.   10
  For nature crescent does not grow alone
  In thews and bulk, but as this temple waxes
  The inward service of the mind and soul
  Grows wide withal. Perhaps he loves you now,
  And now no soil nor cautel doth besmirch   15
  The virtue of his will, but you must fear,
  His greatness weighed, his will is not his own.
  For he himself is subject to his birth.
  He may not, as unvalued persons do,
  Carve for himself, for on his choice depends   20
  The safety and health of this whole state,
  And therefore must his choice be circumscribed
  Unto the voice and yielding of that body
  Whereof he is the head. Then if he says he loves
    you,
  It fits your wisdom so far to believe it   25
  As he in his particular act and place
  May give his saying deed, which is no further
  Than the main voice of Denmark goes withal.
  Then weigh what loss your honor may sustain
  If with too credent ear you list his songs,   30
  Or lose your heart, or your chaste treasure open
  To his unmastered importunity.
  Fear it, Ophelia, fear it, my dear sister,

7 *primy* of the springtime 9 *perfume and suppliance* filling sweetness
11 *crescent* growing 12 *this temple* the body 15 *cautel* deceit 16
will desire 17 *greatness weighed* high position considered 23 *yielding*
assent 30 *credent* credulous

And keep you in the rear of your affection,
35 Out of the shot and danger of desire.
The chariest maid is prodigal enough
If she unmask her beauty to the moon.
Virtue itself scapes not calumnious strokes.
The canker galls the infants of the spring
40 Too oft before their buttons be disclosed,
And in the morn and liquid dew of youth
Contagious blastments are most imminent.
Be wary then; best safety lies in fear.
Youth to itself rebels, though none else near.
45 *Ophelia.* I shall the effect of this good lesson keep
As watchman to my heart, but, good my brother,
Do not as some ungracious pastors do,
Show me the steep and thorny way to heaven,
Whiles like a puffed and reckless libertine
50 Himself the primrose path of dalliance treads
And recks not his own rede.

Enter Polonius.

Laertes.   O, fear me not.
I stay too long. But here my father comes.
A double blessing is a double grace;
Occasion smiles upon a second leave.
Polonius. Yet here, Laertes? Aboard, aboard, for
55 shame!
The wind sits in the shoulder of your sail,
And you are stayed for. There — my blessing with
thee,
And these few precepts in thy memory
Look thou character. Give thy thoughts no tongue,
60 Nor any unproportioned thought his act.
Be thou familiar, but by no means vulgar.
Those friends thou hast, and their adoption tried,

34 *affection* feelings, which rashly lead forward into dangers   39 *canker* rose worm   *galls* injures   40 *buttons* buds   42 *blastments* blights
51 *recks* regards   *rede* counsel   59 *character* inscribe   60 *unproportioned* unadjusted to what is right

Grapple them unto thy soul with hoops of steel,
But do not dull thy palm with entertainment
Of each new-hatched, unfledged courage. Beware   65
Of entrance to a quarrel; but being in,
Bear't that th' opposèd may beware of thee.
Give every man thine ear, but few thy voice;
Take each man's censure, but reserve thy judg-
    ment.
Costly thy habit as thy purse can buy,   70
But not expressed in fancy; rich, not gaudy,
For the apparel oft proclaims the man,
And they in France of the best rank and station
Are of a most select and generous chief in that.
Neither a borrower nor a lender be,   75
For loan oft loses both itself and friend,
And borrowing dulleth edge of husbandry.
This above all, to thine own self be true,
And it must follow as the night the day
Thou canst not then be false to any man.   80
Farewell. My blessing season this in thee!

Laertes. Most humbly do I take my leave, my lord.

Polonius. The time invites you. Go, your servants
    tend.

Laertes. Farewell, Ophelia, and remember well
    What I have said to you.

Ophelia.   'Tis in my memory locked,   85
And you yourself shall keep the key of it.

Laertes. Farewell.   *Exit Laertes.*

Polonius. What is't, Ophelia, he hath said to you?

Ophelia. So please you, something touching the Lord
    Hamlet.

Polonius. Marry, well bethought.   90
'Tis told me he hath very oft of late
Given private time to you, and you yourself

---

65 *courage* man of spirit, young blood   69 *censure* judgment   74 *chief* eminence   77 *husbandry* thriftiness   81 *season* ripen and make fruitful   83 *tend* wait   90 *Marry* by Mary

Have of your audience been most free and bounte-
ous.

If it be so — as so 'tis put on me,

95   And that in way of caution — I must tell you
You do not understand yourself so clearly
As it behooves my daughter and your honor.
What is between you? Give me up the truth.

Ophelia. He hath, my lord, of late made many
        tenders

100 Of his affection to me.

Polonius. Affection? Pooh! You speak like a green girl,
Unsifted in such perilous circumstance.
Do you believe his tenders, as you call them?

Ophelia. I do not know, my lord, what I should think.

Polonius. Marry, I will teach you. Think yourself a
105   baby
That you have ta'en these tenders for true pay
Which are not sterling. Tender yourself more
        dearly,
Or (not to crack the wind of the poor phrase,
Running it thus) you'll tender me a fool.

110 *Ophelia.* My lord, he hath importuned me with love
In honorable fashion.

Polonius. Ay, fashion you may call it. Go to, go to.

Ophelia. And hath given countenance to his speech,
        my lord,
With almost all the holy vows of heaven.

115 *Polonius.* Ay, springes to catch woodcocks. I do know,
When the blood burns, how prodigal the soul
Lends the tongue vows. These blazes, daughter,
Giving more light than heat, extinct in both

---

99 *tenders* offers 102 *Unsifted* untested 106–9 *tenders . . . Tender
. . . tender* offers . . . hold in regard . . . present (a word play going through three meanings, the last use of the word yielding further
complexity with its valid implications that she will show herself to him
as a fool, will show him to the world as a fool, and may go so far as to
present him with a baby, which would be a fool because "fool" was an
Elizabethan term of endearment especially applicable to an infant as
a "little innocent") 108 *crack . . . of* make wheeze like a horse
driven too hard 112 *Go to* go away, go on (expressing impatience)
115 *springes* snares *woodcocks* birds believed foolish

Even in their promise, as it is a-making,
You must not take for fire. From this time   120
Be something scanter of your maiden presence.
Set your entreatments at a higher rate
Than a command to parley. For Lord Hamlet,
Believe so much in him that he is young,
And with a larger tether may he walk   125
Than may be given you. In few, Ophelia,
Do not believe his vows, for they are brokers,
Not of that dye which their investments show,
But mere implorators of unholy suits,
Breathing like sanctified and pious bawds,   130
The better to beguile. This is for all:
I would not, in plain terms, from this time forth
Have you so slander any moment leisure
As to give words or talk with the Lord Hamlet.
Look to't, I charge you. Come your ways.   135
Ophelia. I shall obey, my lord.   *Exit all.*

ACT I, SCENE IV

Enter Hamlet, Horatio, and Marcellus.

Hamlet. The air bites shrewdly; it is very cold.
Horatio. It is a nipping and an eager air.
Hamlet. What hour now?
Horatio.   I think it lacks of twelve.
Marcellus. No, it is struck.
Horatio. Indeed? I heard it not. It then draws near the
    season   5

122 *entreatments* military negotiations for surrender 123 *parley* confer with a beseiger 127 *brokers* middlemen, panders 128 *investments* clothes 133 *slander* use disgracefully *moment* momentary I, iv, 1 *shrewdly* wickedly 2 *eager* sharp

Wherein the spirit held his wont to walk.

    A flourish of trumpets, and two pieces go off.

What does this mean, my lord?

Hamlet. The king doth wake tonight and takes his
    rouse,

Keeps wassail, and the swaggering upspring reels,

10 And as he drains his draughts of Rhenish down

The kettledrum and trumpet thus bray out

The triumph of his pledge.

Horatio.   Is it a custom?

Hamlet. Ay, marry, is't,

But to my mind, though I am native here

15 And to the manner born, it is a custom

More honored in the breach than the observance.

This heavy-headed revel east and west

Makes us traduced and taxed of other nations.

They clepe us drunkards and with swinish phrase

20 Soil our addition, and indeed it takes

From our achievements, though performed at
    height,

The pith and marrow of our attribute.

So oft it chances in particular men

That (for some vicious mole of nature in them,

25 As in their birth, wherein they are not guilty,

Since nature cannot choose his origin)

By the o'ergrowth of some complexion,

Oft breaking down the pales and forts of reason,

Or by some habit that too much o'erleavens

30 The form of plausive manners — that (these men

---

8 *rouse* carousal 9 *upspring* a German dance 10 *Rhenish* Rhine wine
12 *triumph* achievement, feat (in downing a cup of wine at one
draught) 16 *More . . . observance* better broken than observed 18
taxed of censured by 19 *clepe* call 20 *addition* reputation, title added
as a distinction 22 *attribute* reputation, what is attributed 24 *mole*
blemish, flaw 26 *his* its 27 *complexion* part of the make-up, combination of humors which were thought to be fluids that entered the
body and determined, by their proportions, a person's health and
temperament. The four Shakespearean humors are: mercurial, phleg-
matic, sanguine, and choleric 28 *pales* barriers, fences 29 *o'erleavens*
works change throughout, as yeast ferments dough 30 *plausive* pleasing

Carrying, I say, the stamp of one defect,
Being nature's livery, or fortune's star)
Their virtues else, be they as pure as grace,
As infinite as man may undergo,
Shall in the general censure take corruption   35
From that particular fault. The dram of evil
Doth all the noble substance of a doubt,
To his own scandal.

Enter Ghost.

Horatio.   Look, my lord, it comes.
Hamlet. Angels and ministers of grace defend us!
Be thou a spirit of health or goblin damned,   40
Bring with thee airs from heaven or blasts from
   hell,
Be thy intents wicked or charitable,
Thou com'st in such a questionable shape
That I will speak to thee. I'll call thee Hamlet,
King, father, royal Dane. O, answer me!   45
Let me not burst in ignorance, but tell
Why thy canonized bones, hearsèd in death,
Have burst their cerements, why the sepulchre
Wherein we saw thee quietly interred
Hath oped his ponderous and marble jaws   50
To cast thee up again. What may this mean
That thou, dead corse, again in complete steel,
Revisits thus the glimpses of the moon,
Making night hideous, and we fools of nature
So horridly to shake our disposition   55
With thoughts beyond the reaches of our souls?
Say, why is this? wherefore? what should we do?
                                  Ghost beckons.

---

32 *livery* characteristic equipment or provision *star* make-up as
formed by stellar influence 40 *of health* sound, good *goblin* fiend
47 *canonized* buried with the established rites of the Church 48 *cerements* waxed gravecloths 54 *fools of nature* men made conscious of
natural limitations by a supernatural manifestation

Horatio. It beckons you to go away with it,
   As if it some impartment did desire
   To you alone.
60 *Marcellus.*   Look with what courteous action
   It waves you to a more removèd ground.
   But do not go with it.
Horatio.   No, by no means.
Hamlet. It will not speak. Then will I follow it.
Horatio. Do not, my lord.
Hamlet.   Why, what should be the fear?
65 I do not set my life at a pin's fee,
   And for my soul, what can it do to that,
   Being a thing immortal as itself?
   It waves me forth again. I'll follow it.
Horatio. What if it tempt you toward the flood, my
        lord,
70 Or to the dreadful summit of the cliff
   That beetles o'er his base into the sea,
   And there assume some other horrible form,
   Which might deprive your sovereignty of reason
   And draw you into madness? Think of it.
75 The very place puts toys of desperation,
   Without more motive, into every brain
   That looks so many fathoms to the sea
   And hears it roar beneath.
Hamlet.   It waves me still.
   Go on. I'll follow thee.
Marcellus. You shall not go, my lord.
80 *Hamlet.*   Hold off your hands.
Horatio. Be ruled. You shall not go.
Hamlet.   My fate cries out
   And makes each petty artere in this body
   As hardy as the Nemean lion's nerve.
   Still am I called. Unhand me, gentlemen.

---

71 *beetles* juts out   73 *deprive* take away   *sovereignty of reason* state
of being ruled by reason   75 *toys* fancies   82 *artere* artery   83
Nemean lion a lion slain by Hercules in the performance of one of his
twelve labors   *nerve* sinew

By heaven, I'll make a ghost of him that lets me!   85
I say, away! Go on. I'll follow thee.
                                        Exit Ghost and Hamlet.
Horatio. He waxes desperate with imagination.
Marcellus. Let's follow. 'Tis not fit thus to obey him.
Horatio. Have after. To what issue will this come?
Marcellus. Something is rotten in the state of Den-
    mark.   90
Horatio. Heaven will direct it.
Marcellus.   Nay, let's follow him.   *Exit all.*

ACT I, SCENE V

Enter Ghost and Hamlet.

Hamlet. Whither wilt thou lead me? Speak. I'll go no
    further.
Ghost. Mark me.
Hamlet.   I will.
Ghost.   My hour is almost come,
    When I to sulph'rous and tormenting flames
    Must render up myself.
Hamlet.   Alas, poor ghost!
Ghost. Pity me not, but lend thy serious hearing   5
    To what I shall unfold.
Hamlet.   Speak. I am bound to hear.
Ghost. So art thou to revenge, when thou shalt hear.
Hamlet. What?
Ghost. I am thy father's spirit,
    Doomed for a certain term to walk the night,   10
    And for the day confined to fast in fires,

85 *lets* hinders I, v, 3 *flames* sufferings in purgatory (not hell) 11
fast do penance

Till the foul crimes done in my days of nature
Are burnt and purged away. But that I am forbid
To tell the secrets of my prison house,
15   I could a tale unfold whose lightest word
Would harrow up thy soul, freeze thy young blood,
Make thy two eyes like stars start from their spheres,
Thy knotted and combinèd locks to part,
And each particular hair to stand an end
20   Like quills upon the fretful porpentine.
But this eternal blazon must not be
To ears of flesh and blood. List, list, O, list!
If thou didst ever thy dear father love —

Hamlet. O God!

25   *Ghost.* Revenge his foul and most unnatural murther.

Hamlet. Murther?

Ghost. Murther most foul, as in the best it is,
But this most foul, strange, and unnatural.

Hamlet. Haste me to know't, that I, with wings as swift
30   As meditation or the thoughts of love,
May sweep to my revenge.

Ghost.   I find thee apt,
And duller shouldst thou be than the fat weed
That roots itself in ease on Lethe wharf,
Wouldst thou not stir in this. Now, Hamlet, hear.
35   'Tis given out that, sleeping in my orchard,
A serpent stung me. So the whole ear of Denmark
Is by a forgèd process of my death
Rankly abused. But know, thou noble youth,
The serpent that did sting thy father's life
Now wears his crown.

40   *Hamlet.*   O my prophetic soul!
My uncle?

17 *spheres* transparent revolving shells in each of which, according to
the Ptolemaic astronomy, a planet or other heavenly body was placed
19 *an* on 20 *porpentine* porcupine 21 *eternal blazon* revelation of
eternity 30 *meditation* thought 33 *Lethe* the river in Hades which
brings forgetfulness of past life to a spirit who drinks of it 37 *forgèd
process* falsified official report

Ghost. Ay, that incestuous, that adulterate beast,
  With witchcraft of his wit, with traitorous gifts —
  O wicked wit and gifts, that have the power
  So to seduce! — won to his shameful lust   45
  The will of my most seeming-virtuous queen.
  O Hamlet, what a falling-off was there,
  From me, whose love was of that dignity
  That it went hand in hand even with the vow
  I made to her in marriage, and to decline   50
  Upon a wretch whose natural gifts were poor
  To those of mine!
  But virtue, as it never will be moved,
  Though lewdness court it in a shape of heaven,
  So lust, though to a radiant angel linked,   55
  Will sate itself in a celestial bed
  And prey on garbage.
  But soft, methinks I scent the morning air.
  Brief let me be. Sleeping within my orchard,
  My custom always of the afternoon,   60
  Upon my secure hour thy uncle stole
  With juice of cursed hebona in a vial,
  And in the porches of my ears did pour
  The leperous distilment, whose effect
  Holds such an enmity with blood of man   65
  That swift as quicksilver it courses through
  The natural gates and alleys of the body,
  And with a sudden vigor it doth posset
  And curd, like eager droppings into milk,
  The thin and wholesome blood. So did it mine,   70
  And a most instant tetter barked about
  Most lazarlike with vile and loathsome crust
  All my smooth body.
  Thus was I sleeping by a brother's hand
  Of life, of crown, of queen at once dispatched,   75

---

42 *adulterate* adulterous 54 *shape of heaven* angelic disguise 61 *secure* carefree, unsuspecting 62 *hebona* some poisonous plant 68 *posset* curdle 69 *eager* sour 71 *tetter* eruption *barked* covered as with a bark 72 *lazarlike* leperlike

Cut off even in the blossoms of my sin,
Unhouseled, disappointed, unaneled,
No reck'ning made, but sent to my account
With all my imperfections on my head.
80   O, horrible! O, horrible! Most horrible!
If thou hast nature in thee, bear it not.
Let not the royal bed of Denmark be
A couch for luxury and damnèd incest.
But howsomever thou pursues this act,
85   Taint not thy mind, nor let thy soul contrive
Against thy mother aught. Leave her to heaven
And to those thorns that in her bosom lodge
To prick and sting her. Fare thee well at once.
The glowworm shows the matin to be near
90   And gins to pale his uneffectual fire.
Adieu, adieu, adieu. Remember me.   *Exit.*
Hamlet. O all you host of heaven! O earth! What else?
And shall I couple hell? O fie! Hold, hold, my
            heart,
And you, my sinews, grow not instant old,
95   But bear me stiffly up. Remember thee?
Ay, thou poor ghost, while memory holds a seat
In this distracted globe. Remember thee?
Yea, from the table of my memory
I'll wipe away all trivial fond records,
100   All saws of books, all forms, all pressures past
That youth and observation copied there,
And thy commandment all alone shall live
Within the book and volume of my brain,
Unmixed with baser matter. Yes, by heaven!
105   O most pernicious woman!
O villain, villain, smiling, damnèd villain!
My tables — meet it is I set it down
That one may smile, and smile, and be a villain.

---

77 *Unhouseled* without the Sacrament   *disappointed* unprepared spiri-
tually   *unaneled* without extreme unction   83 *luxury* lust   89 *matin*
morning   97 *globe* head   98 *table* writing tablet, record book   100
saws wise sayings   *forms* mental images, concepts   *pressures* impressions

At least I am sure it may be so in Denmark. *Writes.*
So, uncle, there you are. Now to my word: 110
It is "Adieu, adieu, remember me."
I have sworn't.

Enter Horatio and Marcellus.

Horatio. My lord, my lord!
Marcellus.   Lord Hamlet!
Horatio.   Heavens secure him!
Hamlet. So be it!
Marcellus. Illo, ho, ho, my lord!   115
Hamlet. Hillo, ho, ho, boy! Come, bird, come.
Marcellus. How is't, my noble lord?
Horatio.   What news, my lord?
Hamlet. O, wonderful!
Horatio. Good my lord, tell it.
Hamlet.   No, you will reveal it.
Horatio. Not I, my lord, by heaven.
Marcellus.   Nor I, my lord.   120
Hamlet. How say you then? Would heart of man
    once think it?
But you'll be secret?
Both.   Ay, by heaven, my lord.
Hamlet. There's never a villain dwelling in all Den-
    mark
But he's an arrant knave.
Horatio. There needs no ghost, my lord, come from
    the grave   125
To tell us this.
Hamlet.   Why, right, you are in the right,
And so, without more circumstance at all,
I hold it fit that we shake hands and part:
You, as your business and desires shall point you,
For every man hath business and desire   130
Such as it is, and for my own poor part,
Look you, I'll go pray.

115 *Illo, ho, ho* cry of the falconer to summon his hawk   127 *circum*
stance ceremony

Horatio. These are but wild and whirling words, my
    lord.

Hamlet. I am sorry they offend you, heartily;
    Yes, faith, heartily.

135 *Horatio.*   There's no offense, my lord.

Hamlet. Yes, by Saint Patrick, but there is, Horatio,
    And much offense too. Touching this vision here,
    It is an honest ghost, that let me tell you.
    For your desire to know what is between us,

140   O'ermaster't as you may. And now, good friends,
    As you are friends, scholars, and soldiers,
    Give me one poor request.

Horatio. What is't, my lord? We will.

Hamlet. Never make known what you have seen to-
    night.

Both. My lord, we will not.

Hamlet.   Nay, but swear't.

145 *Horatio.*   In faith,
    My lord, not I.

Marcellus.   Nor I, my lord — in faith.

Hamlet. Upon my sword.

Marcellus.   We have sworn, my lord, already.

Hamlet. Indeed, upon my sword, indeed.

                 Ghost cries under the stage.

Ghost. Swear.

Hamlet. Ha, ha, boy, say'st thou so? Art thou there,
150   truepenny?
    Come on. You hear this fellow in the cellerage.
    Consent to swear.

Horatio.   Propose the oath, my lord.

Hamlet. Never to speak of this that you have seen,
    Swear by my sword.

155 *Ghost.* (*beneath*) Swear.

Hamlet. Hic et ubique? Then we'll shift our ground.
    Come hither, gentlemen,
    And lay your hands again upon my sword.

---

138 *honest* genuine (not a disguised demon)   147 *sword* i.e. upon the
cross formed by the sword hilt   150 *truepenny* honest old fellow   156
Hic et ubique here and everywhere

   Swear by my sword
   Never to speak of this that you have heard.   160
Ghost. (*beneath*) Swear by his sword.
Hamlet. Well said, old mole! Canst work i' th' earth
     so fast?
   A worthy pioner! Once more remove, good friends.
Horatio. O day and night, but this is wondrous
     strange!
Hamlet. And therefore as a stranger give it welcome.   165
   There are more things in heaven and earth, Horatio,
   Than are dreamt of in your philosophy.
   But come:
   Here as before, never, so help you mercy,
   How strange or odd some'er I bear myself   170
   (As I perchance hereafter shall think meet
   To put an antic disposition on),
   That you, at such times seeing me, never shall,
   With arms encumb'red thus, or this head-shake,
   Or by pronouncing of some doubtful phrase,   175
   As "Well, well, we know," or "We could, an if we
     would,"
   Or "If we list to speak," or "There be, an if they
     might,"
   Or such ambiguous giving out, to note
   That you know aught of me — this do swear,
   So grace and mercy at your most need help you.   180
Ghost. (*beneath*) Swear.   *They swear.*
Hamlet. Rest, rest, perturbèd spirit! So, gentlemen,
   With all my love I do commend me to you,
   And what so poor a man as Hamlet is
   May do t' express his love and friending to you,   185
   God willing, shall not lack. Let us go in together,
   And still your fingers on your lips, I pray.
   The time is out of joint. O cursèd spite
   That ever I was born to set it right!
   Nay, come, let's go together.   *Exit all.* 190

163 *pioner* pioneer, miner   167 *your philosophy* this philosophy one
hears about   172 *antic* grotesque, mad   174 *encumb'red* folded   176
an if if   183 *commend* entrust   187 *still* always

ACT II, SCENE I

Enter old Polonius, with his man (Reynaldo).

Polonius. Give him this money and these notes, Reynaldo.

Reynaldo. I will, my lord.

Polonius. You shall do marvellous wisely, good Reynaldo,

Before you visit him, to make inquire

Of his behavior.

5 *Reynaldo.*   My lord, I did intend it.

Polonius. Marry, well said, very well said. Look you,
sir,

Enquire me first what Danskers are in Paris,

And how, and who, what means, and where they
keep,

What company, at what expense; and finding

10 By this encompassment and drift of question

That they do know my son, come you more nearer

Than your particular demands will touch it.

Take you as 'twere some distant knowledge of him,

As thus, "I know his father and his friends,

15 And in part him" — do you mark this, Reynaldo?

II, i, 7 *Danskers* Danes   8 *what means* what their wealth   *keep* dwell
10 *encompassment* circling about   12 *particular demands* definite questions

Reynaldo. Ay, very well, my lord.

Polonius. "And in part him, but," you may say, "not
    well,
  But if't be he I mean, he's very wild
  Addicted so and so." And there put on him
  What forgeries you please; marry, none so rank   20
  As may dishonor him — take heed of that —
  But, sir, such wanton, wild, and usual slips
  As are companions noted and most known
  To youth and liberty.

Reynaldo.   As gaming, my lord.

Polonius. Ay, or drinking, fencing, swearing, quarrel-
    ling,   25
  Drabbing. You may go so far.

Reynaldo. My lord, that would dishonor him.

Polonius. Faith, no, as you may season it in the charge.
  You must not put another scandal on him,
  That he is open to incontinency.   30
  That's not my meaning. But breathe his faults so
    quaintly
  That they may seem the taints of liberty,
  The flash and outbreak of a fiery mind,
  A savageness in unreclaimèd blood,
  Of general assault.

Reynaldo.   But, my good lord —   35

Polonius. Wherefore should you do this?

Reynaldo.   Ay, my lord,
  I would know that.

Polonius.   Marry, sir, here's my drift,
  And I believe it is a fetch of warrant.
  You laying these slight sullies on my son
  As 'twere a thing a little soiled i' th' working,   40
  Mark you,
  Your party in converse, him you would sound,

---

20 *forgeries* invented wrongdoings 26 *Drabbing* whoring 28 *season*
soften 30 *incontinency* unrestrained sexual indulgence 31 *quaintly*
expertly, gracefully 34 *unreclaimèd* untamed 35 *Of general assault*
assailing all young men 38 *fetch of warrant* allowable trick

Having ever seen in the prenominate crimes
The youth you breathe of guilty, be assured
45   He closes with you in this consequence:
"Good sir," or so, or "friend," or "gentleman" —
According to the phrase or the addition
Of man and country —

Reynaldo.   Very good, my lord.

Polonius. And then, sir, does 'a this — 'a does —
50   What was I about to say? By the mass, I was about
to say something! Where did I leave?

Reynaldo. At "closes in the consequence," at "friend
or so," and "gentleman."

Polonius. At "closes in the consequence" — Ay,
marry!
55   He closes thus: "I know the gentleman;
I saw him yesterday, or t'other day,
Or then, or then, with such or such, and, as you say,
There was 'a gaming, there o'ertook in's rouse,
There falling out at tennis"; or perchance,
60   "I saw him enter such a house of sale,"
Videlicet, a brothel, or so forth.
See you now —
Your bait of falsehood takes this carp of truth,
And thus do we of wisdom and of reach,
65   With windlasses and with assays of bias,
By indirections find directions out.
So, by my former lecture and advice,
Shall you my son. You have me, have you not?

Reynaldo. My lord, I have.

Polonius.   God bye ye, fare ye well.
70 *Reynaldo.* Good my lord.

Polonius. Observe his inclination in yourself.

Reynaldo. I shall, my lord.

---

43 *Having ever* if he has ever   *prenominate* aforementioned   45 *closes
with you* follows your lead to a conclusion   *consequence* following
way   47 *addition* title   58 *o'ertook* overcome with drunkenness   *rouse*
carousal   59 *falling out* quarreling   61 *Videlicet* namely   64 *reach*
far-reaching comprehension   65 *windlasses* roundabout courses *assays of bias* devious attacks   66 *directions* ways of procedure   69 *God
bye ye* God be with you, good-bye

Polonius. And let him ply his music.
Reynaldo.   Well, my lord.
Polonius. Farewell.   *Exit Reynaldo.*

Enter Ophelia.

                How now, Ophelia, what's the matter?
Ophelia. O my lord, my lord, I have been so af-
    frighted!   75
Polonius. With what, i' th' name of God?
Ophelia. My lord, as I was sewing in my closet,
    Lord Hamlet, with his doublet all unbraced,
    No hat upon his head, his stockings fouled,
    Ungartered, and down-gyvèd to his ankle,   80
    Pale as his shirt, his knees knocking each other,
    And with a look so piteous in purport
    As if he had been loosèd out of hell
    To speak of horrors — he comes before me.
Polonius. Mad for thy love?
Ophelia.   My lord, I do not know,   85
    But truly I do fear it.
Polonius.   What said he?
Ophelia. He took me by the wrist and held me hard.
    Then goes he to the length of all his arm,
    And with his other hand thus o'er his brow
    He falls to such perusal of my face   90
    As 'a would draw it. Long stayed he so.
    At last, a little shaking of mine arm
    And thrice his head thus waving up and down,
    He raised a sigh so piteous and profound
    As it did seem to shatter all his bulk   95
    And end his being. That done, he lets me go,
    And with his head over his shoulder turned
    He seemed to find his way without his eyes,
    For out o' doors he went without their helps
    And to the last bended their light on me.   100

---

77 *closet* private living-room 78 *doublet* jacket *unbraced* unlaced
80 *down-gyvèd* fallen down like gyves or fetters on a prisoner's legs

Polonius. Come, go with me. I will go seek the king.
  This is the very ecstasy of love,
  Whose violent property fordoes itself
  And leads the will to desperate undertakings
105 As oft as any passion under heaven
  That does afflict our natures. I am sorry.
  What, have you given him any hard words of late?
Ophelia. No, my good lord; but as you did command
  I did repel his letters and denied
  His access to me.
110 *Polonius.*   That hath made him mad.
  I am sorry that with better heed and judgment
  I had not quoted him. I feared he did but trifle
  And meant to wrack thee; but beshrew my jealousy.
  By heaven, it is as proper to our age
115 To cast beyond ourselves in our opinions
  As it is common for the younger sort
  To lack discretion. Come, go we to the king.
  This must be known, which, being kept close,
      might move
  More grief to hide than hate to utter love.
120 Come.   *Exit all.*

ACT II, SCENE II

*Flourish. Enter King and Queen, Rosencrantz, and
Guildenstern (with others).*

King. Welcome, dear Rosencrantz and Guildenstern.

102 *ecstasy* madness 103 *property* quality *fordoes* destroys 112
quoted observed 113 *beshrew* curse 115 *cast beyond ourselves* find
by calculation more significance in something than we ought to 118
close secret *move* cause 119 *to hide . . . love* by such hiding of love
than there would be hate moved by a revelation of it (a violently con-
densed putting of the case which is a triumph of special statement for
Polonius)

Moreover that we much did long to see you,
The need we have to use you did provoke
Our hasty sending. Something have you heard
Of Hamlet's transformation — so call it,   5
Sith nor th' exterior nor the inward man
Resembles that it was. What it should be,
More than his father's death, that thus hath put him
So much from th' understanding of himself,
I cannot dream of. I entreat you both   10
That, being of so young days brought up with him,
And sith so neighbored to his youth and havior,
That you vouchsafe your rest here in our court
Some little time, so by your companies
To draw him on to pleasures, and to gather   15
So much as from occasion you may glean,
Whether aught to us unknown afflicts him thus,
That opened lies within our remedy.

Queen. Good gentlemen, he hath much talked of you,
And sure I am two men there are not living   20
To whom he more adheres. If it will please you
To show us so much gentry and good will
As to expend your time with us awhile
For the supply and profit of our hope,
Your visitation shall receive such thanks   25
As fits a king's remembrance.

Rosencrantz.   Both your majesties
Might, by the sovereign power you have of us,
Put your dread pleasures more into command
Than to entreaty.

Guildenstern.   But we both obey,
And here give up ourselves in the full bent   30
To lay our service freely at your feet,
To be commanded.

II, ii, 2 *Moreover that* besides the fact that 6 *Sith* since 12 *youth
and havior* youthful ways of life 18 *opened* revealed 21 *more adheres*
is more attached 22 *gentry* courtesy 30 *in the full bent* at the limit
of bending (of a bow), to full capacity

King. Thanks, Rosencrantz and gentle Guildenstern.

Queen. Thanks, Guildenstern and gentle Rosencrantz.
35   And I beseech you instantly to visit
        My too much changèd son. — Go, some of you,
        And bring these gentlemen where Hamlet is.

Guildenstern. Heavens make our presence and our
        practices
        Pleasant and helpful to him!

Queen.   Ay, amen!

                            Exit Rosencrantz and Guildenstern
                                    (with some Attendants)

                            Enter Polonius.

Polonius. Th' ambassadors from Norway, my good
40   lord,
        Are joyfully returned.

King. Thou still hast been the father of good news.

Polonius. Have I, my lord? Assure you, my good liege,
        I hold my duty as I hold my soul,
45   Both to my God and to my gracious king
        And I do think — or else this brain of mine
        Hunts not the trail of policy so sure
        As it hath used to do — that I have found
        The very cause of Hamlet's lunacy.

50 *King.* O, speak of that! That do I long to hear.

Polonius. Give first admittance to th' ambassadors.
        My news shall be the fruit to that great feast.

King. Thyself do grace to them and bring them in.

                                            Exit Polonius.

        He tells me, my dear Gertrude, he hath found
55   The head and source of all your son's distemper.

Queen. I doubt it is no other but the main,
        His father's death and our o'erhasty marriage.

King. Well, we shall sift him.

42 *still* always   52 *fruit* dessert   53 *grace* honor   56 *doubt* suspect

Enter Ambassadors (Voltemand and Cornelius), with
    Polonius.

                              Welcome, my good friends.
    Say, Voltemand, what from our brother Norway?
Voltemand. Most fair return of greetings and desires.   60
    Upon our first, he sent out to suppress
    His nephew's levies, which to him appeared
    To be a preparation 'gainst the Polack,
    But better looked into, he truly found
    It was against your highness, whereat grieved.   65
    That so his sickness, age, and impotence
    Was falsely borne in hand, sends out arrests
    On Fortinbras; which he in brief obeys,
    Receives rebuke from Norway, and in fine
    Makes vow before his uncle never more   70
    To give th' assay of arms against your majesty.
    Whereon old Norway, overcome with joy,
    Gives him threescore thousand crowns in annual
        fee
    And his commission to employ those soldiers,
    So levied as before, against the Polack,   75
    With an entreaty, herein further shown,
                                        Gives a paper
    That it might please you to give quiet pass
    Through your dominions for this enterprise,
    On such regards of safety and allowance
    As therein are set down.
King.   It likes us well;   80
    And at our more considered time we'll read,
    Answer, and think upon this business.
    Meantime we thank you for your well-took labor.
    Go to your rest; at night we'll feast together.
    Most welcome home!   *Exit Ambassadors.*
Polonius.   This business is well ended.   85

61 *our first* our first words about the matter 67 *borne in hand* deceived 69 *in fine* in the end 71 *assay* trial 79 *regards* terms 81
considered time convenient time for consideration

My liege and madam, to expostulate
What majesty should be, what duty is,
Why day is day, night night, and time is time,
Were nothing but to waste night, day, and time.
90   Therefore, since brevity is the soul of wit,
And tediousness the limbs and outward flourishes,
I will be brief. Your noble son is mad.
Mad call I it, for, to define true madness,
What is't but to be nothing else but mad?
But let that go.
95 *Queen.*   More matter, with less art.
Polonius. Madam, I swear I use no art at all.
That he is mad, 'tis true: 'tis true 'tis pity,
And pity 'tis 'tis true — a foolish figure.
But farewell it, for I will use no art.
100   Mad let us grant him then, and now remains
That we find out the cause of this effect
Or rather say, the cause of this defect,
For this effect defective comes by cause.
Thus it remains, and the remainder thus.
105   Perpend.
I have a daughter (have while she is mine),
Who in her duty and obedience, mark,
Hath given me this. Now gather, and surmise.
                                    Reads the letter.
"To the celestial, and my soul's idol, the most beau-
110 tified Ophelia," —
That's an ill phrase, a vile phrase; "beautified" is a
vile phrase. But you shall hear. Thus: *Reads.*
"In her excellent white bosom, these, &c."
Queen. Came this from Hamlet to her?
115 *Polonius.* Good madam, stay awhile. I will be faithful.
                                              Reads.
            "Doubt thou the stars are fire;
                Doubt that the sun doth move;
                Doubt truth to be a liar;

---

86 *expostulate* discuss   90 *wit* understanding   98 *figure* figure in rhe-
toric   105 *Perpend* ponder   118 *Doubt* suspect

But never doubt I love.

"O dear Ophelia, I am ill at these numbers. I   120
have not art to reckon my groans, but that I love
thee best, O most best, believe it. Adieu.

"Thine evermore, most dear lady,
whilst this machine is to him, HAMLET."

This in obedience hath my daughter shown me,   125
And more above hath his solicitings,
As they fell out by time, by means, and place,
All given to mine ear.

King.   But how hath she
Received his love?

Polonius.   What do you think of me?

King. As of a man faithful and honorable.   130

Polonius. I would fain prove so. But what might you
    think,
When I had seen this hot love on the wing
(As I perceived it, I must tell you that,
Before my daughter told me), what might you
Or my dear majesty your queen here, think,   135
If I had played the desk or table book,
Or given my heart a winking, mute and dumb,
Or looked upon this love with idle sight?
What might you think? No, I went round to work
And my young mistress thus I did bespeak: 140
"Lord Hamlet is a prince, out of thy star.
This must not be." And then I prescripts gave her,
That she should lock herself from his resort,
Admit no messengers, receive no tokens.
Which done, she took the fruits of my advice,   145
And he, repellèd, a short tale to make,
Fell into a sadness, then into a fast,
Thence to a watch, thence into a weakness,
Thence to a lightness, and, by this declension,

120 *numbers* verses   124 *machine* body   *to* attached to   126 *above* besides   136 *desk or table book* i.e. silent receiver   137 *winking* i.e.
closed by heart to   139 *round* roundly, plainly   141 *star* condition determined by stellar influence   142 *prescripts* instructions   148 *watch*
sleepless state   149 *lightness* lightheadedness

150   Into the madness wherein now he raves,
         And all we mourn for.
    King.   Do you think 'tis this?
    Queen. It may be, very like.
    Polonius. Hath there been such a time — I would
         fain know that —
         That I have positively said " 'Tis so,"
         When it proved otherwise?
155 *King.*   Not that I know.
    Polonius. (*pointing to his head and shoulder*) Take
         this from this, if this be otherwise.
         If circumstances lead me, I will find
         Where truth is hid, though it were hid indeed
         Within the center.
    King.   How may we try it further?
    Polonius. You know sometimes he walks for hours
160   together
         Here in the lobby.
    Queen.   So he does indeed.
    Polonius. At such a time I'll loose my daughter to
         him.
         Be you and I behind an arras then.
         Mark the encounter. If he love her not,
165   And be not from his reason fallen thereon,
         Let me be no assistant for a state
         But keep a farm and carters.
    King.   We will try it.

              Enter Hamlet reading a book.

    Queen. But look where sadly the poor wretch comes
         reading.
    Polonius. Anyway, I do beseech you both, away.
                   Exit King and Queen with Attendants.

---

159 *center* center of the Ptolemaic universe where the Earth is believed
to be the center of the universe, with the sun, moon, and planets revolving around it 163 *arras* hanging tapestry 165 *thereon* on that
account

I'll board him presently. O, give me leave.   170
How does my good Lord Hamlet?

Hamlet. Well, God-a-mercy.

Polonius. Do you know me, my lord?

Hamlet. Excellent well. You are a fishmonger.   175

Polonius. Not I, my lord.

Hamlet. Then I would you were so honest a man.

Polonius. Honest, my lord?

Hamlet. Ay, sir. To be honest, as this world goes, is
    to be one man picked out of ten thousand.

Polonius. That's very true, my lord.   180

Hamlet. For if the sun breed maggots in a dead dog,
    being a good kissing carrion — Have you a daugh-
    ter?

Polonius. I have, my lord.

Hamlet. Let her not walk i' th' sun. Conception is a
    blessing, but as your daughter may conceive, friend, 185
    look to't.

Polonius. (*aside*) How say you by that? Still harping
    on my daughter. Yet he knew me not at first. 'A
    said I was a fishmonger. 'A is far gone, far gone.
    And truly in my youth I suffered much extremity   190
    for love, very near this. I'll speak to him again. —
    What do you read, my lord?

Hamlet. Words, words, words.

Polonius. What is the matter, my lord?

Hamlet. Between who?   195

Polonius. I mean the matter that you read, my lord.

Hamlet. Slanders, sir, for the satirical rogue says here
    that old men have grey beards, that their faces are
    wrinkled, their eyes purging thick amber and plum-
    tree gum, and that they have a plentiful lack of   200
    wit, together with most weak hams. All which, sir,
    though I most powerfully and potently believe, yet
    I hold it not honesty to have it thus set down, for

---

170 *board* accost *presently* at once   172 *God-a-mercy* thank you
(literally, "God have mercy!")   174 *fishmonger* seller of prostitutes,
procurer (a cant term used here with a glance at the fishing Polonius
is doing when he offers Ophelia as bait)   182 *good kissing carrion*
good bit of flesh for kissing   195 *Between who* matter for a quarrel
between what persons (Hamlet's willful misunderstanding)

you yourself, sir, should be old as I am if, like a
205 crab, you could go backward.

Polonius. (*aside*) Though this be madness, yet there
is method in't. — Will you walk out of the air, my
lord?

Hamlet. Into my grave?

210 *Polonius.* Indeed, that's out of the air. (*aside*) How
pregnant sometimes his replies are! a happiness
that often madness hits on, which reason and sanity
could not so prosperously be delivered of. I will
leave him and suddenly contrive the means of
215 meeting between him and my daughter. — My
honorable lord, I will most humbly take my leave
of you.

Hamlet. You cannot, sir, take from me anything that
I will more willingly part withal — except my life,
220 except my life, except my life.

Enter Guildenstern and Rosencrantz.

Polonius. Fare you well, my lord.

Hamlet. These tedious old fools!

Polonius. You go to seek the Lord Hamlet. There he
is.

Rosencrantz. (*to Polonius*) God save you, sir!

Exit Polonius.

225 *Guildenstern.* My honored lord!

Rosencrantz. My most dear lord!

Hamlet. My excellent good friends! How dost thou,
Guildenstern? Ah, Rosencrantz! Good lads, how
do ye both?

230 *Rosencrantz.* As the indifferent children of the earth.

Guilderstern. Happy in that we are not over-happy.
On Fortune's cap we are not the very button.

Hamlet. Nor the soles of her shoe?

Rosencrantz. Neither, my lord.

Hamlet. Then you live about her waist, or in the   235
    middle of her favors?

Guildenstern. Faith, her privates we.

Hamlet. In the secret parts of Fortune? O, most true!
    she is a strumpet. What news?

Rosencrantz. None, my lord, but that the world's   240
    grown honest.

Hamlet. Then is doomsday near. But your news is not
    true. Let me question more in particular. What
    have you, my good friends, deserved at the hands
    of Fortune that she sends you to prison hither?   245

Guildenstern. Prison, my lord?

Hamlet. Denmark's a prison.

Rosencrantz. Then is the world one.

Hamlet. A goodly one; in which there are many con-
    fines, wards, and dungeons, Denmark being one o'   250
    th' worst.

Rosencrantz. We think not so, my lord.

Hamlet. Why, then 'tis none to you, for there is noth-
    ing either good or bad but thinking makes it so. To
    me it is a prison.   255

Rosencrantz. Why, then your ambition makes it one.
    'Tis too narrow for your mind.

Hamlet. O God, I could be bounded in a nutshell
    and count myself a king of infinite space, were it
    not that I have bad dreams.   260

Guildenstern. Which dreams indeed are ambition,
    for the very substance of the ambitious is merely
    the shadow of a dream.

Hamlet. A dream itself is but a shadow.

Rosencrantz. Truly, and I hold ambition of so airy   265
    and light a quality that it is but a shadow's shadow.

Hamlet. Then are our beggars bodies, and our mon-
    archs and outstretched heroes the beggars' shadows.

237 *privates* ordinary men in private, not public, life (with obvious
play upon the sexual term "private parts")   249–50 *confines* places of
imprisonment   250 *wards* cells   267 *bodies* solid substances, not shadows (because beggars lack ambition)   268 *outstretched* elongated as
shadows (with a corollary implication of far reaching with respect to
the ambitions that make both heroes and monarchs into shadows)

        Shall we to th' court? for, by my fay, I cannot rea-
270   son.

     Both. We'll wait upon you.

     Hamlet. No such matter. I will not sort you with the
        rest of my servants, for, to speak to you like an
        honest man, I am most dreadfully attended. But
275   in the beaten way of friendship, what make you at
        Elsinore?

     Rosencrantz. To visit you, my lord; no other occasion.

     Hamlet. Beggar that I am, I am even poor in thanks,
        but I thank you; and sure, dear friends, my thanks
280   are too dear a halfpenny. Were you not sent for? Is
        it your own inclining? Is it a free visitation? Come,
        come, deal justly with me. Come, come. Nay,
        speak.

     Guildenstern. What should we say, my lord?

285   *Hamlet.* Why, anything — but to th' purpose. You
        were sent for, and there is a kind of confession in
        your looks, which your modesties have not craft
        enough to color. I know the good king and queen
        have sent for you.

290   *Rosencrantz.* To what end, my lord?

     Hamlet. That you must teach me. But let me con-
        jure you by the rights of our fellowship, by the
        consonancy of our youth, by the obligation of our
        ever-presented love, and by what more dear a better
295   proposer can charge you withal, be even and direct
        with me whether you were sent for or no.

     Rosencrantz. (*aside to Guildenstern*) What say you?

     Hamlet. (*aside*) Nay then, I have an eye of you. — If
        you love me, hold not off.

300   *Guildenstern.* My lord, we were sent for.

     Hamlet. I will tell you why. So shall my anticipation
        prevent your discovery, and your secrecy to the king
        and queen moult no feather. I have of late — but

269 *fay* faith   271 *wait upon* attend   275 *make* do   280 *a halfpenny* at
a halfpenny   293 *consonancy* accord (in sameness of age)   295 *proposer* propounder   *withal* with   *even* straight   302 *prevent* forestall
discovery disclosure   303 *moult no feather* be left whole

wherefore I know not — lost all my mirth, forgone
all custom of exercises; and indeed, it goes so heav-   305
ily with my disposition that this goodly frame the
earth seems to me a sterile promontory; this most
excellent canopy, the air, look you, this brave o'er-
hanging firmament, this majestical roof fretted
with golden fire — why, it appeareth nothing to me   310
but a foul and pestilent congregation of vapors.
What a piece of work is a man, how noble in reason, how infinite in faculties, in form and moving
how express and admirable, in action how like an
angel, in apprehension how like a god: the beauty   315
of the world, the paragon of animals! And yet to
me what is this quintessence of dust? Man delights
not me — nor woman neither, though by your smiling you seem to say so.

Rosencrantz. My lord, there was no such stuff in my   320
thoughts.

Hamlet. Why did ye laugh then, when I said "Man
delights not me"?

Rosencrantz. To think, my lord, if you delight not in
man, what lenten entertainment the players shall   325
receive from you. We coted them on the way, and
hither are they coming to offer you service.

Hamlet. He that plays the king shall be welcome —
his majesty shall have tribute of me, the adven-
turous knight shall use his foil and target, the lover   330
shall not sigh gratis, the humorous man shall end
his part in peace, the clown shall make those laugh
whose lungs are tickle o' th' sere, and the lady shall
say her mind freely, or the blank verse shall halt
for't. What players are they?   335

Rosencrantz. Even those you were wont to take such
delight in, the tragedians of the city.

---

309 *firmament* sky *fretted* decorated with fretwork 314 *express* well
framed 317 *quintessence* fifth or last and finest essence (an alchemical
term) 325 *lenten* scanty 326 *coted* overtook 330 *foil and target*
sword and shield 331 *humorous man* eccentric character dominated
by one of the humors 333 *tickle o' th' sere* hair-triggered for the dis-
charge of laughter (*sere*: part of a gunlock) 334 *halt* go lame

Hamlet. How chances it they travel? Their residence,
both in reputation and profit, was better both ways.

340 *Rosencrantz.* I think their inhibition comes by the
means of the later innovation.

Hamlet. Do they hold the same estimation they did
when I was in the city? Are they so followed?

Rosencrantz. No indeed, are they not.

345 *Hamlet.* How comes it? Do they grow rusty?

Rosencrantz. Nay, their endeavor keeps in the wonted
pace, but there is, sir, an eyrie of children, little
eyases, that cry out on the top of question and are
most tyrannically clapped for't. These are now the

350 fashion, and so berattle the common stages (so they
call them) that many wearing rapiers are afraid of
goosequills and dare scarce come thither.

Hamlet. What, are they children? Who maintains
'em? How are they escoted? Will they pursue the

355 quality no longer than they can sing? Will they not
say afterwards, if they should grow themselves to
common players (as it is most like, if their means
are no better), their writers do them wrong to make
them exclaim against their own succession?

360 *Rosencrantz.* Faith, there has been much to do on
both sides, and the nation holds it no sin to tarre
them to controversy. There was, for a while, no
money bid for argument unless the poet and the
player went to cuffs in the question.

365 *Hamlet.* Is't possible?

Guildenstern. O, there has been much throwing
about of brains.

338 *residence* residing at the capital 340 *inhibition* impediment to
acting in residence 341 *innovation* new fashion of having companies
of boy actors play on the "private" stage; political upheaval
347 *eyrie* nest 348 *eyases* nestling hawks *on the top of question*
above others on matter of dispute 350 *berattle* berate *common
stages* "public" theatres of the "common" players, who were organized
in companies mainly composed of adult actors (allusion being made
to the "War of the Theatres" in Shakespeare's London) 352 *goosequills* pens (of satirists who made out that the London public stage
showed low taste) 354 *escoted* supported 355 *quality* profession of
acting *sing* i.e. with unchanged voices 361 *tarre* incite 363 *argument* matter of a play

Hamlet. Do the boys carry it away?

Rosencrantz. Ay, that they do, my lord — Hercules
and his load too.   370

Hamlet. It is not very strange, for my uncle is King
of Denmark, and those that would make mows at
him while my father lived give twenty, forty, fifty,
a hundred ducats apiece for his picture in little.
'Sblood, there is something in this more than   375
natural, if philosophy could find it out.

A flourish.

Guildenstern. There are the players.

Hamlet. Gentlemen, you are welcome to Elsinore.
Your hands, come then. Th' appurtenance of welcome is fashion and ceremony. Let me comply   380
with you in this garb, lest my extent to the players
(which I tell you must show fairly outwards) should
more appear like entertainment than yours. You are
welcome. But my uncle-father and aunt-mother are
deceived.   385

Guildenstern. In what, my dear lord?

Hamlet. I am but mad north-north-west. When the
wind is southerly I know a hawk from a handsaw.

Enter Polonius.

Polonius. Well be with you, gentlemen.

Hamlet. Hark you, Guildenstern — and you too —   390
at each ear a hearer. That great baby you see there
is not yet out of his swaddling clouts.

Rosencrantz. Happily he is the second time come to
them, for they say an old man is twice a child.

370 *load* i.e. the whole world (with a topical reference to the sign of
the Globe Theatre, a representation of Hercules bearing the world on
his shoulders)   372 *mows* grimaces   375 *'Sblood* by God's blood, a
common Elizabethan oath   381 *garb* fashion   *extent* showing of welcome   388 *hawk* mattock or pickaxe (also called "hack"; here used
apparently with a play on *hawk:* a bird)   *handsaw* carpenter's tool
(apparently with a play on some corrupt form of *hernshaw:* heron, a
bird often hunted with the hawk)   392 *clauts* clothes   393 *Happily*
haply, perhaps

395 *Hamlet.* I will prophesy he comes to tell me of the
       players. Mark it. — You say right, sir; a Monday
       morning, 'twas then indeed.

Polonius. My lord, I have news to tell you.

Hamlet. My lord, I have news to tell you. When
400   Roscius was an actor in Rome —

Polonius. The actors are come hither, my lord.

Hamlet. Buzz, buzz.

Polonius. Upon my honor —

Hamlet. Then came each actor on his ass —

405 *Polonius.* The best actors in the world, either for
       tragedy, comedy, history, pastoral, pastoral-comical,
       historical-pastoral, scene individable, or poem un-
       limited. Seneca cannot be too heavy, nor Plautus
410   too light. For the law of writ and the liberty, these
       are the only men.

Hamlet. O Jephthah, judge of Israel, what a treasure
       hadst thou!

Polonius. What treasure had he, my lord?

415 *Hamlet.* Why,

> "One fair laughter, and no more,
> The which he lovèd passing well."

Polonius. (*aside*) Still on my daughter.

Hamlet. Am I not i' th' right, old Jephthah?

420 *Polonius.* If you call me Jephthah, my lord, I have a
       daughter that I love passing well.

Hamlet. Nay, that follows not.

Polonius. What follows then, my lord?

Hamlet. Why,

> "As by lot, God wot,"·

425   and then, you know,

> "It came to pass, as most like it was."

400 *Roscius* the greatest of Roman comic actors   408 *scene individ-able* drama observing the unities   *poem unlimited* drama not observing the unities   409 *Seneca* Roman writer of tragedies   *Plautus* Roman writer of comedies   410 *law of writ* orthodoxy determined by critical rules of the drama   *liberty* freedom from such orthodoxy   412 *Jephthah* the compelled sacrificer of a dearly beloved daughter (Judges II)   417 *passing* surpassingly (verses quoted being from a ballad on Jephthah)

The first row of the pious chanson will show you
more, for look where my abridgment comes.

Enter the Players.

You are welcome, masters, welcome, all. — I am
glad to see thee well. — Welcome, good friends. —   430
O, old friend, why, thy face is valanced since I saw
thee last. Com'st thou to beard me in Denmark?
— What, my young lady and mistress? By'r Lady,
your ladyship is nearer to heaven than when I saw
you last by the altitude of a chopine. Pray God   435
your voice, like a piece of uncurrent gold, be not
cracked within the ring. — Masters, you are all
welcome. We'll e'en to't like French falconers, fly
at anything we see. We'll have a speech straight.
Come, give us a taste of your quality. Come, a   440
passionate speech.

Player. What speech, my good lord?

Hamlet. I heard thee speak me a speech once, but it
was never acted, or if it was, not above once, for
the play, I remember, pleased not the million;   445
'twas caviary to the general, but it was (as I received
it, and others, whose judgments in such matters
cried in the top of mine) an excellent play, well
digested in the scenes, set down with as much
modesty as cunning. I remember one said there   450
were no sallets in the lines to make the matter
savory, nor no matter in the phrase that might in-
dict the author of affectation, but called it an
honest method, as wholesome as sweet, and by very
much more handsome than fine. One speech in't I   455
chiefly loved. 'Twas Aeneas' tale to Dido, and there-
about of it especially where he speaks of Priam's

427 *row* stanza *chanson* song 428 *my abridgment* that which shortens my talk 431 *valanced* fringed (with a beard) 433 *young lady* boy
who plays women's parts 435 *chopine* women's thick-soled shoe 436
uncurrent not legal tender 437 *within the ring* from the edge through
the line circling the design on the coin (with a play on *ring:* a sound)
446 *caviary* caviare *general* multitude 448 *in the top of* more
authoritatively than 451 *sallets* salads, highly seasoned passages

slaughter. If it live in your memory, begin at this
line — let me see, let me see:

460   "The rugged Pyrrhus, like th' Hyrcanian beast
        — "

'Tis not so; it begins with Pyrrhus:

        "The rugged Pyrrhus, he whose sable arms,
        Black as his purpose, did the night resemble
465   When he lay couchèd in the ominous horse,
        Hath now this dread and black complexion
            smeared
        With heraldry more dismal. Head to foot
        Now is he total gules, horridly tricked
        With blood of fathers, mothers, daughters, sons
470   Baked and impasted with the parching streets,
        That lend a tyrannous and a damnèd light
        To their lord's murther. Roasted in wrath and
            fire,
        And thus o'ersizèd with coagulate gore,
        With eyes like carbuncles, the hellish Pyrrhus
475   Old grandsire Priam seeks."

So, proceed you.

Polonius. Fore God, my lord, well spoken, with good
accent and good discretion.

Player.   "Anon he finds him,
        Striking too short at Greeks. His antique sword,
480   Rebellious to his arm, lies where it falls,
        Repugnant to command. Unequal matched,
        Pyrrhus at Priam drives, in rage strikes wide,
        But with the whiff and wind of his fell sword
        Th' unnervèd father falls. Then senseless Ilium,
485   Seeming to feel this blow, with flaming top
        Stoops to his base, and with a hideous crash

___

457-58 *Priam's slaughter* i.e. at the fall of Troy   460 *Hyrcanian beast*
tiger   463 *sable* black   465 *ominous* fateful   *horse* the wooden horse
by which the Greeks gained entrance to Troy   467 *dismal* ill-omened
468 *gules* red (heraldic term)   *tricked* decorated in color (heraldic
term)   470 *parching* i.e. because Troy was burning   473 *o'ersizèd*
covered as with size, a glutinous material used for filling pores of
plaster, etc.   *coagulate* clotted   483 *fell* cruel   484 *senseless* without
feeling   486 *his* its

Takes prisoner Pyrrhus' ear. For lo! his sword,
Which was declining on the milky head
Of reverend Priam, seemed i' th' air to stick
So as a painted tyrant Pyrrhus stood,   490
And like a neutral to his will and matter
Did nothing.
But as we often see, against some storm,
A silence in the heavens, the rack stand still,
The bold winds speechless, and the orb below   495
As hush as death, anon the dreadful thunder
Doth rend the region, so after Pyrrhus' pause,
Arousèd vengeance sets him new awork,
And never did the Cyclops' hammers fall
On Mars's armor, forged for proof eterne,   500
With less remorse than Pyrrhus' bleeding sword
Now falls on Priam.
Out, out, thou strumpet Fortune! All you gods,
In general synod take away her power,
Break all the spokes and fellies from her wheel, 505
And bowl the round nave down the hill of
    heaven,
As low as to the fiends."

Polonius. This is too long.

Hamlet. It shall to the barber's, with your beard. —
Prithee say on. He's for a jig or a tale of bawdry, 510
or he sleeps. Say on; come to Hecuba.

Player. "But who (ah woe!) had seen the mobled
    queen — "

Hamlet. "The mobled queen"?

Polonius. That's good. "Mobled queen" is good.   515

Player. "Run barefoot up and down, threat'ning the
    flames

---

490 *painted* pictured 491 *will and matter* purpose and its realization
(between which he stands motionless) 493 *against* just before 494
rack clouds 497 *region* sky 499 *Cyclops* gigantic workmen with one
huge eye in the middle of their foreheads, who made armor in the
smithy of Vulcan 500 *proof eterne* eternal protection 505 *fellies* seg-
ments of the rim 506 *nave* hub 510 *jig* short comic piece with singing and dancing often presented after a play 512 *mobled* muffled

With bisson rheum; a clout upon that head
Where late the diadem stood, and for a robe,
About her lank and all o'erteemèd loins,
520   A blanket in the alarm of fear caught up —
Who this had seen, with tongue in venom
    steeped
'Gainst Fortune's state would treason have pro-
    nounced.
But if the gods themselves did see her then,
When she saw Pyrrhus make malicious sport
525   In mincing with his sword her husband's limbs,
The instant burst of clamor that she made
(Unless things mortal move them not at all)
Would have made milch the burning eyes of
    heaven
And passion in the gods."

530 *Polonius.* Look, whe'r he has not turned his color,
and has tears in's eyes. Prithee no more.

Hamlet. 'Tis well. I'll have thee speak out the rest of
this soon. — Good my lord, will you see the players well bestowed? Do you hear? Let them be well
535   used, for they are the abstract and brief chronicles
of the time. After your death you were better have
a bad epitaph than their ill report while you live.

Polonius. My lord, I will use them according to their
desert.

540 *Hamlet.* God's bodkin, man, much better! Use every
man after his desert, and who shall scape whipping?
Use them after your own honor and dignity. The
less they deserve, the more merit is in your bounty.
Take them in.

545 *Polonius.* Come, sirs.

Hamlet. Follow him, friends. We'll hear a play tomor-

---

517 *bisson rheum* blinding tears   *clout* cloth   519 *o'erteemèd* over-
productive of children   522 *state* government of worldly events   528
milch tearful (milk-giving)   *eyes* i.e. stars   530 *whe'r* whether   534
bestowed lodged   540 *God's bodkin* by God's little body

row. (*aside to Player*) Dost thou hear me, old
friend? Can you play *The Murther of Gonzago?*

Player. Ay, my lord.

Hamlet. We'll ha't tomorrow night. You could for a   550
need study a speech of some dozen or sixteen lines
which I would set down and insert in't, could you
not?

Player. Ay, my lord.

Hamlet. Very well. Follow that lord, and look you   555
mock him not. — My good friends, I'll leave you
till night. You are welcome to Elsinore.

    Exit Polonius and Players.

Rosencrantz. Good my lord.

                  Exit Polonius and Players.

Hamlet. Ay, so, God bye to you. — Now I am alone.
O, what a rogue and peasant slave am I!   560
Is it not monstrous that this player here,
But in a fiction, in a dream of passion,
Could force his soul so to his own conceit
That from her working all his visage wanned,
Tears in his eyes, distraction in his aspect,   565
A broken voice, and his whole function suiting
With forms to his conceit? And all for nothing,
For Hecuba!
What's Hecuba to him, or he to Hecuba,
That he should weep for her? What would he do   570
Had he the motive and the cue for passion
That I have? He would drown the stage with tears
And cleave the general ear with horrid speech,
Make mad the guilty and appal the free,
Confound the ignorant, and amaze indeed   575
The very faculties of eyes and ears.
Yet I,

---

563 *conceit* conception, idea   566 *function* action of bodily powers

A dull and muddy-mettled rascal, peak
Like John-a-dreams, unpregnant of my cause,
580   And can say nothing. No, not for a king,
Upon whose property and most dear life
A damned defeat was made. Am I a coward?
Who calls me villain? breaks my pate across?
Plucks off my beard and blows it in my face?
585   Tweaks me by the nose? gives me the lie i' th' throat
As deep as to the lungs? Who does me this?
Ha, 'swounds, I should take it, for it cannot be
But I am pigeon-livered and lack gall
To make oppression bitter, or ere this
590   I should ha' fatted all the region kites
With this slave's offal. Bloody, bawdy villain!
Remorseless, treacherous, lecherous, kindless
    villain!
O, vengeance!
Why, what an ass am I! This is most brave,
595   That I, the son of a dear father murthered,
Prompted to my revenge by heaven and hell,
Must like a whore unpack my heart with words
And fall a-cursing like a very drab,
A stallion! Fie upon't, foh! About, my brains.
600   Hum —
I have heard that guilty creatures sitting at a play
Have by the very cunning of the scene
Been struck so to the soul that presently
They have proclaimed their malefactions.
605   For murther, though it have no tongue, will speak
With most miraculous organ. I'll have these players
Play something like the murther of my father
Before mine uncle. I'll observe his looks.
I'll tent him to the quick. If 'a do blench,

---

578 *muddy-mettled* dull-spirited *peak* mope 579 *John-a-dreams* a
sleepy dawdler *unpregnant* barren of realization 587 *'swounds* by
God's wounds 588 *pigeon-livered* of dovelike gentleness 590 *region
kites* kites of the air 591 *offal* guts 592 *kindless* unnatural 599
stallion prostitute (male or female) 603 *presently* immediately 609
tent probe *blench* flinch

I know my course. The spirit that I have seen   610
May be a devil, and the devil hath power
T' assume a pleasing shape, yea, and perhaps
Out of my weakness and my melancholy,
As he is very potent with such spirits,
Abuses me to damn me. I'll have grounds   615
More relative than this. The play's the thing
Wherein I'll catch the conscience of the king.   *Exit.*

615 *Abuses* deludes   616 *relative* pertinent

ACT III, SCENE I

*Enter King, Queen, Polonius, Ophelia,
Rosencrantz, Guildenstern, Lords.*

King. And can you by no drift of conference
    Get from him why he puts on this confusion,
    Grating so harshly all his days of quiet
    With turbulent and dangerous lunacy?
Rosencrantz. He does confess he feels himself dis-
5   tracted,
    But from what cause 'a will by no means speak.
Guildenstern. Nor do we find him forward to be
    sounded,
    But with a crafty madness keeps aloof
    When we would bring him on to some confession
    Of his true state.
10 *Queen.*   Did he receive you well?
Rosencrantz. Most like a gentleman.
Guildenstern. But with much forcing of his disposi-
    tion.
Rosencrantz. Niggard of question, but of our demands
    Most free in his reply.
Queen.   Did you assay him
    To any pastime?
15 *Rosencrantz.* Madam, it so fell out that certain players

III, i, 1 *drift of conference* direction of conversation 14 *assay* try to
win

74

We o'erraught on the way. Of these we told him,
And there did seem in him a kind of joy
To hear of it. They are here about the court,
And, as I think, they have already order   20
This night to play before him.
Polonius.   'Tis most true,
And he beseeched me to entreat your majesties
To hear and see the matter.
King. With all my heart, and it doth much content me
To hear him so inclined.   25
Good gentlemen, give him a further edge
And drive his purpose into these delights.
Rosencrantz. We shall, my lord.
                    Exit Rosencrantz and Guildenstern.
King.   Sweet Gertrude, leave us too,
For we have closely sent for Hamlet hither,
That he, as 'twere by accident, may here   30
Affront Ophelia.
Her father and myself (lawful espials)
Will so bestow ourselves that, seeing unseen,
We may of their encounter frankly judge
And gather by him, as he is behaved,   35
If't be th' affliction of his love or no
That thus he suffers for.
Queen.   I shall obey you. —
And for your part, Ophelia, I do wish
That your good beauties be the happy cause
Of Hamlet's wildness. So shall I hope your virtues 40
Will bring him to his wonted way again,
To both your honors.
Ophelia.   Madame, I wish it may.
                                Exit Queen.
Polonius. Ophelia, walk you here. — Gracious, so
    please you,
We will bestow ourselves. — (*to Ophelia*) Read on
    his book,

45   That show of such an exercise may color
        Your loneliness. We are oft to blame in this,
        'Tis too much proved, that with devotion's visage
        And pious action we do sugar o'er
        The devil himself.

King.   (aside) O, 'tis too true.
        How smart a lash that speech doth give my con-
50   science!
        The harlot's cheek, beautied with plast'ring art,
        Is not more ugly to the thing that helps it
        Than is my deed to my most painted word.
        O heavy burthen!

55 Polonius. I hear him coming. Let's withdraw, my lord.
                                        Exit King and Polonius.

                        Enter Hamlet.

    Hamlet. To be, or not to be — that is the question:
        Whether 'tis nobler in the mind to suffer
        The slings and arrows of outrageous fortune
        Or to take arms against a sea of troubles
60   And by opposing end them. To die, to sleep —
        No more — and by a sleep to say we end
        The heartache, and the thousand natural shocks
        That flesh is heir to. 'Tis a consummation
        Devoutly to be wished. To die, to sleep —
65   To sleep — perchance to dream: ay, there's the rub,
        For in that sleep of death what dreams may come
        When we have shuffled off this mortal coil,
        Must give us pause. There's the respect
        That makes calamity of so long life.
70   For who would bear the whips and scorns of time,
        Th' oppressor's wrong, the proud man's contumely
        The pangs of despised love, the law's delay,
        The insolence of office, and the spurns

45 *exercise* religious exercise (the book being obviously one of devotion)   *color* give an appearance of naturalness to   52 *to* compared to
65 *rub* obstacle (literally, obstruction encountered by a bowler's ball)
67 *shuffled off* cast off as an encumbrance   *coil* to-do, turmoil   68 *respect* consideration   69 *of so long life* so long-lived

That patient merit of th' unworthy takes,
When he himself might his quietus make   75
With a bare bodkin? Who would fardels bear,
To grunt and sweat under a weary life,
But that the dread of something after death,
The undiscovered country, from whose bourn
No traveller returns, puzzles the will,   80
And makes us rather bear those ills we have
Than fly to others that we know not of?
Thus conscience does make cowards of us all,
And thus the native hue of resolution
Is sicklied o'er with the pale cast of thought,   85
And enterprises of great pitch and moment
With this regard their currents turn awry
And lose the name of action. — Soft you now,
The fair Ophelia! — Nymph, in thy orisons
Be all my sins remembered.

Ophelia.   Good my lord,   90
How does your honor for this many a day?

Hamlet. I humbly thank you, well, well, well.

Ophelia. My lord, I have remembrances of yours
That I have longèd long to redeliver.
I pray you, now receive them.

Hamlet.   No. not I,   95
I never gave you aught.

Ophelia. My honored lord, you know right well you
          did,
And with them words of so sweet breath composed
As made the things more rich. Their perfume lost,
Take these again, for to the noble mind   100
Rich gifts wax poor when givers prove unkind.
There, my lord.

Hamlet. Ha, ha! Are you honest?

Ophelia. My lord?

Hamlet. Are you fair?   105

---

75 *quietus* settlement (literally, release from debt) 76 *bodkin* dagger
fardels burdens 79 *bourn* confine, region 86 *pitch* height (of a soaring falcon's flight) 87 *regard* consideration 89 *orisons* prayers (because of the book of devotion she reads)

Ophelia. What means your lordship?

Hamlet. That if you be honest and fair, your honesty
should admit no discourse to your beauty.

Ophelia. Could beauty, my lord, have better com-
110 merce than with honesty?

Hamlet. Ay, truly; for the power of beauty will sooner
transform honesty from what it is to a bawd than
the force of honesty can translate beauty into his
likeness. This was sometime a paradox, but now
115 the time gives it proof. I did love you once.

Ophelia. Indeed, my lord, you made me believe so.

Hamlet. You should not have believed me, for virtue
cannot so inoculate our old stock but we shall relish
of it. I loved you not.

120 *Ophelia.* I was the more deceived.

Hamlet. Get thee to a nunnery. Why wouldst thou be
a breeder of sinners? I am myself indifferent honest,
but yet I could accuse me of such things that it
were better my mother had not borne me: I am
125 very proud, revengeful, ambitious, with more of-
fenses at my beck than I have thoughts to put them
in, imagination to give them shape, or time to act
them in. What should such fellows as I do crawling
between earth and heaven? We are arrant knaves
130 all; believe none of us. Go thy ways to a nunnery.
Where's your father?

Ophelia. At home, my lord.

Hamlet. Let the doors be shut upon him, that he may
play the fool nowhere but in's own house. Farewell.

135 *Ophelia.* O, help him, you sweet heavens!

Hamlet. If thou dost marry, I'll give thee this plague
for thy dowry: be thou as chaste as ice, as pure as
snow, thou shalt not escape calumny. Get thee to a
nunnery. Go, farewell. Or if thou wilt needs marry,
140 marry a fool, for wise men know well enough what

---

103 *honest* chaste   109–10 *commerce* intercourse   114 *paradox* idea
contrary to common opinion   118 *inoculate* graft   *relish* have a flavor
(because of original sin)   122 *indifferent honest* moderately respect-
able

monsters you make of them. To a nunnery, go, and
quickly too. Farewell.

Ophelia. O heavenly powers, restore him!

Hamlet. I have heard of your paintings too, well
enough. God hath given you one face, and you make   145
yourselves another. You jig, you amble, and you
lisp; you nickname God's creatures and make your
wantonness your ignorance. Go to, I'll no more
on't; it hath made me mad. I say we will have no
more marriage. Those that are married already —   150
all but one — shall live. The rest shall keep as they
are. To a nunnery, go.   *Exit.*

Ophelia. O, what a noble mind is here o'erthrown!
The courtier's, soldier's, scholar's, eye, tongue,
    sword,
Th' expectancy and rose of the fair state,   155
The glass of fashion and the mould of form,
Th' observed of all observers, quite, quite down!
And I, of ladies most deject and wretched,
That sucked the honey of his music vows,
Now see that noble and most sovereign reason   160
Like sweet bells jangled, out of time and harsh,
That unmatched form and feature of blown youth
Blasted with ecstacy. O, woe is me
T' have seen what I have seen, see what I see!

Enter King and Polonius.

King. Love? His affections do not that way tend,   165
Nor what he spake, though it lacked form a little,
Was not like madness. There's something in his
    soul
O'er which his melancholy sits on brood,
And I do doubt the hatch and the disclose

141 *monsters* i.e. men wearing horns given by unfaithful wives,
cuckolds 148 *wantonness* affectation *your ignorance* a matter for
which you offer the excuse that you don't know any better 155 *expectancy and rose* fair hope 156 *glass* mirror 165 *affections* emotions
169 *doubt* fear

170 Will be some danger; which for to prevent,
I have in quick determination
Thus set it down: he shall with speed to England
For the demand of our neglected tribute,
Haply the seas, and countries different,
175 With variable objects, shall expel
This something-settled matter in his heart,
Whereon his brains still beating puts him thus
From fashion of himself. What think you on't?

Polonius. It shall do well. But yet do I believe
180 The origin and commencement of his grief
Sprung from neglected love. — How now, Ophelia?
You need not tell us what Lord Hamlet said.
We heard it all. — My lord, do as you please,
But if you hold it fit, after the play
185 Let his queen mother all alone entreat him
To show his grief. Let her be round with him,
And I'll be placed, so please you, in the ear
Of all their conference. If she find him not,
To England send him, or confine him where
Your wisdom best shall think.

190 *King.*   It shall be so.
Madness in great ones must not unwatched go.

Exit all.

❧

ACT III, SCENE II

Enter Hamlet and three of the Players.

Hamlet. Speak the speech, I pray you, as I pronounced
it to you, trippingly on the tongue. But if you

---

176 *something-settled* somewhat settled   186 *round* plain-spoken   III,
ii, 2 *trippingly* easily

mouth it, as many of our players do, I had as lief
the town crier spoke my lines. Nor do not saw the
air too much with your hand, thus, but use all   5
gently, for in the very torrent, tempest, and (as I
may say) whirlwind of your passion, you must ac-
quire and beget a temperance that may give it
smoothness. O, it offends me to the soul to hear a
robustious periwig-pated fellow tear a passion to   10
tatters, to very rags, to split the ears of the groundlings, who for the most part are capable of nothing
but inexplicable dumb shows and noise. I would
have such a fellow whipped for o'erdoing Termagant. It out-herods Herod. Pray you avoid it.   15

Player. I warrant your honor.

Hamlet. Be not too tame neither, but let your own
discretion be your tutor. Suit the action to the
word, the word to the action, with this special observance, that you o'erstep not the modesty of na-   20
ture. For anything so overdone is from the purpose
of playing, whose end, both at the first and now,
was and is, to hold, as 'twere, the mirror up to nature, to show virtue her own feature, scorn her own
image, and the very age and body of the time his   25
form and pressure. Now this overdone, or come
tardy off, though it make the unskillful laugh, cannot but make the judicious grieve, the censure of
the which one must in your allowance o'erweigh a
whole theatre of others. O, there be players that I   3
have seen play, and heard others praise, and that
highly (not to speak it profanely), that neither having th' accent of Christians, nor the gait of Christian, pagan, nor man, have so strutted and bellowed

10 *robustious* boisterous   *periwig-pated* wig-wearing (after the custom
of actors)   11-12 *groundlings* spectators who paid least and stood
on the ground in the pit or yard of the theatre   13 *dumb shows* actions without words, forecasting dramatic matter to follow (the play
presented later in this scene giving an old-fashioned example)   14-15
Termagant a Saracen "god" in medieval romance and drama   15
Herod the raging tyrant of old Biblical plays   21 *from* apart from
26 *pressure* impressed or printed character   26-27 *come tardy off*
brought off slowly and badly   28-29 *the censure of the which one* the
judgment of even one of whom

35   that I have thought some of Nature's journeymen
      had made men, and not made them well, they
      imitated humanity so abominably.

Player. I hope we have reformed that indifferently
      with us, sir.

40   *Hamlet.* O, reform it altogether! And let those that
      play your clowns speak no more than is set down for
      them, for there be of them that will themselves
      laugh, to set on some quantity of barren spectators
      to laugh too, though in the mean time some neces-
45   sary question of the play be then to be considered.
      That's villainous and shows a most pitiful ambition
      in the fool that uses it. Go make you ready.

                                    Exit Players.

Enter Polonius, Guildenstern, and Rosencrantz.

      How now, my lord? Will the king hear this piece of
      work?

50   *Polonius.* And the queen too, and that presently.
      Hamlet. Bid the players make haste.

                                    Exit Polonius.

      Will you two help to hasten them?
      Rosencrantz. Ay, my lord.

                        Exit Guildenstern and Rosencrantz.

      Hamlet. What, ho, Horatio!

Enter Horatio.

55   *Horatio.* Here, sweet lord, at your service.
      Hamlet. Horatio, thou art e'en as just a man
          As e'er my conversation coped withal.
      Horatio. O, my dear lord —
      Hamlet.   Nay, do not think I flatter.
          For what advancement may I hope from thee,

35 *journeymen* workmen not yet masters of their trade   38 *indifferently* fairly well   42 *of them* some of them   50 *presently* at once   57
conversaiton coped withal intercourse with men encountered

That no revenue hast but thy good spirits   60
To feed and clothe thee? Why should the poor be
    flattered?
No, let the candied tongue lick absurd pomp,
And crook the pregnant hinges of the knee
Where thrift may follow fawning. Dost thou hear?
Since my dear soul was mistress of her choice   65
And could of men distinguish her election,
S' hath sealed thee for herself, for thou hast been
As one in suff'ring all that suffers nothing,
A man that Fortune's buffets and rewards
Hast ta'en with equal thanks; and blest are those   70
Whose blood and judgment are so well commeddled
That they are not a pipe for Fortune's finger
To sound what stop she please. Give me that man
That is not passion's slave, and I will wear him
In my heart's core, ay, in my heart of heart,   75
As I do thee. Something too much of this —
There is a play tonight before the king.
One scene of it comes near the circumstance
Which I have told thee, of my father's death.
I prithee, when thou seest that act afoot,   80
Even with the very comment of thy soul
Observe my uncle. If his occulted guilt
Do not itself unkennel in one speech,
It is a damnèd ghost that we have seen,
And my imaginations are as foul   85
As Vulcan's stithy. Give him heedful note,
For I mine eyes will rivet to his face,
And after we will both our judgments join
In censure of his seeming.
Horatio.   Well, my lord.
If 'a steal aught the whilst this play is playing,   90
And scape detecting, I will pay the theft.

63 *pregnant* quick to move   64 *thrift* profit   67 *sealed* marked   71
blood passion   *commeddled* mixed together   81 *the very . . . soul*
thy deepest sagacity   82 *occulted* hidden   84 *damnèd ghost* evil spirit,
devil   86 *stithy* smithy   89 *censure of* sentence upon

*Enter Trumpets and Kettledrums, King, Queen,
Polonius, Ophelia, Rosencrantz, Guildenstern,
and other Lords attendant.*

Hamlet. They are coming to the play. I must be idle.
   Get you a place.

King. How fares our cousin Hamlet?

95 *Hamlet.* Excellent, i' faith, of the chameleon's dish. I
   eat the air, promise-crammed. You cannot feed ca-
   pons so.

King. I have nothing with this answer, Hamlet. These
   words are not mine.

100 *Hamlet.* No, nor mine now. (*to Polonius*) My lord,
   you played once i' th' university, you say?

Polonius. That did I, my lord, and was accounted a
   good actor.

Hamlet. What did you enact?

105 *Polonius.* I did enact Julius Caesar. I was killed i' th'
   Capitol; Brutus killed me.

Hamlet. It was a brute part of him to kill so capital a
   calf there. Be the players ready?

Rosencrantz. Ay, my lord. They stay upon your pa-
110 tience.

Queen. Come hither, my dear Hamlet, sit by me.

Hamlet. No, good mother. Here's metal more attrac-
   tive.

Polonius. (*to the King*) O ho! do you mark that?

115 *Hamlet.* Lady, shall I lie in your lap?

                              He lies at Ophelia's feet.

Ophelia. No, my lord.

Hamlet. I mean, my head upon your lap?

Ophelia. Ay, my lord.

Hamlet. Do you think I meant country matters?

---

92 *be idle* be foolish, act the madman   94 *cousin* nephew   95 *chameleon's dish* i.e. air (which was believed the chameleon's food; Hamlet
willfully takes *fares* in the sense of "feeds")   99 *not mine* not for me
as the asker of my question   109–10 *stay upon your patience* await
your indulgence   119 *country matters* rustic goings-on, barnyard mat-
ing

Ophelia. I think nothing, my lord.   120

Hamlet. That's a fair thought to lie between maids'
legs.

Ophelia. What is, my lord?

Hamlet. Nothing.

Ophelia. You are merry, my lord.   125

Hamlet. Who, I?

Ophelia. Ay, my lord.

Hamlet. O God, your only jig-maker! What should a
man do but be merry? For look you how cheerfully
my mother looks, and my father died within's two   130
hours.

Ophelia. Nay, 'tis twice two months, my lord.

Hamlet. So long? Nay then, let the devil wear black,
for I'll have a suit of sables. O heavens! die two
months ago, and not forgotten yet? Then there's   135
hope a great man's memory may outlive his life half
a year. But, by'r Lady, he must build churches then,
or else shall 'a suffer not thinking on, with the
hobby-horse, whose epitaph is "For O, for O, the
hobby-horse is forgot!"

The trumpets sound. Dumb show follows:

*Enter a King and a Queen (very lovingly), the Queen
embracing him, and he her. She kneels; and makes
show of protestation unto him. He takes her up, and
declines his head upon her neck. He lies him down
upon a bank of flowers. She, seeing him asleep, leaves
him. Anon come in another man: takes off his crown,
kisses it, pours poison in the sleeper's ears, and leaves
him. The Queen returns, finds the King dead, makes
passionate action. The poisoner, with some three or
four, come in again, seem to condole with her. The*

128 *jig-maker* writer of jigs   134 *sables* black furs (luxurious garb, not
for mourning)   139 *hobby-horse* traditional figure strapped round the
waist of a performer in May games and morris dances

dead body is carried away. The poisoner woos the
Queen with gifts; she seems harsh awhile, but in the
end accepts love.   *Exit all.*

Ophelia. What means this, my lord?

Hamlet. Marry, this is miching mallecho; it means
mischief.

Ophelia. Belike this show imports the argument of the
145   play.

Enter Prologue.

Hamlet. We shall know by this fellow. The players
cannot keep counsel; they'll tell all.

Ophelia. Will 'a tell us what this show meant?

Hamlet. Ay, or any show that you'll show him. Be not
150   you ashamed to show, he'll not shame to tell you
what it means.

Ophelia. You are naught, you are naught. I'll mark the
play.

Prologue. For us and for our tragedy,
155   Here stooping to your clemency,
             We beg your hearing patiently.   *Exit.*

Hamlet. Is this a prologue, or the posy of a ring?

Ophelia. 'Tis brief, my lord.

Hamlet. As woman's love.

Enter two Players as King and Queen.

160 *King.* Full thirty times hath Phoebus' cart gone round
             Neptune's salt wash and Tellus' orbèd ground,
             And thirty dozen moons with borrowed sheen
             About the world have times twelve thirties been,
             Since love our hearts, and Hymen did our hands,
165   Unite commutual in most sacred bands,

142 *miching mallecho* sneaking iniquity 152 *naught* indecent 157
posy brief motto in rhyme ("poesy") *ring* finger ring 160 *Phoebus'
cart* the sun's chariot 161 *Tellus* Roman goddess of the earth 162
borrowed i.e. taken from the sun 164 *Hymen* Greek god of marriage
165 *commutual* mutually

Queen. So many journeys may the sun and moon
  Make us again count o'er ere love be done!
  But woe is me, you are so sick of late,
  So far from cheer and from your former state,
  That I distrust you. Yet, though I distrust,   170
  Discomfort you, my lord, it nothing must.
  For women fear too much, even as they love,
  And women's fear and love hold quantity,
  In neither aught, or in extremity.
  Now what my love is, proof hath made you know,   175
  And as my love is sized, my fear is so.
  Where love is great, the littlest doubts are fear;
  Where little fears grow great, great love grows there.

King. Faith, I must leave thee, love, and shortly too;
  My operant powers their functions leave to do.   180
  And thou shalt live in this fair world behind,
  Honored, beloved, and haply one as kind
  For husband shalt thou —

Queen.   O, confound the rest!
  Such love must needs be treason in my breast.
  In second husband let me be accurst!   185
  None wed the second but who killed the first.

Hamlet. (aside) That's wormwood.

Queen. The instances that second marriage move
  Are base respects of thrift, but none of love.
  A second time I kill my husband dead   190
  When second husband kisses me in bed.

King. I do believe you think what now you speak,
  But what we do determine oft we break.
  Purpose is but the slave to memory,
  Of violent birth, but poor validity,   195
  Which now like fruit unripe sticks on the tree,
  But fall unshaken when they mellow be.
  Most necessary 'tis that we forget
  To pay ourselves what to ourselves is debt.

---

170 *distrust you* fear for you 173 *quantity* proportion 180 *operant powers* active bodily forces 187 *wormwood* a bitter herb 188 *instances* motives 194 *slave to* i.e. dependent upon for life 195 *validity* strength

200 What to ourselves in passion we propose,
The passion ending, doth the purpose lose.
The violence of either grief or joy
Their own enactures with themselves destroy.
Where joy most revels, grief doth most lament;
205 Grief joys, joy grieves, on slender accident.
This world is not for aye, nor 'tis not strange
That even our loves should with our fortunes change,
For 'tis a question left us yet to prove,
Whether love lead fortune, or else fortune love.
210 The great man down, you mark his favorite flies,
The poor advanced makes friends of enemies;
And hitherto doth love on fortune tend,
For who not needs shall never lack a friend,
And who in want a hollow friend doth try,
215 Directly seasons him his enemy.
But, orderly to end where I begun,
Our wills and fates do so contrary run
That our devices still are overthrown;
Our thoughts are ours, their ends none of our own.
220 So think thou wilt no second husband wed,
But die thy thoughts when thy first lord is dead.

Queen. Nor earth to me give food, nor heaven light,
Sport and repose lock from me day and night,
To desperation turn my trust and hope,
225 An anchor's cheer in prison be my scope,
Each opposite that blanks the face of joy
Meet what I would have well, and it destroy,
Both here and hence pursue me lasting strife,
If, once a widow, ever I be wife!

230 *Hamlet.* If she should break it now!

King. 'Tis deeply sworn. Sweet, leave me here awhile.
My spirits grow dull, and fain I would beguile
The tedious day with sleep.

203 *enactures* fulfillments   215 *seasons him* ripens him into   218 *still*
always   225 *anchor's* hermit's   226 *blanks* blanches, makes pale   228
hence in the next world

Queen.   Sleep rock thy brain, *He sleeps.*
    And never come mischance between us twain!

                                     Exit.

Hamlet. Madam, how like you this play?   235
Queen. The lady doth protest too much, methinks.
Hamlet. O, but she'll keep her word.
King. Have you heard the argument? Is there no
    offense in't?
Hamlet. No, no, they do but jest, poison in jest; no   240
    offense i' th' world.
King. What do you call the play?
Hamlet. *The Mousetrap.* Marry, how? Tropically.
    This play is the image of a murther done in Vienna.
    Gonzago is the duke's name; his wife, Baptista. You 245
    shall see anon. 'Tis a knavish piece of work, but
    what o' that? Your majesty, and we that have free
    souls, it touches us not. Let the galled jade winch;
    our withers are unwrung.

                   Enter Lucianus.

    This is one Lucianus, nephew to the king.   250
Ophelia. You are as good as a chorus, my lord.
Hamlet. I could interpret between you and your love,
    if I could see the puppets dallying.
Ophelia. You are keen, my lord, you are keen.
Hamlet. It would cost you a groaning to take off my   255
    edge.
Ophelia. Still better, and worse.
Hamlet. So you must take your husband's. — Begin,
    murtherer. Leave thy damnable faces and begin.
    Come, the croaking raven doth bellow for revenge.   260
Lucianus. Thoughts black, hands apt, drugs fit, and
    time agreeing,

238 *argument* plot summary   243 *Tropically* in the way of a trope or
figure (with a play on "trapically")   247 *free* guiltless   248 *galled*
sore-backed *jade* horse *winch* wince   249 *withers* shoulders   251
chorus in a play who explain the action   253 *puppets* i.e. you and
your lover as in a puppet show

Confederate season, else no creature seeing,
Thou mixture rank, of midnight weeds collected,
265   With Hecate's ban thrice blasted, thrice infected,
Thy natural magic and dire property
On wholesome life usurps immediately.

>   *Pours the poison in his ears.*

Hamlet. 'A poisons him i' th' garden for his estate.
His name's Gonzago. The story is extant, and writ-
270   ten in very choice Italian. You shall see anon how
the murtherer gets the love of Gonzago's wife.

Ophelia. The king rises.

Hamlet. What, frighted with false fire?

Queen. How fares my lord?

275   *Polonius.* Give o'er the play.

King. Give me some light. Away!

Polonius. Lights, lights, lights!

>   *Exit all but Hamlet and Horatio.*

Hamlet. Why, let the strucken deer go weep,
The hart ungallèd play.
280   For some must watch, while some must sleep;
Thus runs the world away.

Would not this, sir, and a forest of feathers — if
the rest of my fortunes turn Turk with me — with
two Provincial roses on my razed shoes, get me a
285   fellowship in a cry of players, sir?

Horatio. Half a share.

Hamlet. A whole one, I.
For thou dost know, O Damon dear,
This realm dismantled was
290   Of Jove himself; and now reigns here
A very, very — peacock.

Horatio. You might have rhymed.

Hamlet. O good Horatio, I'll take the ghost's word for
a thousand pound. Didst perceive?

---

263 *Confederate season* the occasion being my ally   265 *Hecate* goddess of witchcraft and black magic   *ban* curse   273 *false fire* of a gun
charged with powder but no shot, a blank-discharge   282 *feathers*
plumes for actors' costumes   283 *turn Turk* turn renegade, like a
Christian turning Mohammedan   284 *Provincial roses* ribbon rosettes
razed decorated with cut patterns   285 *cry* pack

Horatio. Very well, my lord.   295
Hamlet. Upon the talk of the poisoning?
Horatio. I did very well note him.
Hamlet. Aha! Come, some music! Come, the re-
corders!

> For if the king like not the comedy,   300
> Why then, belike he likes it not, perdy.

Come, some music!

Enter Rosencrantz and Guildenstern.

Guildenstern. Good my lord, vouchsafe me a word
with you.
Hamlet. Sir, a whole history.   305
Guildenstern. The king, sir —
Hamlet. Ay, sir, what of him?
Guildenstern. Is in his retirement marvellous dis-
tempered.
Hamlet. With drink, sir?   310
Guildenstern. No, my lord, with choler.
Hamlet. Your wisdom should show itself more richer
to signify this to the doctor, for for me to put him
to his purgation would perhaps plunge him into
more choler.   315
Guildenstern. Good my lord, put your discourse into
some frame, and start not so wildly from my affair.
Hamlet. I am tame, sir; pronounce.
Guildenstern. The queen, your mother, in most
great affliction of spirit hath sent me to you.   320
Hamlet. You are welcome.
Guildenstern. Nay, good my lord, this courtesy is not
of the right breed. If it shall please you to make me
a wholesome answer, I will do your mother's com-

298–99 *recorders* musical instruments of the flute class 301 *perdy* by
God ("par dieu") 308–9 *distempered* out of temper, vexed (twisted
by Hamlet into "deranged") 311 *choler* anger (twisted by Hamlet
into "biliousness") 317 *frame* logical order

325 mandment. If not, your pardon and my return shall
be the end of my business.

Hamlet. Sir, I cannot.

Rosencrantz. What, my lord?

Hamlet. Make you a wholesome answer; my wit's dis-
330 eased. But, sir, such answer as I can make, you
shall command, or rather, as you say, my mother.
Therefore no more, but to the matter. My mother,
you say —

Rosencrantz. Then thus she says: your behavior hath
335 struck her into amazement and admiration.

Hamlet. O wonderful son, that can so stonish a
mother! But is there no sequel at the heels of this
mother's admiration? Impart.

Rosencrantz. She desires to speak with you in her
340 closet ere you go to bed.

Hamlet. We shall obey, were she ten times our mother.
Have you any further trade with us?

Rosencrantz. My lord, you once did love me.

Hamlet. And do still, by these pickers and stealers.

345 *Rosencrantz.* Good my lord, what is your cause of distemper? You do surely bar the door upon your own
liberty, if you deny your griefs to your friend.

Hamlet. Sir, I lack advancement.

Rosencrantz. How can that be, when you have the
350 voice of the king himself for your succession in
Denmark?

Hamlet. Ay, sir, but "while the grass grows" — the
proverb is something musty.

Enter the Player with recorders.

O, the recorders. Let me see one. To withdraw

335 *admiration* wonder 340 *closet* private room 344 *pickers and
stealers* i.e. hands 352 *while the grass grows* a proverb, ending: "the
horse starves" *withdraw* step aside

with you — why do you go about to recover the 355
  wind of me, as if you would drive me into a toil?
Guildenstern. O my lord, if my duty be too bold, my
  love is too unmannerly.
Hamlet. I do not well understand that. Will you play
  upon this pipe?   360
Guildenstern. My lord, I cannot.
Hamlet. I pray you.
Guildenstern. Believe me, I cannot.
Hamlet. I do beseech you.
Guildenstern. I know no touch of it, my lord.   365
Hamlet. It is as easy as lying. Govern these ventages
  with your fingers and thumb, give it breath with
  your mouth, and it will discourse most eloquent
  music. Look you, these are the stops.
Guildenstern. But these cannot I command to any 370
  utt'rance of harmony. I have not the skill.
Hamlet. Why, look you now, how unworthy a thing
  you make of me! You would play upon me, .you
  would seem to know my stops, you would pluck out
  the heart of my mystery, you would sound me from 375
  my lowest note to the top of my compass; and there
  is much music, excellent voice, in this little organ,
  yet cannot you make it speak. 'Sblood, do you think
  I am easier to be played on than a pipe? Call me
  what instrument you will, though you can fret me, 380
  you cannot play upon me.

Enter Polonius.

God bless you, sir!
Polonius. My lord, the queen would speak with you,
  and presently.
Hamlet. Do you see yonder cloud that's almost in 385
  shape of a camel?

355-56 *recover the wind* come up to windward like a hunter *toil*
snare 358 *is too unmannerly* leads me beyond the restraint of good
manners 366 *ventages* holes, vents 380 *fret* irritate (with a play on
the fret-fingering of certain stringed musical instruments) 384 *presently* at once

Polonius. By th' mass and 'tis, like a camel indeed.

Hamlet. Methinks it is like a weasel.

Polonius. It is backed like a weasel.

390 *Hamlet.* Or like a whale.

Polonius. Very like a whale.

Hamlet. Then I will come to my mother by and by.
   (*aside*) They fool me to the top of my bent. — I
   will come by and by.

395 *Polonius.* I will say so.   *Exit.*

Hamlet. "By the by" is easily said. Leave me, friends.
                                      Exit all but Hamlet.

   'Tis now the very witching time of night,
   When churchyards yawn, and hell itself breathes out
   Contagion to this world. Now could I drink hot
400   blood
   And do such bitter business as the day
   Would quake to look on. Soft, now to my mother.
   O heart, lose not they nature; let not ever
   The soul of Nero enter this firm bosom.
405 Let me be cruel, not unnatural;
   I will speak daggers to her, but use none.
   My tongue and soul in this be hypocrites:
   How in my words somever she be shent,
   To give them seals never, my soul, consent!   *Exit.*

---

392 *by and by* immediately   404 *Nero* murderer of his mother   408
shent reproved   409 *seals* authentications in actions

ACT III, SCENE III

Enter King, Rosencrantz, and Guildenstern.

King. I like him not, nor stands it safe with us
    To let his madness range. Therefore prepare you.
    I your commission will forthwith dispatch,
    And he to England shall along with you.
    The terms of our estate may not endure   5
    Hazard so near's as doth hourly grow
    Out of his brows.
Guildenstern.   We will ourselves provide.
    Most holy and religious fear it is
    To keep those many many bodies safe
    That live and feed upon your majesty.   10
Rosencrantz. The single and peculiar life is bound
    With all the strength and armor of the mind
    To keep itself from noyance, but much more
    That spirit upon whose weal depends and rests
    The lives of many. The cess of majesty   15
    Dies not alone, but like a gulf doth draw
    What's near it with it; or 'tis a massy wheel
    Fixed on the summit of the highest mount,
    To whose huge spokes ten thousand lesser things
    Are mortised and adjoined, which when it falls,   20
    Each small annexment, petty consequence,
    Attends the boist'rous ruin. Never alone
    Did the king sigh, but with a general groan.
King. Arm you, I pray you, to this speedy voyage,
    For we will fetters put upon this fear,   25
    Which now goes too free-footed.

III, iii, 5 *terms* circumstances *estate* royal position 7 *brows* effronteries (apparently with an implication of knitted brows) 11 *peculiar* individual 13 *noyance* harm 15 *cess* cessation, decease 16 *gulf* whirlpool 22 *Attends* joins in (like a royal attendant) 24 *Arm* prepare

Rosencrantz.
                                                We will haste us.
                                                Exit Gentelmen.

Enter Polonius.

Polonius. My lord, he's going to his mother's closet.
    Behind the arras I'll convey myself
        To hear the process. I'll warrant she'll tax him
            home,
30   And, as you said, and wisely was it said,
        'Tis meet that some more audience than a mother,
        Since nature makes them partial, should o'erhear
        The speech, of vantage. Fare you well, my liege.
        I'll call upon you ere you go to bed
33   And tell you what I know.

33   *King.*   Thanks, dear my lord.
                                        Exit Polonius.

        O, my offense is rank, it smells to heaven;
        It hath the primal eldest curse upon't,
        A brother's murther. Pray can I not,
        Though inclination be as sharp as will.
40   My stronger guilt defeats my strong intent,
        And like a man to double business bound
        I stand in pause where I shall first begin,
        And both neglect. What if this cursèd hand
        Were thicker than itself with brother's blood,
45   Is there not rain enough in the sweet heavens
        To wash it white as snow? Whereto serves mercy
        But to confront the visage of offense?
        And what's in prayer but this twofold force,
        To be forestallèd ere we come to fall,
50   Or pardoned being down? Then I'll look up.
        My fault is past. But, O, what form of prayer
        Can serve my turn? "Forgive me my foul murther"?
        That cannot be, since I am still possessed

---

29 *process* proceedings   *tax him home* thrust home in reprimanding
him   33 *of vantage* from an advantageous position   37 *primal eldest
curse* that of Cain, who also murdered a brother   47 *offense* sin

Of those effects for which I did the murther,
My crown, mine own ambition, and my queen.   55
May one be pardoned and retain th' offense?
In the corrupted currents of this world
Offense's gilded hand may shove by justice,
And oft 'tis seen the wicked prize itself
Buys out the law. But 'tis not so above.   60
There is no shuffling; there the action lies
In his true nature, and we ourselves compelled,
Even to the teeth and forehead of our faults,
To give in evidence. What then? What rests?
Try what repentance can. What can it not?   65
Yet what can it when one cannot repent?
O wretched state! O bosom black as death!
O limèd soul, that struggling to be free
Art more engaged! Help, angels! Make assay.
Bow, stubborn knees, and, heart with strings of
    steel,   70
Be soft as sinews of the new-born babe.
All may be well.   *He kneels.*

Enter Hamlet.

Hamlet. Now might I do it pat, now 'a is a-praying,
And now I'll do't. And so 'a goes to heaven,
And so am I revenged. That would be scanned.   75
A villain kills my father, and for that
I, his sole son, do this same villain send
To heaven.
Why, this is hire and salary, not revenge.
'A took my father grossly, full of bread,   80
With all his crimes broad blown, as flush as May;
And how his audit stands, who knows save heaven?

54 *effects* things acquired 58 *gilded* gold-laden 61 *shuffling* sharp
practice, double-dealing *action* legal proceeding (in heaven's court)
63 *teeth and forehead* face-to-face recognition 68 *limèd* caught in
birdlime, a gluey material spread as a bird-snare 69 *engaged* em-
bedded *assay* an attempt 73 *pat* opportunely 80 *grossly* in a state
of gross unpreparedness *bread* i.e. worldly sense gratification 81
broad blown fully blossomed *flush* vigorous 82 *audit* account

But in our circumstance and course of thought,
'Tis heavy with him; and am I then revenged,
85 To take him in the purging of his soul,
When he is fit and seasoned for his passage?
No.
Up, sword, and know thou a more horrid hent.
When he is drunk asleep, or in his rage,
90 Or in th' incestuous pleasure of his bed,
At game a-swearing, or about some act
That has no relish of salvation in't —
Then trip him, that his heels may kick at heaven,
And that his soul may be as damned and black
95 As hell, whereto it goes. My mother stays.
This physic but prolongs thy sickly days.   *Exit.*
King. (*rises*) My words fly up, my thoughts remain
    below. Words without thoughts never to heaven go.
                                            Exit.

❧

ACT III, SCENE IV

Enter Queen Gertrude and Polonius.

Polonius. 'A will come straight. Look you lay home to
    him.
Tell him his pranks have been too broad to bear
    with,
And that your grace hath screened and stood be-
    tween
Much heat and him. I'll silence me even here.
5 Pray you be round with him.
Hamlet. (*within*) Mother, mother, mother!
Queen. I'll warrant you; fear me not. Withdraw; I
    hear him coming. *Polonius hides behind the arras.*

88 *more horrid hent* grasping by me on a more horrid occasion 92
relish flavor III, iv, 1 *lay* thrust 2 *broad* unrestrained 5 *round*
plain-spoken

Enter Hamlet.

Hamlet. Now, mother, what's the matter?
Queen. Hamlet, thou hast thy father much offended.   10
Hamlet. Mother, you have my father much offended.
Queen. Come, come, you answer with an idle tongue.
Hamlet. Go, go, you question with a wicked tongue.
Queen. Why, how now, Hamlet?
Hamlet.   What's the matter now?
Queen. Have you forgot me?
Hamlet.   No, by the rood, not so!   15
    You are the queen, your husband's brother's wife,
    And (would it were not so) you are my mother.
Queen. Nay, then I'll set those to you that can speak.
Hamlet. Come, come, and sit you down. You shall not
    budge.
    You go not till I set up up a glass   20
    Where you may see the inmost part of you.
Queen. What wilt thou do? Thou wilt not murther
    me? Help, ho!
Polonius. (*behind*) What, ho! help!
Hamlet. (*draws*) How now? a rat? Dead for a ducat,
    dead!
    Makes a pass through the arras and kills Polonius.
Polonius. (*behind*) O, I am slain!
Queen.   O me, what hast thou done?   25
Hamlet. Nay, I know not. Is it the king?
Queen. O, what a rash and bloody deed is this!
Hamlet. A bloody deed—almost as bad, good
    mother,
    As kill a king, and marry with his brother.
Queen. As kill a king?
Hamlet.   Ay, lady, it was my word.   30
    Lifts up the arras and sees Polonius.
    Thou wretched, rash, intruding fool, farewell!
    I took thee for thy better. Take thy fortune.
    Thou find'st to be too busy is some danger.—

12 *idle* foolish 15 *rood* cross

Leave wringing of your hands. Peace, sit you down
35 And let me wring your heart, for so I shall
If it be made of penetrable stuff,
If damnèd custom have not brazed it so
That it is proof and bulwark against sense.

Queen. What have I done that thou dar'st wag thy
     tongue
In noise so rude against me?

40 *Hamlet.*   Such an act
That blurs the grace and blush of modesty,
Calls virtue hypocrite, takes off the rose
From the fair forehead of an innocent love,
And set a blister there, makes marriage vows
45 As false as dicers' oaths. O, such a deed
As from the body of contraction plucks
The very soul, and sweet religion makes
A rhapsody of words! Heaven's face does glow,
And this solidity and compound mass,
50 With heated visage, as against the doom,
Is thought-sick at the act.

Queen.   Ay me, what act,
That roars so loud and thunders in the index?

Hamlet. Look here upon this picture, and on this,
The counterfeit presentment of two brothers.
55 See what a grace was seated on this brow:
Hyperion's curls, the front of Jove himself,
An eye like Mars, to threaten and command,
A station like the herald Mercury
New lighted on a heaven-kissing hill —
60 A combination and a form indeed
Where every god did seem to set his seal
To give the world assurance of a man.
This was your husband. Look you now what follows.
Here is your husband, like a mildewed ear

37 *custom* habit *brazed* hardened like brass 38 *proof* armor *sense*
feeling 44 *blister* brand (of degradation) 46 *contraction* the marriage contract 47 *religion* i.e. sacred marriage vows 49 *compound
mass* the earth as compounded of the four elements 50 *against* in expectation of *doom* Day of Judgment 52 *index* table of contents preceding the body of a book 54 *counterfeit presentment* portrayed representation 56 *Hyperion* the sun god *front* forehead 58 *station*
attitude in standing

Blasting his wholesome brother. Have you eyes?   65
Could you on this fair mountain leave to feed,
And batten on this moor? Ha! have you eyes?
You cannot call it love, for at your age
The heyday in the blood is tame, it's humble,
And waits upon the judgment, and what judgment   70
Would step from this to this? Sense sure you have,
Else could you not have motion, but sure that sense
Is apoplexed, for madness would not err,
Nor sense to ecstasy was ne'er so thralled
But it reserved some quantity of choice   75
To serve in such a difference. What devil was't
That thus hath cozened you at hoodman-blind?
Eyes without feeling, feeling without sight,
Ears without hands or eyes, smelling sans all,
Or but a sickly part of one true sense   80
Could not so mope.
O shame, where is thy blush? Rebellious hell,
If thou canst mutine in a matron's bones,
To flaming youth let virtue be as wax
And melt in her own fire. Proclaim no shame   85
When the compulsive ardor gives the charge,
Since frost itself as actively doth burn,
And reason panders will.
Queen.   O Hamlet, speak no more.
Thou turn'st mine eyes into my very soul,
And there I see such black and grainèd spots   90
As will not leave their tinct.
Hamlet.   Nay, but to live
In the rank sweat of an enseamèd bed,
Stewed in corruption, honeying and making love
Over the nasty sty—
Queen.   O, speak to me no more.
These words like daggers enter in mine ears.   95
No more, sweet Hamlet.
Hamlet.   A murtherer and a villain,

67 *batten* feed greedily   72 *motion* desire, impulse   77 *cozened* cheated
hoodman-blind blindman's buff   79 *sans* without   83 *mutine* mutiny
88 *panders will* acts as procurer for desire   90 *grainèd* dyed in grain
91 *tinct* color   92 *enseamèd* grease-laden

A slave that is not twentieth part the tithe
Of your precedent lord, a vice of kings,
A cutpurse of the empire and the rule,
100   That from a shelf the precious diadem stole
And put it in his pocket —
Queen.   No more.

Enter the Ghost in his nightgown.

Hamlet. A king of shreds and patches —
Save me and hover o'er me with your wings,
You heavenly guards! What would your gracious
figure?
105   *Queen.* Alas, he's mad.
Hamlet. Do you not come your tardy son to chide,
That, lapsed in time and passion, lets go by
Th' important acting of your dread command?
O, say!
110   *Ghost.* Do not forget. This visitation
Is but to whet thy almost blunted purpose.
But look, amazement on thy mother sits.
O, step between her and her fighting soul!
Conceit in weakest bodies strongest works.
Speak to her, Hamlet.
115   *Hamlet.*   How is it with you, lady?
Queen. Alas, how is't with you,
That you do bend your eye on vacancy,
And with th' incorporal air do hold discourse?
Forth at your eyes your spirits wildly peep,
120   And as the sleeping soldiers in th' alarm
Your bedded hairs like life in excrements
Start up and stand an end. O gentle son,
Upon the heat and flame of thy distemper
Sprinkle cool patience. Whereon do you look?

---

98 *tithe* tenth part 99 *vice* clownish rogue (like the Vice of the
morality plays) 100 *cutpurse* skulking thief 102 *s.d. nightgown*
dressing gown 108 *lapsed . . . passion* having let the moment slip
and passion cool 114 *Conceit* imagination 118 *incorporal* bodiless
121 *excrements* outgrowths 122 *an* on 123 *distemper* mental disorder

Hamlet. On him, on him! Look you, how pale he
    glares!   125
  His form and cause conjoined, preaching to sfones,
  Would make them capable. — Do not look upon
    me,
  Lest with this piteous action you convert
  My stern effects. Then what I have to do
  Will want true color — tears perchance for blood.   130
Queen. To whom do you speak this?
Hamlet.   Do you see nothing there?
Queen. Nothing at all; yet all that is I see.
Hamlet. Nor did you nothing hear?
Queen.   No, nothing but ourselves.
Hamlet. Why, look you there! Look how it steals away!
  My father, in his habit as he lived!   135
  Look where he goes even now out at the portal!

                          Exit Ghost.

Queen. This is the very coinage of your brain.
  This bodiless creation ecstasy
  Is very cunning in.
Hamlet.   Ecstasy?
  My pulse as yours doth temperately keep time   140
  And makes as healthful music. It is not madness
  That I have uttered. Bring me to the test,
  And I the matter will reword, which madness
  Would gambol from. Mother, for love of grace,
  Lay not that flattering unction to your soul,   145
  That not your trespass but my madness speaks.
  It will but skin and film the ulcerous place
  Whiles rank corruption, mining all within,
  Infects unseen. Confess yourself to heaven,
  Repent what's past, avoid what is to come,   150
  And do not spread the compost on the weeds
  To make them ranker. Forgive me this my virtue.
  For in the fatness of these pursy times

---

127 *capable* susceptible 129 *effects* manifestations of emotion and
purpose 144 *gambol* shy (like a startled horse) 145 *unction* ointment 148 *mining* undermining 151 *compost* fertilizing mixture 153
fatness slackness *pursy* corpulent

Virtue itself of vice must pardon beg,
155   Yea, curb and woo for leave to do him good.
        Queen. O Hamlet, thou hast cleft my heart in twain.
        Hamlet. O, throw away the worser part of it,
        And live the purer with the other half.
        Good night — but go not to my uncle's bed.
160   Assume a virtue, if you have it not.
        That monster custom, who all sense doth eat,
        Of habits devil, is angel yet in this,
        That to the use of actions fair and good
        He likewise gives a frock or livery
165   That aptly is put on. Refrain tonight,
        And that shall lend a kind of easiness
        To the next abstinence; the next more easy;
        For use almost can change the stamp of nature,
        And either . . . the devil, or throw him out
170   With wondrous potency. Once more, good night,
        And when you are desirous to be blest,
        I'll blessing beg of you. — For this same lord,
        I do repent; but heaven hath pleased it so,
        To punish me with this, and this with me,
175   That I must be their scourge and minister.
        I will bestow him and will answer well
        The death I gave him. So again, good night.
        I must be cruel only to be kind.
        Thus bad begins, and worse remains behind.
        One word more, good lady.
180   *Queen.*   What shall I do?
        Hamlet. Not this, by no means, that I bid you do:
        Let the bloat king tempt you again to bed,
        Pinch wanton on your cheek, call you his mouse,
        And let him, for a pair of reechy kisses,
185   Or paddling in your neck with his damned fingers,
        Make you to ravel all this matter out,
        That I essentially am not in madness,

155 *curb* bow to   164 *livery* characteristic dress (accompanying the suggestion of "garb" in *habits*)   168 *use* habit *stamp* impression, form   176 *bestow* stow, hide   179 *behind* to come   182 *bloat* bloated with sense gratification   184 *reechy* filthy   186 *ravel . . . out* disentangle

But mad in craft. 'Twere good you let him know,
For who that's but a queen, fair, sober, wise,
Would from a paddock, from a bat, a gib,   190
Such dear concernings hide? Who would do so?
No, in despite of sense and secrecy,
Unpeg the basket on the house's top.
Let the birds fly, and like the famous ape,
To try conclusions, in the basket creep   195
And break your own neck down.

Queen. Be thou assured, if words be made of breath,
    And breath of life, I have no life to breathe
    What thou hast said to me.

Hamlet. I must to England; you know that?

Queen.   Alack,   200
    I had forgot. 'Tis so concluded on.

Hamlet. There's letters sealed, and my two school-
    fellows,
Whom I will trust as I will adders fanged,
They bear the mandate; they must sweep my way
And marshal me to knavery. Let it work.   205
For 'tis the sport to have the enginer
Hoist with his own petar, and 't shall go hard
But I will delve one yard below their mines
And blow them at the moon. O, 'tis most sweet
When in one line two crafts directly meet.   210
This man shall set me packing.
I'll lug the guts into the neighbor room.
Mother, good night. Indeed, this counsellor
Is now most still, most secret, and most grave,
Who was in life a foolish prating knave.   215
Come, sir, to draw toward an end with you.
Good night, mother.

      Exit the Queen. Then exit Hamlet, tugging in
                        Polonius

---

190 *paddock* toad   *gib* tomcat   191 *dear concernings* matters of great
personal significance   194 *famous ape* one in a story now unknown
195 *conclusions* experiments   204 *mandate* order   206 *enginer* engi-
neer, constructor of military engines or works   207 *Hoist* blown up
petar petard, bomb, or mine   211 *packing* traveling in a hurry (with a
play upon his "packing" or shouldering of Polonius' body and also
upon his "packing" in the sense of "plotting" or "contriving")

ACT IV, SCENE I

*Enter King and Queen, with Rosencrantz and
Guildenstern.*

King. There's matter in these sighs. These profound
heaves
You must translate; 'tis fit we understand them.
Where is your son?
Queen. Bestow this place on us a little while.

                    Exit Rosencrantz and Guildenstern.
5   Ah, mine own lord, what have I seen tonight!
King. What, Gertrude? How does Hamlet?
Queen. Mad as the sea and wind when both contend
Which is the mightier. In his lawless fit,
Behind the arras hearing something stir,
10   Whips out his rapier, cries, "A rat, a rat!"
And in this brainish apprehension kills
The unseen good old man.
King.   O heavy deed!
It had been so with us, had we been there.
His liberty is full of threats to all,
15   To you yourself, to us, to every one.
Alas, how shall this bloody deed be answered?
It will be laid to us, whose providence
Should have kept short, restrained, and out of haunt

IV, i, 11 *brainish apprehension* headstrong conception 17 *providence*
foresight 18 *haunt* association with others

106

This mad young man. But so much was our love
We would not understand what was most fit,   20
But, like the owner of a foul disease,
To keep it from divulging, let it feed
Even on the pith of life. Where is he gone?
Queen. To draw apart the body he hath killed;
O'er whom his very madness, like some ore   25
Among a mineral of metals base,
Shows itself pure. 'A weeps for what is done.
King. O Gertrude, come away!
The sun no sooner shall the mountains touch
But we will ship him hence, and this vile deed   30
We must with all our majesty and skill
Both countenance and excuse. Ho, Guildenstern!

Enter Rosencrantz and Guildenstern.

Friends both, go join you with some further aid.
Hamlet in madness hath Polonius slain,
And from his mother's closet hath he dragged him.   35
Go seek him out; speak fair, and bring the body
Into the chapel. I pray you haste in this.
                    Exit Rosencrantz and Guildenstern.
Come, Gertrude, we'll call up our wisest friends
And let them know both what we mean to do
And what's untimely done . . .   40
Whose whisper o'er the world's diameter,
As level as the cannon to his blank
Transports his poisoned shot, may miss our name
And hit the woundless air. O, come away!
My soul is full of discord and dismay.   *Exit all.*   45

---

22 *divulging* becoming known   25 *ore* vein of gold   26 *mineral* mine
42 *As level* with as direct aim   *blank* mark, central white spot on a
target

❧

ACT IV, SCENE II

Enter Hamlet.

Hamlet. Safely stowed.

Gentlemen. (*within*) Hamlet! Lord Hamlet!

Hamlet. But soft, what noise? Who calls on Hamlet?
O, here they come.

Enter Rosencrantz, Guildenstern, and others.

5 *Rosencrantz.* What have you done, my lord, with the
dead body?

Hamlet. Compounded it with dust, whereto 'tis kin.

Rosencrantz. Tell us where 'tis, that we may take it
thence

10 And bear it to the chapel.

Hamlet. Do not believe it.

Rosencrantz. Believe what?

Hamlet. That I can keep your counsel and not mine
own. Besides, to be demanded of a sponge, what

15 replication should be made by the son of a king?

Rosencrantz. Take you me for a sponge, my lord?

Hamlet. Ay, sir, that soaks up the king's countenance,
his rewards, his authorities. But such officers do
the king best service in the end. He keeps them, like

20 an ape, in the corner of his jaw, first mouthed, to
be last swallowed. When he needs what you have
gleaned, it is but squeezing you and, sponge, you
shall be dry again.

Rosencrantz. I understand you not, my lord.

IV, ii, 15 *replication* reply   17 *countenance* favor

Hamlet. I am glad of it. A knavish speech sleeps in a   25
    foolish ear.

Rosencrantz. My lord, you must tell us where the body
    is and go with us to the king.

Hamlet. The body is with the king, but the king is
    not with the body. The king is a thing —   30

Guildenstern. A thing, my lord?

Hamlet. Of nothing. Bring me to him. Hide fox, and
    all after.   *Exit all.*

⚜

ACT IV, SCENE III

Enter King, and two or three.

King. I have sent to seek him and to find the body.
    How dangerous is it that this man goes loose!
    Yet must not we put the strong law on him;
    He's loved of the distracted multitude,
    Who like not in their judgment, but their eyes,   5
    And where 'tis so, th' offender's scourge is weighed,
    But never the offense. To bear all smooth and even,
    This sudden sending him away must seem
    Deliberate pause. Diseases desperate grown
    By desperate appliance are relieved,   10
    Or not at all.

Enter Rosencrantz, Guildenstern, and all the rest.

               How now? What hath befallen?

Rosencrantz. Where the dead body is bestowed, my
    lord,

25 *sleeps in* means nothing to   32 *Of nothing* (cf. Prayer Book, Psalm
144: 4, "Man is like a thing of naught: his time passeth away like a
shadow")   32–33 *Hide . . . after* (apparently well-known words from
some game of hide-and-seek)   IV, iii, 4 *distracted* confused   6 *scourge*
punishment   9 *Deliberate pause* something done with much deliberation

We cannot get from him.

King.   But where is he?

Rosencrantz. Without, my lord; guarded, to know
  your pleasure.

King. Bring him before us.

15 *Rosencrantz.*   Ho! Bring in the lord.

They enter with Hamlet.

King. Now, Hamlet, where's Polonius?

Hamlet. At supper.

King. At supper? Where?

Hamlet. Not where he eats, but where 'a is eaten. A
20 certain convocation of politic worms are e'en at him.
 Your worm is your only emperor for diet. We fat
 all creatures else to fat us, and we fat ourselves for
 maggots. Your fat king and your lean beggar is but
 variable service — two dishes, but to one table.
25 That's the end.

King. Alas, alas!

Hamlet. A man may fish with the worm that hath eat
 of a king, and eat of the fish that hath fed of that
 worm.

30 *King.* What dost thou mean by this?

Hamlet. Nothing but to show you how a king may go
 a progress through the guts of a beggar.

King. Where is Polonius?

Hamlet. In heaven. Send thither to see. If your mes-
35 senger find him not there, seek him i' th' other
 place yourself. But if indeed you find him not
 within this month, you shall nose him as you go up
 the stairs into the lobby.

King. (*to Attendants*) Go seek him there.

40 *Hamlet.* 'A will stay till you come.   *Exit Attendants.*

King. Hamlet, this deed, for thine especial safety,

20 *politic worms* political and craftily scheming worms (such as Polonius might well attract)   21 *diet* food and drink (perhaps with a play
upon a famous "convocation," the Diet of Worms opened by the Emperor Charles V on January 28, 1521, before which Luther appeared)
24 *variable service* different servings of one food   31 *progress* royal
journey of state

Which we do tender as we dearly grieve
For that which thou hast done, must send thee
   hence
With fiery quickness. Therefore prepare thyself.
The bark is ready and the wind at help,   45
Th' associates tend, and everything is bent
For England.

Hamlet.   For England?

King.   Ay, Hamlet.

Hamlet.   Good.

King. So is it, if thou knew'st our purposes.

Hamlet. I see a cherub that sees them. But come, for
   England! Farewell, dear mother.   50

King. Thy loving father, Hamlet.

Hamlet. My mother — father and mother is man and
   wife, man and wife is one flesh, and so, my mother.
   Come, for England!   *Exit.*

King. Follow him at foot; tempt him with speed
   aboard.   55
Delay it not; I'll have him hence tonight.
Away! for everything is sealed and done
That else leans on th' affair. Pray you make haste.
                   Exit all but the King.
And, England, if my love thou hold'st at aught —
As my great power thereof may give thee sense,   60
Since yet thy cicatrice looks raw and red
After the Danish sword, and thy free awe
Pays homage to us — thou mayst not coldly set
Our sovereign process, which imports at full
By letters congruing to that effect   65
The present death of Hamlet. Do it, England,
For like the hectic in my blood he rages,
And thou must cure me. Till I know 'tis done,
Howe'er my haps, my joys were ne'er begun.   *Exit.*

42 *tender* hold dear   *dearly* intensely 46 *tend* wait *bent* set in readiness (like a bent bow) 49 *cherub* one of the cherubin (angels with a distinctive quality of knowledge) 55 *at foot* at heel, close 59 *leans on* is connected with 59 *England* King of England 62 *free awe* voluntary show of respect 63 *set* esteem 64 *process* formal command 65 *congruing* agreeing 66 *present* instant 67 *hectic* a continuous fever 69 *haps* fortunes

ACT IV, SCENE IV

Enter Fortinbras with his Army over the stage.

Fortinbras. Go, captain, from me greet the Danish
    king.
    Tell him that by his license Fortinbras
    Craves the conveyance of a promised march
    Over his kingdom. You know the rendezvous.
5   If that his majesty would aught with us,
    We shall express our duty in his eye;
    And let him know so.
Captain.   I will do't, my lord.
Fortinbras. Go softly on.   *Exit all but the Captain.*

Enter Hamlet, Rosencrantz, Guildenstern, and others.

Hamlet. Good sir, whose powers are these?
10 *Captain.* They are of Norway, sir.
    Hamlet. How purposed, sir, I pray you?
    Captain. Against some part of Poland.
    Hamlet. Who commands them, sir?
    Captain. The nephew to old Norway, Fortinbras.
15 *Hamlet.* Goes it against the main of Poland, sir,
    Or for some frontier?
    Captain. Truly to speak, and with no addition,
    We go to gain a little patch of ground
    That hath in it no profit but the name.
20   To pay five ducats, five, I would not farm it,
    Nor will it yield to Norway or the Pole
    A ranker rate, should it be sold in fee.

IV, iv, 3 *conveyance* escort 6 *eye* presence 8 *softly* slowly 9 *powers*
forces 15 *main* main body 17 *additton* exaggeration 20 *To pay* i.e.
for a yearly rental of 22 *ranker* more abundant *in fee* outright

Hamlet. Why, then the Polack never will defend it.

Captain. Yes, it is already garrisoned.

Hamlet. Two thousand souls and twenty thousand
    ducats   25
  Will not debate the question of this straw.
  This is th' imposthume of much wealth and peace,
  That inward breaks, and shows no cause without
  Why the man dies. I humbly thank you, sir.

Captain. God bye you, sir.   *Exit.*

Rosencrantz.   Will't please you go, my lord?   30

Hamlet. I'll be with you straight. Go a little before.
                        Exit all but Hamlet.

  How all occasions do inform against me
  And spur my dull revenge! What is a man,
  If his chief good and market of his time
  Be but to sleep and feed? A beast, no more.   35
  Sure he that made us with such large discourse,
  Looking before and after, gave us not
  That capability and godlike reason
  To fust in us unused. Now, whether it be
  Bestial oblivion, or some craven scruple   40
  Of thinking too precisely on th' event —
  A thought which, quartered, hath but one part wis-
    dom
  And ever three parts coward — I do not know
  Why yet I live to say, "This thing's to do,"
  Sith I have cause, and will, and strength, and means   45
  To do't. Examples gross as earth exhort me.
  Witness this army of such mass and charge,
  Led by a delicate and tender prince,
  Whose spirit, with divine ambition puffed,
  Makes mouths at the invisible event,   50
  Exposing what is mortal and unsure
  To all that fortune, death, and danger dare,
  Even for an eggshell. Rightly to be great

27 *imposthume* abscess 32 *inform* take shape 34 *market of* compen-
sation for 36 *discourse* power of thought 39 *fust* grow mouldy 40
oblivion forgetfulness 41 *event* outcome 46 *gross* large and evident
47 *charge* expense 50 *Makes mouths* makes faces scornfully

Is not to stir without great argument,
55 But greatly to find quarrel in a straw
When honor's at the stake. How stand I then,
That have a father killed, a mother stained,
Excitements of my reason and my blood,
And let all sleep, while to my shame I see
60 The imminent death of twenty thousand men
That for a fantasy and trick of fame
Go to their graves like beds, fight for a plot
Whereon the numbers cannot try the cause,
Which is not tomb enough and continent
65 To hide the slain? O, from this time forth,
My thoughts be bloody, or be nothing worth!   *Exit.*

⊱⊰

ACT IV, SCENE V

Enter Horatio, Queen Gertrude, and a Gentleman.

Queen. I will not speak with her.
Gentleman. She is importunate, indeed distract.
Her mood will needs be pitied.
Queen.   What would she have?
Gentleman. She speaks much of her father, says she hears
There's tricks i' th' world, and hems, and beats her
5   heart,
Spurns enviously at straws, speaks things in doubt
That carry but half sense. Her speech is nothing,
Yet the unshapèd use of it doth move

---

55 *greatly . . . straw* to recognize the great argument even in some small matter 61 *fantasy* fanciful image *trick* toy 63 *try the cause* find space in which to settle the issue by battle 64 *continent* receptacle IV, v, 2 *distract* insane 5 *tricks* deceits 6 *Spurns enviously* kicks spitefully, takes offense *straws* trifles 8 *unshapèd use* disordered manner

The hearers to collection; they aim at it,
And botch the words up fit to their own thoughts,   10
Which, as her winks and nods and gestures yield
  them,
Indeed would make one think there might be
  thought,
Though nothing sure, yet much unhappily.
Horatio. 'Twere good she were spoken with, for she
  may stew
Dangerous conjectures in ill-breeding minds.   15
Queen. Let her come in.   *Exit Gentleman.*
  (*aside*) To my sick soul (as sin's true nature is)
Each toy seems prologue to some great amiss.
So full of artless jealousy is guilt
It spills itself in fearing to be split.   20

Enter Ophelia (distracted).

Ophelia. Where is the beauteous majesty of Denmark?
Queen. How now, Ophelia?
Ophelia. How should I your true-love know
  From another one?   *She sings.* 25
          By his cockle hat and staff
          And his sandal shoon.
Queen. Alas, sweet lady, what imports this song?
Ophelia. Say you? Nay, pray you mark.
          He is dead and gone, lady,
            He is 'dead and gone;   30
          At his head a grass-green turf,
            At his heels a stone.
          O, ho!
Queen. Nay, but Ophelia —
Ophelia. Pray you mark.   35
  (*Sings*) White his shroud as the mountain snow —

---

9 *collection* attempts at shaping meaning *aim* guess 10 *botch* patch
18 *toy* trifle *amiss* calamity 19 *artless* unskillfully managed *jealousy*
suspicion 20 *spills* destroys 25 *cockle hat* hat bearing a cockle shell,
worn by a pilgrim who had been to the shrine of St. James of Com-
postela 26 *shoon* shoes

Enter King.

Queen. Alas, look here, my lord.

Ophelia.   Larded all with sweet flowers;   Song.
                Which bewept to the grave did not go
40   With true-love showers.

King. How do you, pretty lady?

Ophelia. Well, God dild you! They say the owl was a
     baker's daughter. Lord, we know what we are, but
     know not what we may be. God be at your table!

45 *King.* Conceit upon her father.

Ophelia. Pray let's have no words of this, but when
     they ask you what it means, say you this:

                Tomorrow is Saint Valentine's day. Song.
                All in the morning betime,
50   And I a maid at your window,
                To be your Valentine.

                Then up he rose and donned his clo'es
                And dupped the chamber door,
                Let in the maid, that out a maid
55   Never departed more.

King. Pretty Ophelia!

Ophelia. Indeed, la, without an oath, I'll make an end
     on't:

     (Sings) By Gis and by Saint Charity,
                Alack, and fie for shame!
60   Young men will do't if they come to't.
                By Cock, they are to blame.
                Quoth she, "Before you tumbled me,
                You promised me to wed."

     He answers:

65   "So would I 'a' done, by yonder sun,
                An thou hadst not come to my bed."

38 *Larded* garnished   42 *dild* yield, repay   *the owl* an owl into which,
according to a folktale, a baker's daughter was transformed because
of her failure to show wholehearted generosity when Christ asked for
bread in the baker's shop   45 *Conceit* thought   49 *betime* early   53
dupped opened   58 *Gis* Jesus   61 *Cock* God

King. How long hath she been thus?

Ophelia. I hope all will be well. We must be patient,
  but I cannot choose but weep to think they would
  lay him i' th' cold ground. My brother shall know   70
  of it; and so I thank you for your good counsel.
  Come, my coach! Good night, ladies, good night.
  Sweet ladies, good night, good night.   *Exit.*

King. Follow her close; give her good watch, I pray
   you.   *Exit Horatio.*

O, this is the poison of deep grief; it springs   75
All from her father's death — and now behold!
O Gertrude, Gertrude,
When sorrows come, they come not single spies,
But in battalions: first, her father slain;
Next, your son gone, and he most violent author   80
Of his own just remove; the people muddied,
Thick and unwholesome in their thoughts and whis-
     pers
For good Polonius' death, and we have done but
     greenly
In hugger-mugger to inter him; poor Ophelia
Divided from herself and her fair judgment,   85
Without the which we are pictures or mere beasts;
Last, and as much containing as all these,
Her brother is in secret come from France,
Feeds on his wonder, keeps himself in clouds,
And wants not buzzers to infect his ear   90
With pestilent speeches of his father's death,
Wherein necessity, of matter beggared,
Will nothing stick our person to arraign
In ear and ear. O my dear Gertrude, this,
Like to a murd'ring piece, in many places   95
Gives me superfluous death.   *A noise within.*

---

81 *muddled* stirred up and confused   83 *greenly* foolishly   84 *hugger-mugger* secrecy and disorder   89 *clouds* obscurity   90 *wants* lacks *buzzers* whispering talebearers   92 *of matter beggared* unprovided with facts   93 *nothing stick* in no way hesitate   *arraign* accuse   95 *murd'ring piece* cannon loaded with shot meant to scatter

Enter a Messenger.

Queen.   Alack, what noise is this?
King. Attend, where are my Switzers? Let them guard
    the door.
    What is the matter?
Messenger   Save yourself, my lord.
    The ocean, overpeering of his list,
100 Eats not the flats with more impiteous haste
    Than young Laertes, in a riotous head,
    O'erbears your officers. The rabble call him lord,
    And, as the world were now but to begin,
    Antiquity forgot, custom not known,
105 The ratifiers and props of every word,
    They cry, "Choose we! Laertes shall be king!"
    Caps, hands, and tongues applaud it to the clouds,
    "Laertes shall be king! Laertes king!"
                     A noise within.

Queen. How cheerfully on the false trail they cry!
110 O, this is counter, you false Danish dogs!
King. The doors are broke.

Enter Laertes with others.

Laertes. Where is this king? — Sirs, stand you all
    without.
All. No, let's come in.
Laertes.   I pray you give me leave.
All. We will, we will.
115 **Laertes.** I thank you. Keep the door.
                      Exit his Followers.
    O thou vile king,
    Give me my father.
Queen.   Calmly, good Laertes.
Laertes. That drop of blood that's calm proclaims me
    bastard,

97 *Switzers* hired Swiss guards 99 *overpeering of* rising to look over
and pass beyond *list* boundary 100 *impiteous* pitiless 101 *head*
armed force 105 *word* promise 110 *counter* hunting backward on the
trail

Cries cuckold to my father, brands the harlot
Even here between the chaste unsmirched brows   120
Of my true mother.

King.   What is the cause, Laertes,
That thy rebellion looks so giantlike?
Let him go, Gertrude. Do not fear our person.
There's such divinity doth hedge a king
That treason can but peep to what it would,   125
Acts little of his will. Tell me, Laertes,
Why thou art thus incensed. Let him go, Gertrude.
Speak, man.

Laertes. Where is my father?

King.   Dead.

Queen.   But not by him.

King. Let him demand his fill.   130

Laertes. How come he dead? I'll not be juggled with.
To hell allegiance, vows to the blackest devil,
Conscience and grace to the profoundest pit!
I dare damnation. To this point I stand,
That both the worlds I give to negligence,   135
Let come what comes, only I'll be revenged
Most throughly for my father.

King.   Who shall stay you?

Laertes. My will, not all the world's.
And for my means, I'll husband them so well
They shall go far with little.

King.   Good Laertes,   140
If you desire to know the certainty
Of your dear father, is't writ in your revenge
That swoopstake you will draw both friend and foe,
Winner and loser?

Laertes. None but his enemies.

King.   Will you know them then?   145

Laertes. To his good friends thus wide I'll ope my
   arms

---

123 *fear* fear for 125 *peep to* i.e. through the barrier 135 *both the
worlds* whatever may result in this world or the next *give to negligence* disregard 137 *throughly* thoroughly 143 *swoopstake* sweep-
stake, taking all stakes on the gambling table

And like the kind life-rend'ring pelican
Repast them with my blood.
King.   Why, now you speak
Like a good child and a true gentleman.
150 That I am guiltless of your father's death,
And am most sensibly in grief for it,
It shall as level to your judgment 'pear
As day does to your eye.
                    A *noise within:* "Let her come in."
Laertes. How now? What noise is that?

Enter Ophelia.

155 O heat, dry up my brains; tears seven times salt
Burn out the sense and virtue of mine eye!
By heaven, thy madness shall be paid by weight
Till our scale turn the beam. O rose of May,
Dear maid, kind sister, sweet Ophelia!
160 O heavens, is't possible a young maid's wits
Should be as mortal as an old man's life?
(Nature is fine in love, and where 'tis fine,
It sends some precious instance of itself
After the thing it loves.)
165 *Ophelia.* They bore him barefaced on the bier   Song.
            Hey non nony, nony, hey nony
            And in his grave rained many a tear —
Fare you well, my dove!
Laertes. Hadst thou thy wits, and didst persuade revenge,
170 It could not move thus.
Ophelia. You must sing "A-down, a-down, and you call
    him a-down-a." O, how the wheel becomes it! It is
    the false steward, that stole his master's daughter.
Laertes. This nothing's more than matter.

147 *life-rend'ring* life-yielding (because the mother pelican supposedly
took blood from her breast with her bill to feed her young) 151 *sensibly* feelingly 152 *level* plain 158 *beam* bar of a balance 162 *fine*
refined to purity 163 *instance* token 172 *wheel* burden, refrain 174
more than matter more meaningful than sane speech

Ophelia. There's rosemary, that's for remembrance. 175
    Pray you, love, remember. And there is pansies,
    that's for thoughts.

Laertes. A document in madness, thoughts and re-
    membrance fitted.

Ophelia. There's fennel for you, and columbines. 180
    There's rue for you, and here's some for me. We
    may call it herb of grace o' Sundays. O, you must
    wear your rue with a difference. There's a daisy. I
    would give you some violets, but they withered all
    when my father died. They say 'a made a good end. 185
    (Sings) For bonny sweet Robin is all my joy.

Laertes. Thought and affliction, passion, hell itself,
    She turns to favor and to prettiness.

Ophelia. And will 'a not come again?   *Song.*
        And will 'a not come again? 190
           No, no, he is dead;
           Go to thy deathbed;
        He never will come again.

        His bread was as white as snow,
        All flaxen was his poll. 195
           He is gone, he is gone,
           And we cast away moan.
        God 'a' mercy on his soul!
    And of all Christian souls, I pray God. God bye you.
                                     Exit.

Laertes. Do you see this, O God? 200

King. Laertes, I must commune with your grief,
    Or you deny me right. Go but apart,
    Make choice of whom your wisest friends you will,
    And they shall hear and judge 'twixt you and me.
    If by direct or by collateral hand 205
    They find us touched, we will our kingdom give,

---

178 *document* lessson   180 *fennel* symbol of flattery   *columbines* symbol of thanklessness   181 *rue* symbol of repentance   183 *daisy* symbol
of dissembling   184 *violets* symbol of faithfulness   188 *favor* charm
195 *poll* head   199 *of* on   205 *collateral* indirect   206 *touched* i.e.
with the crime

Our crown, our life, and all that we call ours,
To you in satisfaction; but if not,
Be you content to lend your patience to us,
210 And we shall jointly labor with your soul
To give it due content.

Laertes.   Let this be so.
His means of death, his obscure funeral —
No trophy, sword, nor hatchment o'er his bones,
No noble rite nor formal ostentation —
15 Cry to be heard, as 'twere from heaven to earth,
That I must call't in question.

King.   So you shall;
And where th' offense is, let the great axe fall.
I pray you go with me.   *Exit all*

❧

ACT IV, SCENE VI

Enter Horatio and others.

Horatio. What are they that would speak with me?
Gentleman. Seafaring men, sir. They say they have
letters for you.   *Exit Attendant.*
Horatio. Let them come in.
I do not know from what part of the world
5 I should be greeted, if not from Lord Hamlet.

Enter Sailors.

Sailor. God bless you, sir.
Horatio. Let him bless thee too.

213 *trophy* memorial   *hatchment* coat of arms   214 *ostentation* ceremony   216 *That* so that

Sailor. 'A shall, sir, an't please him. There's a letter
   for you, sir — it came from th' ambassador that was
   bound for England — if your name be Horatio, as   10
   I am let to know it is.

Horatio. (*reads the letter*) "Horatio, when thou shalt
   have overlooked this, give the fellows some means
   to the king. They have letters for him. Ere we were
   two days old at sea, a pirate of very warlike appoint-   15
   ment gave us chase. Finding ourselves too slow of
   sail, we put on a compelled valor, and in the grapple
   I boarded them. On the instant they got clear of
   our ship; so I alone became their prisoner. They
   have dealt with me like thieves of mercy, but they   20
   knew what they did: I am to do a good turn for
   them. Let the king have the letters I have sent, and
   repair thou to me with as much speed as thou
   wouldest fly death. I have words to speak in thine
   ear will make thee dumb; yet are they much too   25
   light for the bore of the matter. These good fellows
   will bring thee where I am. Rosencrantz and Guildenstern hold their course for England. Of them I
   have much to tell thee. Farewell.

        "He that thou knowest thine, HAMLET."   30
   Come, I will give you way for these your letters,
   And do't the speedier that you may direct me
   To him from whom you brought them.   *Exit all.*

IV, vi, 13 *overlooked* surveyed, scanned   *means* i.e. of access   15–16
appointment equipment   20 *thieves of mercy* merciful thieves   26 *bore*
caliber (as of a gun)

❧

ACT IV, SCENE VII

Enter King and Laertes.

King. Now must your conscience my acquittance seal,
    And you must put me in your heart for friend,
    Sith you have heard, and with a knowing ear,
    That he which hath your noble father slain
    Pursued my life.

5 *Laertes.*   It well appears. But tell me
    Why you proceeded not against these feats
    So crimeful and so capital in nature,
    As by your safety, wisdom, all things else,
    You mainly were stirred up.

    King.   O, for two special reasons,
10 Which may to you perhaps seem much unsinewed,
    But yet to me they're strong. The queen his mother
    Lives almost by his looks, and for myself —
    My virtue or my plague, be it either which —
    She is so conjunctive to my life and soul
15 That, as the star moves not but in his sphere,
    I could not but by her. The other motive
    Why to a public count I might not go
    Is the great love the general gender bear him,
    Who, dipping all his faults in their affection,
20 Would, like the spring that turneth wood to stone,
    Convert his gyves to graces; so that my arrows,
    Too slightly timbered for so loud a wind,
    Would have reverted to my bow again,
    And not where I had aimed them.

IV, vii, 6 *feats* deeds 7 *capital* punishable by death 9 *mainly* power-
fully 14 *conjunctive* closely united 17 *count* trial, accounting 18
general gender common people 21 *gyves* fetters

Laertes. And so have I a noble father lost,   25
  A sister driven into desp'rate terms,
  Whose worth, if praises may go back again,
  Stood challenger on mount of all the age
  For her perfections. But my revenge will come.
King. Break not your sleeps for that. You must not
      think   30
  That we are made of stuff so flat and dull
  That we can let our beard be shook with danger,
  And think it pastime. You shortly shall hear more.
  I loved your father, and we love ourself,
  And that, I hope, will teach you to imagine —   35

Enter a Messenger with letters.

  How now? What news?
Messenger.   Letters, my lord, from Hamlet:
  These to your majesty, this to the queen.
King. From Hamlet? Who brought them?
Messenger. Sailors, my lord, they say; I saw them not.
  They were given me by Claudio; he received them   40
  Of him that brought them.
King.   Laertes, you shall hear them. —
  Leave us.   *Exit Messenger.*
  (*Reads*) "High and mighty, you shall know I am set
  naked on your kingdom. Tomorrow shall I beg
  leave to see your kingly eyes; when I shall (first   45
  asking your pardon thereunto) recount the occasion
  of my sudden and more strange return.

                                          HAMLET."

  What should this mean? Are all the rest come back?
  Or is it some abuse, and no such thing?   50
Laertes. Know you the hand?
King.   'Tis Hamlet's character. "Naked"!

26 *terms* circumstances   27 *back again* i.e. to her better circumstances
28 *on mount* on a height   44 *naked* destitute   50 *abuse* imposture   51
character handwriting

And in a postscript here, he says "alone."
Can you devise me?

Laertes. I am lost in it, my lord. But let him come.
55   It warms the very sickness in my heart
That I shall live and tell him to his teeth,
"Thus diddest thou."

King.   If it be so, Laertes
(As how should it be so? how otherwise?),
Will you be ruled by me?

Laertes.   Ay, my lord,
60   So you will not o'errule me to a peace.

King. To thine own peace. If he be now returned
As checking at his voyage, and that he means
No more to undertake it, I will work him
To an exploit now ripe in my device,
65   Under the which he shall not choose but fall;
And for his death no wind of blame shall breathe,
But even his mother shall uncharge the practice
And call it accident.

Laertes.   My lord, I will be ruled;
The rather if you could devise it so
That I might be the organ.

70 *King.*   It falls right.
You have been talked of since your travel much,
And that in Hamlet's hearing, for a quality
Wherein they say you shine. Your sum of parts
Did not together pluck such envy from him
75   As did that one, and that, in my regard,
Of the unworthiest siege.

Laertes.   What part is that, my lord?

King. A very riband in the cap of youth,
Yet needful too, for youth no less becomes
The light and careless livery that it wears
80   Than settled age his sables and his weeds,
Importing health and graveness. Two months since
Here was a gentleman of Normandy.

53 *devise* explain to 61 *checking at* turning aside from (like a falcon
turning from its quarry for other prey) 67 *uncharge the practice*
acquit the stratagem of being a plot 70 *organ* instrument 76 *siege*
seat, rank 77 *riband* decoration 79 *livery* distinctive attire 80 *sables*
dignified robes richly furred with sable *weeds* distinctive garments
81 *health* welfare, prosperity

I have seen myself, and served against the French,
And they can well on horseback, but this gallant
Had witchcraft in't. He grew into his seat,   85
And to such wondrous doing brought his horse
As had he been incorpsed and deminatured
With the brave beast. So far he topped my thought
That I, in forgery of shapes and tricks,
Come short of what he did.

Laertes.   A Norman was't?   90

King. A Norman.

Laertes. Upon my life, Lamord.

King.   The very same

Laertes. I know him well. He is the brooch indeed
And gem of all the nation.

King. He made confession of you,   95
And gave you such a masterly report
For art and exercise in your defense,
And for your rapier most especial,
That he cried out 'twould be a sight indeed
If one could match you. The scrimers of their na-   100
tion
He swore had neither motion, guard, nor eye,
If you opposed them. Sir, this report of his
Did Hamlet so envenom with his envy
That he could nothing do but wish and beg
Your sudden coming o'er to play with you.   105
Now, out of this —

Laertes.   What out of this, my lord?

King. Laertes, was your father dear to you?
Or are you like the painting of a sorrow,
A face without a heart?

Laertes.   Why ask you this?

King. Not that I think you did not love your father,   110
But that I know love is begun by time,
And that I see, in passages of proof,

---

84 *can well* can perform well 87 *incorpsed* made one body *deminatured* made sharer of nature half and half (as man shares with
horse in the centaur) 88 *topped* excelled *thought* imagination of
possibilities 89 *forgery* invention 93 *brooch* ornament 95 *made confession* admitted the rival accomplishments 100 *scrimers* fencers 112
passages of proof incidents of experience

Time qualifies the spark and fire of it.
There lives within the very flame of love
115 A kind of wick or snuff that will abate it,
And nothing is at a like goodness still,
For goodness, growing to a plurisy,
Dies in his own too much. That we would do
We should do when we would, for this "would"
   changes,
120 And hath abatements and delays as many
As there are tongues, are hands, are accidents,
And then this "should" is like a spendthrift sigh,
That hurts by easing. But to the quick o' th'
   ulcer —
Hamlet comes back; what would you undertake
125 To show yourself your father's son in deed
More than in words?

Laertes.   To cut his throat i' th' church!

King. No place indeed should murther sanctuarize;
Revenge should have no bounds. But, good Laertes,
Will you do this? Keep close within your chamber.
130 Hamlet returned shall know you are come home.
We'll put on those shall praise your excellence
And set a double varnish on the fame
The Frenchman gave you, bring you in fine to-
   gether
And wager on your heads. He, being remiss,
135 Most generous, and free from all contriving,
Will not peruse the foils, so that with ease,
Or with a little shuffling, you may choose
A sword unbated, and, in a pass of practice,
Requite him for your father.

Laertes.   I will do't,
140 And for that purpose I'll anoint my sword.
I bought an unction of a mountebank,

---

113 *qualifies* weakens 115 *snuff* unconsumed portion of the burned
wick 116 *still* always 117 *plurisy* excess 123 *hurts* i.e. shortens life
by drawing blood from the heart (as was believed) *quick* sensitive
flesh 127 *sancturize* protect from punishment, give sanctuary to 131
put on instigate 133 *in fine* finally 134 *remiss* negligent 136 *persue*
scan 138 *unbated* not blunted *pass of practice* thrust made effective
by trickery 141 *unction* ointment *mountebank* quack-doctor

So mortal that, but dip a knife in it,
Where it draws blood no cataplasm so rare,
Collected from all simples that have virtue
Under the moon, can save the thing from death   145
That is but scratched withal. I'll touch my point
With this contagion, that, if I gall him slightly,
It may be death.

King.   Let's further think of this,
Weigh what convenience both of time and means
May fit us to our shape. If this should fail,   150
And that our drift look through our bad perform-
ance,
'Twere better not assayed. Therefore this project
Should have a back or second, that might hold
If this did blast in proof. Soft, let me see.
We'll make a solemn wager on your cunnings —   155
I ha't!
When in your motion you are hot and dry —
As make your bouts more violent to that end —
And that he calls for drink, I'll have preferred him
A chalice for the nonce, whereon but sipping,   160
If he by chance escape your venomed stuck,
Our purpose may hold there. — But stay, what
noise?

Enter Queen.

Queen. One woe doth tread upon another's heel,
So fast they follow. Your sister's drowned, Laertes.
Laetes. Drowned! O, where?   165
Queen. There is a willow grows askant the brook,
That shows his hoar leaves in the glassy stream.
Therewith fantastic garlands did she make
Of crowflowers, nettles, daisies, and long purples,
That liberal shepherds give a grosser name,   170

143 *cataplasm* poultice   144 *simples* herbs   146 *withal* with it   147
gall scratch   150 *shape* plan   151 *drift* intention   *look* show   154
blast in proof burst during trial (like a faulty cannon)   159 *preferred*
offered   160 *nonce* occasion   161 *stuck* thrust   166 *askant* alongside
167 *hoar* gray   170 *liberal* free-spoken, licentious

But our cold maids do dead men's fingers call them.
There on the pendent boughs her crownet weeds
Clamb'ring to hang, an envious sliver broke,
When down her weedy trophies and herself
175   Fell in the weeping brook. Her clothes spread wide,
And mermaidlike awhile they bore her up,
Which time she chanted snatches of old lauds,
As one incapable of her own distress,
Or like a creature native and indued
180   Unto that element. But long it could not be
Till that her garments, heavy with their drink,
Pulled the poor wretch from her melodious lay
To muddy death.
Laertes.   Alas, then she is drowned?
Queen. Drowned, drowned.
185   *Laertes.* Too much of water hast thou, poor Ophelia,
And therefore I forbid my tears; but yet
It is our trick; nature her custom holds,
Let shame say what it will. When these are gone,
The woman will be out. Adieu, my lord.
190   I have a speech o' fire, that fain would blaze
But that this folly drowns it.   *Exit.*
King.   Let's follow, Gertrude.
How much I had to do to calm his rage!
Now fear I this will give it start again;
Therefore let's follow.   *Exit all.*

---

172 *crownet* coronet, woven into a crown   177 *lauds* hymns   178 *incapable of* insensible to   179 *indued* endowed   187 *trick* way (i.e. to shed tears when sorrowful)   189 *woman* unmanly part of nature

ACT V, SCENE I

Enter two Clowns.

Clown. Is she to be buried in Christian burial when
she willfully seeks her own salvation?

Other. I tell thee she is. Therefore make her grave
straight. The crowner hath sate on her, and finds it
Christian burial.   5

Clown. How can that be, unless she drowned herself
in her own defense?

Other. Why, 'tis found so.

Clown. It must be *se offendendo*; it cannot be else.
For here lies the point: if I drown myself wittingly,   10
it argues an act, and an act hath three branches —
it is to act, to do, and to perform. Argal, she
drowned herself wittingly.

Other. Nay, but hear you, Goodman Delver.

Clown. Give me leave. Here lies the water — good.   15
Here stands the man — good. If the man go to this
water and drown himself, it is, will he nill he, he
goes, mark you that. But if the water come to him
and drown him, he drowns not himself. Argal, he
that is not guilty of his own death shortens not his   20
own life.

V, i, s.d. *Clowns* rustics   1 *in Christian burial* in consecrated ground
with the prescribed service of the Church (a burial denied to suicides)
4 *straight* straightway, at once   *crowner* coroner   9 *se offendendo* a
clownish transformation of *se defendendo,* "in self-defense"   12 *Argal*
for *ergo,* "therefore"   14 *Delver* Digger   17 *will he nill he* willy-nilly

Other. But is this law?

Clown. Ay marry, is't — crowner's quest law.

Other. Will you ha' the truth on't? If this had not
been a gentlewoman, she should have been buried
out o' Christian burial.

Clown. Why, there thou say'st. And the more pity
that great folk should have count'nance in this world
to drown or hang themselves more than their even-
Christen. Come, my spade. There is no ancient
gentlemen but gard'ners, ditchers, and grave-makers.
They hold up Adam's profession.

Other. Was he a gentleman?

Clown. 'A was the first that ever bore arms.

Other. Why, he had none.

Clown. What, art a heathen? How dost thou understand the Scripture? The Scripture says Adam
digged. Could he dig without arms? I'll put another
question to thee. If thou answerest me not to the
purpose, confess thyself —

Other. Go to.

Clown. What is he that builds stronger than either
the mason, the shipwright, or the carpenter?

Other. The gallows-maker, for that frame outlives a
thousand tenants.

Clown. I like thy wit well, in good faith. The gallows
does well. But how does it well? It does well to
those that do ill. Now thou dost ill to say the gallows is built stronger than the church. Argal, the
gallows may do well to thee. To't again, come.

Other. Who builds stronger than a mason, a shipwright, or a carpenter?

Clown. Ay, tell me that, and unyoke.

Other. Marry, now I can tell.

Clown. To't.

Other. Mass, I cannot tell.

---

23 *quest* inquest 27 *thou say'st* you have it right 28 *count'nance*
privilege 29–30 *even-Christen* fellow Christian 35 *had none* i.e. had
no gentleman's coat of arms 53 *unyoke* i.e. unharness your powers
of thought after a good day's work 56 *Mass* by the Mass

Clown. Cudgel thy brains no more about it, for your
dull ass will not mend his pace with beating. And
when you are asked this question next, say "a grave-
maker." The houses he makes last till doomsday.   60
Go, get thee in, and fetch me a stoup of liquor.

Exit Other Clown.

Enter Hamlet and Horatio (as Clown digs and sings).

In youth when I did love, did love,   *Song.*
   Methought it was very sweet
To contract — O — the time for — a — my
   behove,
   O, methought there — a — was nothing —   65
   a — meet.

Hamlet. Has this fellow no feeling of his business,
 that 'a sings at grave-making?
Horatio. Custom hath made it in him a property of
easiness.   70
Hamlet. 'Tis e'en so. The hand of little employment
hath the daintier sense.
Clown. But age with his stealing steps   *Song.*
   Hath clawed me in his clutch,
   And hath slipped me intil the land,   75
   As if I had never been such.

Throws up a skull.

Hamlet. That skull had a tongue in it, and could sing
once. How the knave jowls it to the ground, as if
'twere Cain's jawbone, that did the first murther!
This might be the pate of a politician, which this   80
ass now o'erreaches; one that would circumvent
God, might it not?
Horatio. It might, my lord.
Hamlet. Or of a courtier, which could say "Good
morrow, sweet lord! How dost thou, sweet lord?"   85

61 *stoup* large mug 64 *behove* behoof, benefit 69 *property* peculiarity 70 *easiness* easy acceptability 72 *daintier sense* more delicate
feeling (because the hand is less calloused) 75 *intil* into 78 *jowls*
hurls 80 *politician* crafty schemer 81 *o'erreaches* gets the better of
(with a play upon the literal meaning)

This might be my Lord Such-a-one, that praised my
Lord Such-a-one's horse when 'a meant to beg it,
might it not?

Horatio. Ay, my lord.

90 *Hamlet.* Why, e'en so, and now my Lady Worm's,
chapless, and knocked about the mazzard with a
sexton's spade. Here's fine revolution, an we had the
trick to see't. Did these bones cost no more the
breeding but to play at loggets with 'em? Mine
95 ache to think on't.

Clown. A pickaxe and a spade, a spade,   *Song.*
          For and a shrouding sheet.
          O, a pit of clay for to be made
          For such a guest is meet.

                                        Throws up another skull.

100 *Hamlet.* There's another. Why may not that be the
skull of a lawyer? Where be his quiddities now, his
quillities, his cases, his tenures, and his tricks? Why
does he suffer this mad knave now to knock him
about the sconce with a dirty shovel, and will not
105 tell him of his action of battery? Hum! This fellow
might be in's time a great buyer of land, with his
statutes, his recognizances, his fines, his double
vouchers, his recoveries. Is this the fine of his fines,
and the recovery of his recoveries, to have his fine
110 pate full of fine dirt? Will his vouchers vouch him
no more of his purchases, and double ones too,
than the length and breadth of a pair of indentures?
The very conveyances of his lands will scarcely lie
in this box, and must th' inheritor himself have no
115 more, ha?

---

91 *chapless* lacking the lower chap or jaw   *mazzard* head   94 *loggets*
small pieces of wood thrown in a game   97 *For and* and   101 *quiddities* subtleties (from scholastic "quidditas," meaning the distinctive
nature of anything)   102 *quillities* nice distinctions   *tenures* holdings
of property   104 *sconce* head   107 *statutes, recognizances* legal documents or bonds acknowledging debt   107-8 *fines, recoveries* modes of
converting estate tail into fee simple   *vouchers* persons vouched or
called on to warrant a title   *fine* end (introducing a word play involv-
ing four meanings of "fine")   112 *pair of indentures* deed or legal
agreement in duplicate   113 *conveyances* deeds

Horatio. Not a jot more, my lord.

Hamlet. Is not parchment made of sheepskins?

Horatio. Ay, my lord, and of calveskins too.

Hamlet. They are sheep and claves which seek out
    assurance in that. I will speak to this fellow. Whose   120
    grave's this, sirrah?

Clown. Mine, sir.

    (*Sings*) O, a pit of clay for to be made
               For such a guest is meet.

Hamlet. I think it be thine indeed, for thou liest in't.   125

Clown. You lie out on't, sir, and therefore 'tis not
    yours. For my part, I do not lie in't, yet it is mine.

Hamlet. Thou dost lie in't, to be in't and say it is
    thine. 'Tis for the dead, not for the quick; there-
    fore thou liest.   130

Clown. 'Tis a quick lie, sir; 'twill away again from me
    to you.

Hamlet. What man dost thou dig it for?

Clown. For no man, sir.

Hamlet. What woman then?   135

Clown. For none neither.

Hamlet. Who is to be buried in't?

Clown. One that was a woman, sir; but, rest her soul,
    she's dead.

Hamlet. How absolute the knave is! We must speak   140
    by the card, or equivocation will undo us. By the
    Lord, Horatio, this three years I have taken note of
    it, the age is grown so picked that the toe of the
    peasant comes so near the heel of the courtier he
    galls his kibe.— How long hast thou been a grave-   145
    maker?

Clown. Of all the days i' th' year, I came to't that day
    that our last king Hamlet overcame Fortinbras.

Hamlet. How long is that since?

Clown. Cannot you tell that? Every fool can tell that.   150

129 *quick* living   140 *absolute* positive   141 *by the card* by the card
on which the points of the mariner's compass are marked, absolutely
to the point   *equivocation* ambiguity   143 *picked* refined, spruce   145
galls chafes   *kibe* chilblain

It was the very day that young Hamlet was born —
he that is mad, and sent into England.

Hamlet. Ay, marry, why was he sent into England?

Clown. Why, because 'a was mad. 'A shall recover his
155 wits there; or, if 'a do not, 'tis no great matter there.

Hamlet. Why?

Clown. 'Twill not be seen in him there. There the
men are as mad as he.

Hamlet. How came he mad?

160 *Clown.* Very strangely, they say.

Hamlet. How strangely?

Clown. Faith, e'en with losing his wits.

Hamlet. Upon what ground?

Clown. Why, here in Denmark. I have been sexton
165 here, man and boy, thirty years.

Hamlet. How long will a man lie i' th' earth ere he
rot?

Clown. Faith, if 'a be not rotten before 'a die (as we
have many pocky corses now-a-days that will scarce
170 hold the laying in), 'a will last you some eight year
or nine year. A tanner will last you nine year.

Hamlet. Why he more than another?

Clown. Why, sir, his hide is so tanned with his trade
that 'a will keep out water a great while, and your
175 water is a sore decayer of your whoreson dead body.
Here's a skull now hath lien you i' th' earth three-
and twenty years.

Hamlet. Whose was it?

Clown. A whoreson mad fellow's it was. Whose do
180 you think it was?

Hamlet. Nay, I know not.

Clown. A pestilence on him for a mad roguel 'A
poured a flagon of Rhenish on my head once. This
same skull, sir, was — sir — Yorick's skull, the
185 king's jester.

---

169 *pocky* rotten (literally, corrupted by pox, or syphilis)   183 *Rhenish* Rhine wine

Hamlet. This?

Clown. E'en that.

Hamlet. Let me see. (*Takes the skull.*) Alas, poor
Yorick! I knew him, Horatio, a fellow of infinite
jest, of most excellent fancy. He hath borne me on   190
his back a thousand times. And now how abhorred
in my imagination it is! My gorge rises at it. Here
hung those lips that I have kissed I know not how
oft. Where be your gibes now? Your gambols, your
songs, your flashes of merriment that were wont to   195
set the table on a roar? Not one now to mock your
own grinning? Quite chapfall'n? Now get you to
my lady's chamber, and tell her, let her paint an
inch thick, to this favor she must come. Make her
laugh at that. Prithee, Horatio, tell me one thing.   200

Horatio. What's that, my lord?

Hamlet. Dost thou think Alexander looked o' this
fashion i' th' earth?

Horatio. E'en so.

Hamlet. And smelt so? Pah!   *Puts down the skull.* 205

Horatio. E'en so, my lord.

Hamlet. To what base uses we may return, Horatio!
Why may not imagination trace the noble dust of
Alexander till 'a find it stopping a bunghole?

Horatio. 'Twere to consider too curiously, to consider 210
so.

Hamlet. No, faith, not a jot, but to follow him thither
with modesty enough, and likelihood to lead it; as
thus: Alexander died, Alexander was buried, Alexander returneth to dust; the dust is earth; of earth 215
we make loam; and why of that loam whereto he
was converted might they not stop a beer barrel?
Imperious Caesar, dead and turned to clay,
Might stop a hole to keep the wind away.
O, that that earth which kept the world in awe   220

197 *chapfall'n* lacking the lower chap, or jaw (with a play on the sense
"down in the mouth," "dejected") 199 *favor* countenance, aspect
210 *curiously* minutely 213 *modesty* moderation 218 *Imperious* imperial

Should patch a wall t' expel the winter's flaw!
But soft, but soft awhile! Here comes the king —

*Enter King, Queen, Laertes, and the Corse, with
Lords attendant and a Doctor of Divinity as Priest.*

The queen, the courtiers. Who is this they follow?
And with such maimèd rites? This doth betoken
225 The corse they follow did with desp'rate hand
Fordo it own life. 'Twas of some estate.
Couch we awhile, and mark. *Retires with Horatio.*
Laertes. What ceremony else?
Hamlet.   That is Laertes,
A very noble youth. Mark.
230 *Laertes.* What ceremony else?
Doctor. Her obsequies have been as far enlarged
As we have warranty. Her death was doubtful,
And, but that great command o'ersways the order,
She should in ground unsanctified have lodged
235 Till the last trumpet. For charitable prayers,
Shards, flints, and pebbles should be thrown on her.
Yet here she is allowed her virgin crants,
Her maiden strewments, and the bringing home
Of bell and burial.
Laertes. Must there no more be done?
240 *Doctor.*   No more be done.
We should profane the service of the dead
To sing a requiem and such rest to her
As to peace-parted souls.
Laertes.   Lay her i' th' earth,
And from her fair and unpolluted flesh
245 May violets spring! I tell thee, churlish priest,
A minist'ring angel shall my sister be
When thou liest howling.
Hamlet.   What, the fair Ophelia?

221 *flaw* gust of wind 226 *Fordo* destroy *it* its *estate* rank 227
Couch hide 236 *Shards* broken pieces of pottery 237 *crants* garlands
238 *strewments* strewings of the grave with flowers *bringing home*
lay to rest

Queen. Sweets to the sweet! Farewell.
                                        Scatters flowers.
  I hoped thou shouldst have been my Hamlet's wife.
  I thought thy bride-bed to have decked, sweet maid,   250
  And not have strewed thy grave.
Laertes.   O, treble woe
  Fall ten times treble on that cursèd head
  Whose wicked deed thy most ingenious sense
  Deprived thee of! Hold off the earth awhile,
  Till I have caught her once more in mine arms.   255
                                Leaps in the grave.
  Now pile your dust upon the quick and dead
  Till of this flat a mountain you have made
  T' o'ertop old Pelion or the skyish head
  Of blue Olympus.
Hamlet.   (*coming forward*) What is he   260
      whose grief
  Bears such an emphasis? whose phrase of sorrow
  Conjures the wand'ring stars, and makes them stand
  Like wonder-wounded hearers? This is I,
  Hamlet the Dane.   *Leaps in after Laertes.*
Laertes.   The devil take thy soul!
                                Grapples with him.
Hamlet. Thou pray'st not well.   265
  I prithee take thy fingers from my throat,
  For, though I am not splenitive and rash,
  Yet have I in me something dangerous,
  Which let thy wisdom fear. Hold off thy hand.
King. Pluck them asunder.
Queen.   Hamlet, Hamlet!   270
All. Gentlemen!
Horatio.   Good my lord, be quiet.

Attendants part them, and they come out of the grave.

253 *most ingenious* of quickest apprehension 258 *Pelion* a mountain
in Thessaly, like Olympus and also Ossa (the allusion being to the war
in which the Titans fought the gods and attempted to heap Ossa and
Olympus on Pelion, or Pelion and Ossa on Olympus, in order to scale
heaven) 262 *Conjures* charms, puts a spell upon *wand'ring stars*
planets 267 *splenitive* of fiery temper (the spleen being considered
the seat of anger)

Hamlet. Why, I will fight with him upon this theme
    Until my eyelids will no longer wag.

Queen. O my son, what theme?

275 *Hamlet.* I loved Ophelia. Forty thousand brothers
    Could not with all their quantity of love
    Make up my sum. What wilt thou do for her?

King. O, he is mad, Laertes.

Queen. For love of God, forbear him.

280 *Hamlet.* 'Swounds, show me what thou't do.
    Woo't weep? woo't fight? woo't fast? woo't tear
      thyself?
    Woo't drink up esill? eat a crocodile?
    I'll do't. Dost thou come here to whine?
    To outface me with leaping in her grave?

285   Be buried quick with her, and so will I.
    And if thou prate of mountains, let them throw
    Millions of acres on us, till our ground,
    Singeing his pate against the burning zone,
    Make Ossa like a wart! Nay, an thou'lt mouth,
    I'll rant as well as thou.

290 *Queen.*   This is mere madness;
    And thus a while the fit will work on him.
    Anon, as patient as the female dove
    When that her golden couplets are disclosed,
    His silence will sit drooping.

Hamlet.   Hear you, sir.

295 What is the reason that you use me thus?
    I loved you ever. But it is no matter.
    Let Hercules himself do what he may,
    The cat will mew, and dog will have his day.

King. I pray thee, good Horatio, wait upon him.

                          Exit Hamlet and Horatio.

    (*to Laertes*) Strengthen your patience in our last
300   night's speech.
    We'll put the matter to the present push —

280 *'Swounds* Elizabethan oath meaning God's wounds 281 *Woo't*
wilt (thou) 282 *esill* vinegar 285 *quick* alive 290 *mere* absolute
293 *couplets* pair of fledgings *disclosed* hatched 300 *in* by calling to
mind 301 *present push* immediate trial

This grave shall have a living monument.
An hour of quiet shortly shall we see;
Till then in patience our proceeding be.   *Exit all.*

ACT V, SCENE II

Enter Hamlet and Horatio.

Hamlet. So much for this, sir; now shall you see the
  other. You do remember all the circumstance?
Horatio. Remember it, my lord!
Hamlet. Sir, in my heart there was a kind of fighting
  That would not let me sleep. Methought I lay   5
  Worse than the mutines in the bilboes. Rashly,
  And praised be rashness for it — let us know,
  Our indiscretion sometime serves us well
  When our deep plots do pall, and that should learn
    us
  There's a divinity that shapes our ends,   10
  Rough-hew them how we will —
Horatio.   That is most certain.
Hamlet. Up from my cabin,
  My sea-gown scarfed about me, in the dark
  Groped I to find out them, had my desire,
  Fingered their packet, and in fine withdrew   15
  To mine own room again, making so bold,
  My fears forgetting manners, to unseal
  Their grand commission; where I found, Horatio —
  Ah, royal knavery! — an exact command,
  Larded with many several sorts of reasons,   20
  Importing Denmark's health, and England's too,

V, ii, 6 *mutines* mutineers *bilboes* fetters   9 *pall* fail   11 *Rough-hew*
shape roughly in trial form   15 *Fingered* filched   *in fine* finally   20
Larded enriched   21 *Importing* relating to

With, ho! such bugs and goblins in my life,
That on the supervise, no leisure bated,
No, not to stay the grinding of the axe,
My head should be struck off.

25 *Horatio.*   Is't possible?

Hamlet. Here's the commission; read it at more
    leisure.
But wilt thou hear me how I did proceed?

Horatio. I beseech you.

Hamlet. Being thus benetted round with villainies,
30   Or I could make a prologue to my brains,
They had begun the play. I sat me down,
Devised a new commission, wrote it fair.
I once did hold it, as our statists do,
A baseness to write fair, and labored much
35 How to forget that learning, but, sir, now
It did me yeoman's service. Wilt thou know
Th' effect of what I wrote?

Horatio   Ay, good my lord.

Hamlet. An earnest conjuration from the king,
As love between them like the palm might flourish,
40 As peace should still her wheaten garland wear
And stand a comma 'tween their amities,
And many such-like as's of great charge,
That on the view and knowing of these contents,
Without debatement further, more or less,
45 He should the bearers put to sudden death,
Not shriving time allowed.

Horatio.   How was this sealed?

Hamlet. Why, even in that was heaven ordinant.
I had my father's signet in my purse,
Which was the model of that Danish seal,

22 *bugs* bugbears *in my life* to be encountered as dangers if I should
be allowed to live 23 *supervise* perusal *bated* deducted, allowed 30
Or ere 33 *statists* statesmen 34 *fair* with professional clarity (like a
clerk or a scrivener, not like a gentleman) 36 *yeomen's service* stout
service such as yeomen footsoldiers gave as archers 37 *effect* purport
40 *wheaten garland* adornment of fruitful agriculture 41 *comma* con-
nective (because it indicates continuity of thought in a sentence) 42
charge burden (with a double meaning to fit a play that makes "as's"
into "asses") 46 *shriving time* time for confession and absolution 47
ordinant controlling 49 *model* counterpart

Folded the writ up in the form of th' other,   50
Subscribed it, gave't th' impression, placed it safely,
The changeling never known. Now, the next day
Was our sea-fight, and what to this was sequent
Thou know'st already.

Horatio. So Guildenstern and Rosencrantz go to't.   55

Hamlet. Why, man, they did make love to this employment.
They are not near my conscience; their defeat
Does by their own insinuation grow.
'Tis dangerous when the baser nature comes
Between the pass and fell incensèd points   60
Of mighty opposites.

Horatio.   Why, what a king is this!

Hamlet. Does it not, think thee, stand me now
    upon —
He that hath killed my king, and whored my
    mother,
Popped in between th' election and my hopes,
Thrown out his angle for my proper life,   65
And with such coz'nage — is't not perfect con-
    science
To quit him with this arm? And is't not to be
    damned
To let this canker of our nature come
In further evil?

Horatio. It must be shortly known to him from England   70
What is the issue of the business there.

Hamlet. It will be short; the interim is mine,
And a man's life's no more than to say "one."
But I am very sorry, good Horatio,
That to Laertes I forgot myself,   75
For by the image of my cause I see

---

51 *impression* i.e. of the signet   53 *sequent* subsequent   58 *insinuation*
intrusion   60 *pass* thrust   *fell* fierce   62 *stand* rest incumbent   64
election i.e. to the kingship (the Danish kingship being elective)   65
angle fishing line   *proper* own   66 *coz'nage* cozenage, trickery   67 *quit*
repay   68 *canker* cancer, ulcer

The portraiture of his. I'll court his favors.
But sure the bravery of his grief did put me
Into a tow'ring passion.

Horatio.   Peace, who comes here?

Enter Osric, a courtier.

Osric. Your lordship is right welcome back to Den-
80   mark.

Hamlet. I humbly thank you, sir. (*aside to Horatio*)
Dost know this waterfly?

Horatio. (*aside to Hamlet*) No, my good lord.

Hamlet. (*aside to Horatio*) Thy state is the more
85   gracious, for 'tis a vice to know him. He hath much
land, and fertile. Let a beast be lord of beasts,
and his crib shall stand at the king's mess. 'Tis a
chough, but, as I say, spacious in the possession of
dirt.

90   *Osric.* Sweet lord, if your lordship were at leisure, I
should impart a thing to you from his majesty.

Hamlet. I will receive it, sir, with all diligence of
spirit. Put your bonnet to his right use. 'Tis for the
head.

95   *Osric.* I thank your lordship, it is very hot.

Hamlet. No, believe me, 'tis very cold; the wind is
northerly.

Osric. It is indifferent cold, my lord, indeed.

Hamlet. But yet methinks it is very sultry and hot for
100   my complexion.

Osric. Exceedingly, my lord; it is very sultry, as 'twere
— I cannot tell how. But, my lord, his majesty
bade me signify to you that 'a has laid a great wager
on your head. Sir, this is the matter —

105   *Hamlet.* I beseech you remember.

                    Hamlet moves him to put on his hat.

---

78 *bravery* ostentatious display 87 *mess* table 88 *chough* jackdaw,
chatterer 98 *indifferent* somewhat 100 *complexion* temperament 105
remember i.e. remember you have done all that courtesy demands

Osric. Nay, good my lord; for mine ease, in good faith.
Sir, here is newly come to our court Laertes —
believe me, an absolute gentleman, full of most
excellent differences, of very soft society and great
showing. Indeed, to speak feelingly of him, he is   110
the card or calendar of gentry; for you shall find in
him the continent of what part a gentleman would
see.

Hamlet. Sir, his definement suffers no perdition in
you, though, I know, to divide him inventorially   115
would dozy th' arithmetic of memory, and yet but
yaw neither in respect of his quick sail. But, in the
verity of extolment, I take him to be a soul of great
article, and his infusion of such dearth and rareness,
as, to make true diction of him, his semblable is his   120
mirror, and who else would trace him, his umbrage, nothing more.

Osric. Your lordship speaks most infallibly of him.

Hamlet. The concernancy, sir? Why do we wrap the
gentleman in our more rawer breath?   125

Osric. Sir?

Horatio. Is't not possible to understand in another
tongue? You will to't, sir, really.

Hamlet. What imports the nomination of this gentleman?   130

Osric. Of Laertes?

Horatio. (*aside to Hamlet*) His purse is empty already.
All's golden words are spent.

Hamlet. Of him, sir.

Osric. I know you are not ignorant —

106 *for mine ease* i.e. I keep my hat off just for comfort (a conven-
tional polite phrase)   109 *differences* differentiating characteristics,
special qualities   *soft society* gentle manners   109–10 *great showing*
noble appearance   110 *feelingly* appropriately   111 *card* map   *calendar* guide   *gentry* gentlemanliness   112 *continent* all-containing em-
bodiment (with an implication of geographical continent to go with
card)   114 *definement* definition   *perdition* loss   116 *dozy* dizzy, stag-
ger   117 *yaw* hold to a course unsteadily like a ship that steers wild
neither for all that   *in respect of* in comparison with   119 *article*
scope, importance   *infusion* essence   *dearth* scarcity   120 *semblable*
likeness (i.e. only likeness)   121 *trace* follow   121–22 *umbrage* shadow
124 *concernancy* relevance   125 *rawer breath* cruder speech   128 *to't*
i.e. get to an understanding   129 *nomination* mention

Hamlet. I would you did, sir; yet, in faith, if you did,
   it would not much approve me. Well, sir?

Osric. You are not ignorant of what excellence Laertes
   is —

140 *Hamlet.* I dare not confess that, lest I should compare
   with him in excellence; but to know a man well
   were to know himself.

Osric. I mean, sir, for his weapon; but in the impu-
   tation laid on him by them, in his meed he's un-
145 fellowed.

Hamlet. What's his weapon?

Osric. Rapier and dagger.

Hamlet. That's two of his weapons — but well.

Osric. The king, sir, hath wagered with him six Bar-
150 bary horses, against the which he has impawned, as
   I take it, six French rapiers and poniards, with their
   assigns, as girdle, hangers, and so. Three of the
   carriages, in faith, are very dear to fancy, very
   responsive to the hilts, most delicate carriages, and
155 of very liberal conceit.

Hamlet. What call you the carriages?

Horatio. (aside to Hamlet) I knew you must be edified
   by the margent ere you had done.

Osric. The carriages, sir, are the hangers.

160 *Hamlet.* The phrase would be more germane to the
   matter if we could carry a cannon by our sides. I
   would it might be hangers till then. But on! Six
   Barbary horses against six French swords, their assigns, and three liberal-conceited carriages — that's
165 the French bet against the Danish. Why is this all
   impawned, as you call it?

Osric. The king, sir, hath laid, sir, that in a dozen
   passes between yourself and him he shall not exceed you three hits; he hath laid on twelve for nine,

---

137 *approve me* to be my credit   140 *compare* compete   144 *meed*
worth   150 *impawned* staked   152 *assigns* appurtenances   *hangers*
straps by which the sword hangs from the belt   153 *dear to fancy* very
finely designed   154 *responsive* corresponding closely   155 *liberal conceit* tasteful design, refined conception   158 *margent* margin

and it would come to immediate trial if your lord- 170
ship would vouchsafe the answer.

Hamlet. How if I answer no?

Osric. I mean, my lord, the opposition of your person
in trial.

Hamlet. Sir, I will walk here in the hall. If it please 175
his majesty, it is the breathing time of day with me.
Let the foils be brought, the gentleman willing, and
the king hold his purpose, I will win for him an I
can; if not, I will gain nothing but my shame and
the odd hits. 180

Osric. Shall I redeliver you e'en so?

Hamlet. To this effect, sir, after what flourish your
nature will.

Osric. I commend my duty to your lordship.

Hamlet. Yours, yours. (*Exit Osric.*) He does well to 185
commend it himself; there are no tongues else for's
turn.

Horatio. This lapwing runs away with the shell on his
head.

Hamlet. 'A did comply, sir, with his dug before 'a 190
sucked it. Thus has he, and many more of the same
bevy that I know the drossy age dotes on, only got
the tune of the time and, out of an habit of encounter, a kind of yeasty collection, which carries
them through and through the most fanned and 195
winnowed opinions; and do but blow them to their
trial, the bubbles are out.

Enter a Lord.

Lord. My lord, his majesty commended him to you
by young Osric, who brings back to him that you
attend him in the hall. He sends to know if your 200

176 *breathing time* exercise hour 178 *an* if 188 *lapwing* a bird reputed to be so precocious as to run as soon as hatched 190 *comply*
observe formalities of courtesy *dug* mother's nipple 192 *bevy* company *drossy* frivolous 195–96 *fanned and winnowed* select and refined

pleasure hold to play with Laertes, or that you will
take longer time.

Hamlet. I am constant to my purposes; they follow the
king's pleasure. If his fitness speaks, mine is ready;
205   now or whensoever, provided I be so able as now.

Lord. The king and queen and all are coming down.

Hamlet. In happy time.

Lord. The queen desires you to use some gentle entertainment to Laertes before you fall to play.

210 *Hamlet.* She well instructs me.   *Exit Lord.*

Horatio. You will lose this wager, my lord.

Hamlet. I do not think so. Since he went into France
I have been in continual practice. I shall win at the
odds. But thou wouldst not think how ill all's here
215   about my heart. But it is no matter.

Horatio. Nay, good my lord —

Hamlet. It is but foolery, but it is such a kind of gaingiving as would perhaps trouble a woman.

Horatio. If your mind dislike anything, obey it. I will
220   forestall their repair hither and say you are not fit.

Hamlet. Not a whit, we defy augury. There is special
providence in the fall of a sparrow. If it be now, 'tis
not to come; if it be not to come, it will be now; if
it be not now, yet it will come. The readiness is all.
225 Since no man of aught he leaves knows, what is't to
leave betimes? Let be.

*A table prepared. Enter Trumpets, Drums, and
Officers with cushions; King, Queen, Osric, and all
the State, with foils, daggers, and stoups of
wine borne in; and Laertes.*

King. Come, Hamlet, come, and take this hand from
me.   *The King puts Laertes' hand into Hamlet's.*

---

207 *In happy time* I am happy (a polite response)   208–9 *entertainment* words of reception or greeting   217–18 *gaingiving* misgiving   224
all all that matters

Hamlet. Give me your pardon, sir. I have done you
    wrong,

    But pardon't, as you are a gentleman.   230

    This presence knows, and you must needs have
      heard,

    How I am punished with a sore distraction.

    What I have done

    That might your nature, honor, and exception

    Roughly awake, I here proclaim was madness.   235

    Was't Hamlet wronged Laertes? Never Hamlet.

    If Hamlet from himself be ta'en away,

    And when he's not himself does wrong Laertes,

    Then Hamlet does it not, Hamlet denies it.

    Who does it then? His madness. If't be so,   240

    Hamlet is of the faction that is wronged;

    His madness is poor Hamlet's enemy.

    Sir, in this audience,

    Let my disclaiming from a purposed evil

    Free me so far in your most generous thoughts   245

    That I have shot my arrow o'er the house

    And hurt my brother.

Laertes.   I am satisfied in nature,

    Whose motive in this case should stir me most

    To my revenge. But in my terms of honor

    I stand aloof, and will no reconcilement   250

    Till by some elder masters of known honor

    I have a voice and precedent of peace

    To keep my name ungored. But till that time

    I do receive your offered love like love,

    And will not wrong it.

Hamlet.   I embrace it freely,

    And will this brother's wager frankly play.

    Give us the foils. Come on.

Laertes.   Come, one for me.

Hamlet. I'll be your foil, Laertes. In mine ignorance

---

231 *presence* assembly   234 *exception* disapproval   241 *faction* body
of persons taking a side in a contention   247 *nature* natural feeling
249 *terms of honor* position as a man of honor   252 *voice* authoritative
statement   253 *ungored* uninjured.

Your skill shall, like a star i' th' darkest night,
Stick fiery off indeed.

260 *Laertes.*   You mock me, sir.
Hamlet. No, by this hand.
King. Give them the foils, young Osric. Cousin Hamlet,
You know the wager?
Hamlet.   Very well, my lord.
Your grace has laid the odds o' th' weaker side.
265 *King.* I do not fear it, I have seen you both;
But since he is bettered, we have therefore odds.
Laertes. This is too heavy; let me see another.
Hamlet. This likes me well. These foils have all a
length?   *Prepare to play.*
270 *Osric.* Ay, my good lord.
King. Set me the stoups of wine upon that table.
If Hamlet give the first or second hit,
Or quit in answer of the third exchange,
Let all the battlements their ordnance fire.
275 The king shall drink to Hamlet's better breath,
And in the cup an union shall he throw
Richer than that which four successive kings
In Denmark's crown have worn. Give me the cups,
And let the kettle to the trumpet speak,
280 The trumpet to the cannoneer without,
The cannons to the heavens, the heaven to earth,
"Now the king drinks to Hamlet." Come, begin.
                             Trumpets the while.
And you, the judges, bear a wary eye.
Hamlet. Come on, sir.
Laertes.   Come, my lord.   *They play.*
Hamlet.   One.
Laertes.   No.
Hamlet.   Judgment?
Osric. A hit, a very palpable hit.
                    *Drum, trumpets, and shot. Flourish; a piece
                                            goes off.*

258 *foil* setting that displays a jewel advantageously (with a play upon
the meaning "weapon") 260 *Stick fiery off* show in brilliant relief
273 *quit* repay by a hit 276 *union* pearl 279 *kettle* kettledrum

Laertes.   Well, again.   285
King. Stay, give me drink. Hamlet, this pearl is thine.
   Here's to thy health. Give him the cup.
Hamlet. I'll play this bout first; set it by awhile.
   Come. (*They play.*) Another hit. What say you?
Laertes. A touch, a touch; I do confess't.   290
King. Our son shall win.
Queen.   He's fat, and scant of breath.
   Here, Hamlet, take my napkin, rub thy brows.
   The queen carouses to thy fortune, Hamlet.
Hamlet. Good madam!
King.   Gertrude, do not drink.
Queen. I will, my lord; I pray you pardon me.   *Drinks.*   295
King. (*aside*) It is the poisoned cup; it is too late.
Hamlet. I dare not drink yet, madam — by and by.
Queen. Come, let me wipe thy face.
Laertes. My lord, I'll hit him now.
King.   I do not think't.
Laertes. (*aside*) And yet it is almost against my con-   300
   science.
Hamlet. Come for the third, Laertes. You but dally.
   I pray you pass with your best violence;
   I am afeard you make a wanton of me.
Laertes. Say you so? Come on.   *They play.*   305
Osric. Nothing neither way.
Laertes. Have at you now!
In scuffling they change rapiers, and both are wounded
                        with the poisoned weapon.
King.   Part them. They are incensed.
Hamlet. Nay, come — again!   *The Queen falls.*
Osric.   Look to the queen there, ho!
Horatio. They bleed on both sides. How is it, my lord?
Osric. How is't, Laertes?   310
Laertes. Why, as a woodcock to mine own springe,
   Osric.
   I am justly killed with mine own treachery.

---

291 *fat* not physically fit, out of training 292 *napkin* handkerchief
293 *carouses* drinks a toast 304 *wanton* pampered child 311 *wood-*
cock a bird reputed to be stupid and easily trapped *springe* trap

Hamlet. How does the queen?

King.   She sounds to see them bleed.

Queen. No, no, the drink, the drink! O my dear
315   Hamlet! The drink, the drink! I am poisoned.

Hamlet. O villain! Ho! let the door be locked.
Treachery! Seek it out.   *Laertes falls.*

Laertes. It is here, Hamlet. Hamlet, thou art slain;
No med'cine in the world can do thee good.
320   In thee there is not half an hour's life.
The teacherous instrument is in thy hand,
Unbated and envenomed. The foul practice
Hath turned itself on me. Lo, here I lie,
Never to rise again. Thy mother's poisoned.
325   I can no more. The king, the king's to blame.

Hamlet. The point envenomed too?
Then, venom, to thy work.   *Hurts the king.*

All. Treason! treason!

King. O, yet defend me, friends. I am but hurt.

Hamlet. Here, thou incestuous, murd'rous, damnèd
330   Dane,
Drink off this potion. Is thy union here?
Follow my mother.   *King dies.*

Laertes.   He is justly served.
It is a poison tempered by himself.
Exchange forgiveness with me, noble Hamlet.
335   Mine and my father's death come not upon thee,
Nor thine on me!   *Dies.*

Hamlet. Heaven make thee free of it! I follow thee.
I am dead, Horatio. Wretched queen, adieu!
You that look pale and tremble at this chance,
340   That are but mutes or audience to this act,
Had I but time — as this fell sergeant, Death,
Is strict in his arrest — O, I could tell you —
But let it be. Horatio, I am dead;

313 *sounds* swoons   322 *Unbated* unblunted   *practice* stratagem   333
tempered mixed   340 *mutes* actors in a play who speak no lines   341
sergeant sheriff's officer

Thou livest; report me and my cause aright
To the unsatisfied.

Horatio.   Never believe it.   345
I am more an antique Roman than a Dane.
Here's yet some liquor left.

Hamlet.   As th' art a man,
Give me the cup. Let go. By heaven, I'll ha't!
O God, Horatio, what a wounded name,
Things standing thus unknown, shall live behind
  me!   350
If thou didst ever hold me in thy heart,
Absent thee from felicity awhile,
And in this harsh world draw thy breath in pain,
To tell my story.   *A march afar off.*
                    What warlike noise is this?

Osric. Young Fortinbras, with conquest come from
  Poland,   355
To the ambassadors of England gives
This warlike volley.

Hamlet.   O, I die, Horatio!
The potent poison quite o'ercrows my spirit.
I cannot live to hear the news from England,
But I do prophesy th' election lights   360
On Fortinbras. He has my dying voice.
So tell him, with th' occurrents, more and less,
Which have solicited — the rest is silence.   *Dies.*

Horatio. Now cracks a noble heart. Good night, sweet
  prince,
And flights of angels sing thee to thy rest!   365
                                        March within.

Why does the drum come hither?

*Enter Fortinbras, with the Ambassadors and with
    his train of Drum, Colors, and Attendants.*

---

358 *o'ercrows* triumphs over (like a victor in a cockfight)   360 *election*
i.e. to the throne   361 *voice* vote   362 *occurrents* occurrences   363 *solicited* incited, provoked

Fortinbras. Where is this sight?

Horatio.   What is it you would see?
If aught of woe or wonder, cease your search.

Fortinbras. This quarry cries on havoc. O proud
        Death,
370   What feast is toward in thine eternal cell
        That thou so many princes at a shot
        So bloodily hast struck?

Ambassador.   The sight is dismal;
        And our affairs from England come too late.
        The ears are senseless that should give us hearing
375   To tell him his commandment is fulfilled,
        That Rosencrantz and Guildenstern are dead.
        Where should we have our thanks?

Horatio.   Not from his mouth,
        Had it th' ability of life to thank you.
        He never gave commandment for their death.
380   But since, so jump upon this bloody question,
        You from the Polack wars, and you from England,
        Are here arrived, give order that these bodies
        High on a stage be placèd to the view,
        And let me speak to th' yet unknowing world
385   How these things came about. So shall you hear
        Of carnal, bloody, and unnatural acts,
        Of accidental judgments, casual slaughters,
        Of deaths put on by cunning and forced cause,
        And, in this upshot, purposes mistook
390   Fall'n on th' inventors' heads. All this can I
        Truly deliver.

Fortinbras.   Let us haste to hear it,
        And call the noblest to the audience.
        For me, with sorrow I embrace my fortune.

---

369 *quarry* pile of dead (literally, of dead deer gathered after the hunt)
cries on proclaims loudly   *havoc* indiscriminate killing and destruction
such as would follow the order "havoc," or "pillage," given to an
army   370 *toward* forthcoming   380 *jump* precisely   383 *stage* platform   387 *judgments* retributions   *casual* not humanly planned (rein-
forcing *accidental*)   388 *put on* instigated

I have some rights of memory in this kingdom,
Which now to claim my vantage doth invite me.   395
Horatio. Of that I shall have also cause to speak,
And from his mouth whose voice will draw on
    more.
But let this same be presently performed,
Even while men's minds are wild, lest more mis-
    chance
On plots and errors happen.
Fortinbras.   Let four captains   400
Bear Hamlet like a soldier to the stage,
For he was likely, had he been put on,
To have proved most royal; and for his passage
The soldiers' music and the rites of war
Speak loudly for him.   405
Take up the bodies. Such a sight as this
Becomes the field, but here shows much amiss.
Go, bid the soldiers shoot.

> *Exit all, marching; after the which a peal of
>   ordinance are shot off.*

---

394 *of memory* traditional and kept in mind   395 *vantage* advantageous opportunity   397 *more* i.e. more voices, or votes, for the kingship
398 *presently* immediately   400 *On* on the basis of   402 *put on* set to
perform in office   403 *passage* death

The Tragedy of
MACBETH

William Shakespeare

Edited by Alfred Harbage

Note on the text: This edition follows the folio of 1623 (thought to be taken from a playhouse manuscript), as edited for the Pelican Shakespeare series in 1956. Footnotes are from the Pelican Shakespeare edition.

Names of the Actors

Duncan, King of Scotland
Malcolm ⎫
Donalbain ⎭ his sons
Macbeth ⎫
Banquo ⎪
Macduff ⎪
Lennox ⎪
Ross ⎬ noblemen of Scotland
Menteith ⎪
Angus ⎪
Caithness ⎭
Fleance, son to Banquo
Siward, Earl of Northumberland
Young Siward, his son
Seyton, an officer attending on Macbeth
Boy, son to Macduff
A Captain
An English Doctor
A Scottish Doctor
A Porter
An Old Man
Three Murderers
Lady Macbeth
Lady Macduff
A Gentlewoman, attending on Lady Macbeth
The Weird Sisters
Hecate
The Ghost of Banquo
Apparitions
Lord, Officers, Soldiers, Messengers, Attendants

Scene
Scotland and England

ACT I, SCENE I

Thunder and lightning. Enter three Witches.

1. *Witch.* When shall we three meet again?
   In thunder, lightning, or in rain?
2. *Witch.* When the hurlyburly's done,
   When the battle's lost and won.
3. *Witch.* That will be ere the set of sun. 5
1. *Witch.* Where the place?
2. *Witch.* Upon the heath.
3. *Witch.* There to meet with Macbeth.
1. *Witch.* I come, Graymalkin!
2. *Witch.* Paddock calls.
3. *Witch.* Anon!
All. Fair is foul, and foul is fair. 10
 Hover through the fog and filthy air. *Exit all.*

ACT I, SCENE II

*Alarum within. Enter King Duncan, Malcolm,
Donalbain, Lennox, with Attendants, meeting
a bleeding Captain.*

King. What bloody man is that? He can report,
 As seemeth by his plight, of the revolt
 The newest state.

I, i, 8 *Graymalkin* her familiar spirit, a gray cat   9 *Paddock* a toad
Anon at once

Malcolm.   This is the sergeant
     Who like a good and hardy soldier fought
5   'Gainst my captivity. Hail, brave friend!
     Say to the King the knowledge of the broil
     As thou didst leave it.

Captain.   Doubtful it stood,
     As two spent swimmers that do cling together
     And choke their art. The merciless Macdonwald
10   (Worthy to be a rebel, for to that
     The multiplying villainies of nature
     Do swarm upon him) from the Western Isles
     Of kerns and gallowglasses is supplied;
     And Fortune, on his damnèd quarrel smiling,
15   Showed like a rebel's whore. But all's too weak:
     For brave Macbeth (well he deserves that name),
     Disdaining Fortune, with his brandished steel,
     Which smoked with bloody execution,
     Like valor's minion carved out his passage
20   Till he faced the slave;
     Which ne'er shook hands nor bade farewell to him
     Till he unseamed him from the nave to th' chops
     And fixed his head upon our battlements.

King. O valiant cousin! worthy gentleman!

25 *Captain.* As whence the sun 'gins his reflection
     Shipwracking storms and direful thunders break,
     So from that spring whence comfort seemed to come
     Discomfort swells. Mark, King of Scotland, mark.
     No sooner justice had, with valor armed,
30   Compelled these skipping kerns to trust their heels
     But the Norweyan lord, surveying vantage,
     With furbished arms and new supplies of men,
     Began a fresh assault.

King.   Dismayed not this
     Our captains, Macbeth and Banquo?

I, ii, 3 *sergeant* so designated, apparently, as a staff officer; he ranks as
a captain   12 *Western Isles* Hebrides   13 *kerns* Irish bushfighters
gallowglasses Irish regulars, armored infantrymen   19 *minion* darling
22 *nave* navel   31 *surveying vantage* seeing opportunity

Captain.   Yes,
   As sparrows eagles, or the hare the lion.   35
   If I say sooth, I must report they were
   As cannons overcharged with double cracks,
   So they doubly redoubled strokes upon the foe.
   Except they meant to bathe in reeking wounds,
   Or memorize another Golgotha,   40
   I cannot tell—
   But I am faint; my gashes cry for help.
King. So well thy words become thee as thy wounds,
   They smack of honor both. Go get him surgeons.
                     Exit Captain, attended.

Enter Ross and Angus.

   Who comes here?
Malcolm.   The worthy Thane of Ross.   45
Lennox. What a haste looks through his eyes! So
     should he look
   That seems to speak things strange.
Ross.   God save the King!
King. Whence cam'st thou, worthy Thane?
Ross.   From Fife, great King,
   Where the Norweyan banners flout the sky
   And fan our people cold.   50
   Norway himself, with terrible numbers,
   Assisted by that most disloyal traitor
   The Thane of Cawdor, began a dismal conflict,
   Till that Bellona's bridegroom, lapped in proof,
   Confronted him with self-comparisons,   55
   Point against point rebellious, arm 'gainst arm,
   Curbing his lavish spirit: and to conclude,
   The victory fell on us.
King.   Great happiness!
Ross.   That now

37 *cracks* explosives **40** *memorize another Golgotha* make memorable
as another place of the dead **45** *Thane* a Scottish lord **47** *seems to*
seems about to **53** *dismal* ominous **54** *Bellona* goddess of war
lapped in proof clad in proven armor **55** *self-comparisons* canceling
powers **59** *composition* terms of surrender

Sweno, the Norways' king, craves composition;
60 Nor would we deign him burial of his men
Till he disbursèd, at Saint Colme's Inch,
Ten thousand dollars to our general use.

King. No more that Thane of Cawdor shall deceive
Our bosom interest. Go pronounce his present
death
65 And with his former title greet Macbeth.

Ross. I'll see it done.

King. What he hath lost noble Macbeth hath won.

Exit all.

ACT I, SCENE III

Thunder. Enter the three Witches.

1. Witch. Where hast thou been, sister?

2. Witch. Killing swine.

3. Witch. Sister, where thou?

1. Witch. A sailor's wife had chestnuts in her lap
5 And mounched and mounched and mounched.
"Give me," quoth I.
"Aroint thee, witch!" the rump-fed ronyon cries.
Her husband's to Aleppo gone, master o' the'
Tiger:
But in a sieve I'll thither sail
10 And, like a rat without a tail,
I'll do, I'll do, and I'll do.

2. Witch. I'll give thee a wind.

1. Witch. Th' art kind.

3. Witch. And I another.

61 *Inch* island   62 *dollars* Spanish or Dutch coins   64 *bosom interest*
heart's trust   I, iii. 7 *Aroint thee* get thee gone   *rump-fed ronyon* fat-
rumped scab

1 *Witch.* I myself have all the other,   15
   And the very ports they blow,
   All the quarters that they know
   I' th' shipman's card.
   I'll drain him dry as hay.
   Sleep shall neither night nor day   20
   Hang upon his penthouse lid.
   He shall live a man forbid.
   Weary sev'nights, nine times nine,
   Shall he dwindle, peak, and pine.
   Though his bark cannot be lost,   25
   Yet it shall be tempest-tost.
   Look what I have.

2. *Witch.* Show me, show me.

1. *Witch.* Here I have a pilot's thumb,
   Wracked as homeward he did come. *Drum within.*   30

2. *Witch.* A drum, a drum!
   Macbeth doth come.

All. The weird sisters, hand in hand,
   Posters of the sea and land,
   Thus do go about, about,   35
   Thrice to thine, and thrice to mine,
   And thrice again, to make up nine.
   Peace! The charm's wound up.

Enter Macbeth and Banquo.

Macbeth. So foul and fair a day I have not seen.

Banquo. How far is't called to Forres? What are these,   40
   So withered and so wild in their attire
   That look not like th' inhabitants o' th' earth
   And yet are on't? Live you, or are you aught
   That man may question? You seem to understand
     me,   45
   By each at once her choppy finger laying

---

16 *very ports they blow* their power to blow ships to ports 18 *card*
compass card 21 *penthouse lid* eyelid 22 *forbid* accursed 33 *weird*
fate-serving 34 *Posters* swift travelers 44 *question* confer with

Upon her skinny lips. You should be women,
And yet your beards forbid me to interpret
That you are so.

Macbeth.   Speak, if you can. What are you?

1. *Witch.* All hail, Macbeth! Hail to thee, Thane of
50   Glamis!

2. *Witch.* All hail, Macbeth! Hail to thee, Thane of
          Cawdor!

3. *Witch.* All hail, Macbeth, that shalt be King here-
          after!

Banquo. Good sir, why do you start and seem to fear
          Things that do sound so fair? I' th' name of truth,
55   Are ye fantastical, or that indeed
          Which outwardly ye show? My noble partner
          You greet with present grace and great prediction
          Of noble having and of royal hope,
          That he seems rapt withal. To me you speak not.
60   If you can look into the seeds of time
          And say which grain will grow and which will not,
          Speak then to me, who neither beg nor fear
          Your favors nor your hate.

1. *Witch.* Hail!
65 2. *Witch.* Hail!
3. *Witch.* Hail!

1. *Witch.* Lesser than Macbeth, and greater.

2. *Witch.* Not so happy, yet much happier.

3. *Witch.* Thou shalt get kings, though thou be none.
70   So all hail, Macbeth and Banquo!

1. *Witch.* Banquo and Macbeth, all hail!

Macbeth. Stay, you imperfect speakers, tell me more:
          By Sinel's death I know I am Thane of Glamis,
          But how of Cawdor? The Thane of Cawdor lives,
75   A prosperous gentleman; and to be King
          Stands not within the prospect of belief,
          No more than to be Cawdor. Say from whence

---

46 *choppy* chapped   55 *fantastical* creatures of fantasy   57 *grace*
honor   59 *rapt withal* spellbound at the thought   60 *seeds of time*
genesis of events   68 *happy* fortunate   69 *get* beget   72 *imperfect* in-
complete   73 *Sinel* i.e. Macbeth's father

You owe this strange intelligence, or why
Upon this blasted heath you stop our way
With such prophetic greeting. Speak, I charge you.   80
                              Witches vanish.

Banquo. The earth hath bubbles as the water has,
   And these are of them. Whither are they vanished?
Macbeth. Into the air, and what seemed corporal
   melted
   As breath into the wind. Would they had stayed.
Banquo. Were such things here as we do speak about?   85
   Or have we eaten on the insane root
   That takes the reason prisoner?
Macbeth. Your children shall be kings.
Banquo.   You shall be King.
Macbeth. And Thane of Cawdor too. Went it not so?
Banquo. To th' selfsame tune and words. Who's here?   90

Enter Ross and Angus.

Ross. The King hath happily received, Macbeth,
   The news of thy success; and when he reads
   Thy personal venture in the rebels' fight,
   His wonders and his praises do contend
   Which should be thine or his. Silenced with that,   95
   In viewing o'er the rest o' th' selfsame day,
   He finds thee in the stout Norweyan ranks,
   Nothing afeared of what thyself didst make,
   Strange images of death. As thick as tale
   Came post with post, and every one did bear   00
   Thy praises in his kingdom's great defense
   And poured them down before him.
Angus.   We are sent
   To give thee from our royal master thanks;
   Only to herald thee into his sight,
   Not pay thee.   105
Ross. And for an earnest of a greater honor,

83 *corporal* corporeal 86 *insane* madness-inducing 92 *reads* consid-
ers 94–95 *His wonders . . . or his* dumstruck admiration makes him
keep your praises to himself 99 *thick as tale* i.e. as fast as they can
be counted 100 *post with post* messenger after messenger

He bade me, from him, call thee Thane of Cawdor;
In which addition, hail, most worthy Thane,
For it is thine.

Banquo.   What, can the devil speak true?

Macbeth. The Thane of Cawdor lives. Why do you
110   dress me
In borrowed robes?

Angus.   Who was the Thane lives yet,
But under heavy judgment bears that life
Which he deserves to lose. Whether he was com-
     bined
With those of Norway, or did line the rebel
115   With hidden help and vantage, or that with both
He labored in his country's wrack, I know not;
But treasons capital, confessed and proved,
Have overthrown him.

Macbeth.   (*aside*) Glamis, and Thane of Cawdor —
The greatest is behind! (*to Ross and Angus*) Thanks
     for your pains.
(*aside to Banquo*) Do you not hope your children
120   shall be kings,
When those that gave the Thane of Cawdor to me
Promised no less to them?

Banquo.   (*to Macbeth*) That, trusted home,
Might yet enkindle you unto the crown,
Besides the Thane of Cawdor. But 'tis strange:
125   And oftentimes, to win us to our harm,
The instruments of darkness tell us truths,
Win us with honest trifles, to betray's
In deepest consequence. —
Cousins, a word, I pray you.

Macbeth.   (*aside*) Two truths are told,
130   As happy prologues to the swelling act
Of the imperial theme. — I thank you, gentle-
     men. —

---

108 *addition* title 113 *combined* leagued 114 *line* support 115 *vantage* assitance 119 *is behind* is to come 122 *home* all the way 128 *deepest consequence* i.e. in the vital sequel 129 *Cousins* i.e. fellow lords 130–31 *swelling act . . . imperial theme* i.e. stately drama of rise to sovereignty

(*aside*) This supernatural soliciting
Cannot be ill, cannot be good. If ill,
Why hath it given me earnest of success,
Commencing in a truth? I—am Thane of Cawdor. 135
If good, why do I yield to that suggestion
Whose horrid image doth unfix my hair
And make my seated heart knock at my ribs
Against the use of nature? Present fears
Are less than horrible imaginings.   140
My thought, whose murder yet is but fantastical,
Shakes so my single state of man that function
Is smothered in surmise and nothing is
But what is not.

Banquo.   Look how our partner's rapt.

Macbeth. (*aside*) If chance will have me King, why
        chance may crown me   145
Without my stir.

Banquo.   New honors come upon him,
    Like our strange garments, cleave not to their mould
    But with the aid of use.

Macbeth.   (*aside*) Come what come may,
    Time and the hour runs through the roughest day.

Banquo. Worthy Macbeth, we stay upon your leisure. 150

Macbeth. Give me your favor. My dull brain was
        wrought
    With things forgotten. Kind gentlemen, your pains
    Are regist'red where every day I turn
    The leaf to read them. Let us toward the King.
    (*aside to Banquo*) Think upon what hath chanced,
        and at more time,   155
    The interim having weighed, it, let us speak
    Our free hearts each to other.

Banquo.   Very gladly.

Macbeth. Till then, enough. — Come, friends.

                                        Exit all.

132 *soliciting* inviting, beckoning 138 *seated* fixed 139 *use* way 141
fantastical imaginary 142 *single* unaided, weak *function* normal
powers 144 *rapt* bemused 147 *strange* new 151 *favor* pardon 157
Our free hearts our thoughts freely

❧

ACT I, SCENE IV

*Flourish. Enter King Duncan, Lennox, Malcolm,
Donalbain, and Attendants.*

King. Is execution done on Cawdor? Are not
Those in commission yet returned?
Malcolm.   My liege,
They are not yet come back. But I have spoke
With one that saw him die; who did report
5   That very frankly he confessed his treasons,
Implored your Highness' pardon, and set forth
A deep repentance. Nothing in his life
Became him like the leaving it. He died
As one that had been studied in his death
10   To throw away the dearest thing he owed
As 'twere a careless trifle.
King.   There's no art
To find the mind's construction in the face.
He was a gentleman on whom I built
An absolute trust.

Enter Macbeth, Banquo, Ross, and Angus.

O worthiest cousin,
15   The sin of my ingratitude even now
Was heavy on me. Thou art so far before
That swiftest wing of recompense is slow
To overtake thee. Would thou hadst less deserved,

I, iv, 2 *in commission* commissioned to carry out the execution 9
studied rehearsed 10 *before* ahead in deserving 19 *proportion* pre-
ponderance

That the proportion both of thanks and payment
Might have been mine! Only I have left to say,   20
More is thy due than more than all can pay.

Macbeth. The service and the loyalty I owe,
In doing it pays itself. Your Highness' part
Is to receive our duties, and our duties
Are to your throne and state children and servants,   25
Which do but what they should by doing everything
Safe toward your love and honor.

King.   Welcome hither.
I have begun to plant thee and will labor
To make thee full of growing. Noble Banquo,
That hast no less deserved nor must be known   30
No less to have done so, let me enfold thee
And hold thee to my heart.

Banquo.   There if I grow,
The harvest is your own.

King.   My plenteous joys,
Wanton in fullness, seek to hide themselves
In drops of sorrow. Sons, kinsmen, thanes,   35
And you whose places are the nearest, know
We will establish our estate upon
Our eldest, Malcolm, whom we name hereafter
The Prince of Cumberland; which honor must
Not unaccompanied invest him only,   40
But signs of nobleness, like stars, shall shine
On all deservers. From hence to Inverness,
And bind us further to you.

Macbeth. The rest is labor which is not used for you.
I'll be myself the harbinger, and make joyful   45
The hearing of my wife with your approach;
So, humbly take my leave.

King.   My worthy Cawdor!

Macbeth. (aside) The Prince of Cumberland — that
    is a step

---

27 *Safe* fitting   28 *plant* nurture   34 *Wanton* unrestrained

On which I must fall down or else o'erleap,
50 For in my way it lies. Stars, hide your fires;
Let not light see my black and deep desires.
The eye wink at the hand; yet let that be
Which the eye fears, when it is done, to see.   *Exit.*

King. True, worthy Banquo: he is full so valiant,
55 And in his commendations I am fed;
It is a banquet to me. Let's after him,
Whose care is gone before to bid us welcome.
It is a peerless kinsman.   *Flourish. Exit all.*

>%<

ACT I, SCENE V

Enter Lady Macbeth, alone, with a letter.

Lady. (*reads*) "They met me in the day of success; and
I have learned by the perfect'st report they have
more in them than mortal knowledge. When I
burned in desire to question them further, they
5 made themselves air, into which they vanished.
Whiles I stood rapt in the wonder of it, came missives from the King, who all-hailed me Thane of
Cawdor, by which title, before, these weird sisters
saluted me, and referred me to the coming on of
10 time with 'Hail, King that shall be!' This have I
thought good to deliver thee, my dearest partner of
greatness, that thou mightst not lose the dues of
rejoicing by being ignorant of what greatness is
promised thee. Lay it to thy heart, and farewell."

52 *wink at the hand* blind itself to what the hand does   I, v, 6-7
missives messengers

Glamis thou art, and Cawdor, and shalt be   15
What thou art promised. Yet do I fear thy nature.
It is too full o' th' milk of human kindness
To catch the nearest way. Thou wouldst be great,
Art not without ambition, but without
The illness should attend it. What thou wouldst
    highly,   20
That wouldst thou holily; wouldst not play false,
And yet wouldst wrongly win. Thou'ldst have,
    great Glamis,
That which cries "Thus thou must do" if thou have
    it;
And that which rather thou dost fear to do
Than wishest should be undone. Hie thee hither,   25
That I may pour my spirits in thine ear
And chastise with the valor of my tongue
All that impedes thee from the golden round
Which fate and metaphysical aid doth seem
To have thee crowned withal.

Enter Messenger.

                                What is your tidings?   30
Messenger. The King comes here tonight.
Lady.   Thou'rt mad to say it!
Is not thy master with him? who, were't so,
Would have informed for preparation.
Messenger. So please you, it is true. Our Thane is
    coming.
One of my fellows had the speed of him,   35
Who, almost dead for breath, had scarcely more
Than would make up his message.
Lady.   Give him tending;
He brings great news.   *Exit Messenger.*
                  The raven himself is hoarse

20 *illness* ruthlessness   28 *round* crown   29 *metaphysical* supernatural
30 *withal* with   36 *breath* want of breath

That croaks the fatal entrance of Duncan
40   Under my battlements. Come, you spirits
That tend on mortal thoughts, unsex me here,
And fill me from the crown to the toe top-full
Of direst cruelty. Make thick my blood;
Stop up th' access and passage to remorse,
45   That no compunctious visitings of nature
Shake my fell purpose nor keep peace between
Th' effect and it. Come to my woman's breasts
And take my milk for gall, you murd'ring ministers,
Wherever in your sightless substances
50   You wait on nature's mischief. Come, thick night,
And pall thee in the dunnest smoke of hell,
That my keen knife see not the wound it makes,
Nor heaven peep through the blanket of the dark
To cry "Hold, hold!"

Enter Macbeth.

                              Great Glamis! worthy Cawdor!
55   Greater than both, by the all-hail hereafter!
Thy letters have transported me beyond
This ignorant present, and I feel now
The future in the instant.
Macbeth.   My dearest love,
Duncan comes here tonight.
Lady.   And when goes hence?
Macbeth. Tomorrow, as he purposes.
60   *Lady.*   O, never
Shall sun that morrow see!
Your face, my Thane, is as a book where men
May read strange matters. To beguile the time,
Look like the time; bear welcome in your eye,

---

41 *mortal* deadly   44 *remorse* pity   45 *nature* natural feeling   46 *fell*
fierce   46–47 *keep peace . . . and it* i.e. lull it from achieving its end
48 *for gall* in exchange for gall   *ministers* agents   49 *sightless* invisible
50 *wait on* aid   51 *pall thee* shroud thyself   *dunnest* darkest   57 *ignorant* i.e. ordinarily unaware   63 *beguile the time* make sly use of the
occasion

Your hand, your tongue; look like th' innocent
   flower,   65
But be the serpent under't. He that's coming
Must be provided for; and you shall put
This night's great business into my dispatch,
Which shall to all our nights and days to come
Give solely sovereign sway and masterdom.   70
Macbeth. We will speak further.
Lady.   Only look up clear.
To alter favor ever is to fear.
Leave all the rest to me.   *Exit both.*

❧

ACT I, SCENE VI

Hautboys and torches. Enter King Duncan,
Malcolm, Donalbain, Banquo, Lennox Macduff,
Ross, Angus, and Attendants.

King. This castle hath a pleasant seat. The air
   Nimbly and sweetly recommends itself
   Unto our gentle senses.
Banquo.   This guest of summer,
   The temple-haunting martlet, does approve
   By his loved mansionry that the heaven's breath   5
   Smells wooingly here. No jutty, frieze,
   Buttress, nor coign of vantage, but this bird
   Hath made his pendent bed and procreant cradle.
   Where they most breed and haunt, I have observed
   The air is delicate.

---

64 *Look like the time* play up to the occasion   68 *dispatch* swift man-
agement   71 *look up clear* appear untroubled   72 *alter favor* change
countenance   *fear* incur risk   I, vi, S.D. *Hautboys* oboes   1 *seat* site
3 *gentle* soothed   4 *temple-haunting* nesting in church spires   *martlet*
martin, swallow   *approve* prove   5 *loved mansionry* beloved nests   6
jutty projection   7 *coign of vantage* convenient corner   8 *procreant*
breeding

Enter Lady Macbeth.

10 **King.**   See, see, our honored hostess!
The love that follows us sometimes is our trouble,
Which still we thank as love. Herein I teach you
How you shall bid God 'ield us for your pains
And thank us for your trouble.

Lady.   All our service
15 In every point twice done, and then done double,
Were poor and single business to contend
Against those honors deep and broad wherewith
Your Majesty loads our house. For those of old,
And the late dignities heaped up to them,
We rest your hermits.

20 **King.**   Where's the Thane of Cawdor?
We coursed him at the heels and had a purpose
To be his purveyor; but he rides well,
And his great love, sharp as his spur, hath holp him
To his home before us. Fair and noble hostess,
We are your guest tonight.

25 **Lady.**   Your servants ever
Have theirs, themselves, and what is theirs, in
compt,
To make their audit at your Highness' pleasure,
Still to return your own.

King.   Give me your hand.
Conduct me to mine host: we love him highly
30 And shall continue our graces towards him.
By your leave, hostess.   *Exit all.*

11–12 *The love . . . as love* the love that sometimes inconveniences us
we still hold precious 13 *God 'ield us* God reward me 20 *hermits*
beadsmen 22 *purveyor* advance agent of supplies 26 *Have theirs*
have their servants *what is theirs* their possessions *in compt* in trust
28 *Still* always

ACT I, SCENE VII

Hautboys. Torches. Enter a Sewer, and divers
Servants with dishes and service over the stage.
Then enter Macbeth.

Macbeth: If it were done when 'tis done, then 'twere
    well
It were done quickly. If th' assassination
Could trammel up the consequence and catch
With his surcease success, that but this blow
Might be the be-all and the end-all — ; here,   5
But here upon this bank and shoal of time,
We'ld jump the life to come. But in these cases
We still have judgment here, that we but teach
Bloody instructions, which, being taught, return
To plague th' inventor. This even-handed justice   10
Commends th' ingredience of our poisoned chalice
To our own lips. He's here in double trust:
First, as I am his kinsman and his subject,
Strong both against the deed; then, as his host,
Who should against his murderer shut the door,   15
Not bear the knife myself. Besides, this Duncan
Hath borne his faculties so meek, hath been
So clear in his great office, that his virtues
Will plead like angels, trumpet-tongued against
The deep damnation of his taking-off;   20
And pity, like a naked new-born babe
Striding the blast, or heaven's cherubin horsed
Upon the sightless couriers of the air,

I, vii, S.D. *Sewer* chief waiter 1 *done* done with 1–5 *If it were done . . . and the end-all* Macbeth's hopeful prayer that if the murder could be quickly accomplished, then there would be no reverberations, in the form of punishment 7 *jump* risk 9 *instructions* lessons 17 *faculties* powers 18 *clear* untainted 23 *sightless couriers* invisible coursers (the winds)

Shall blow the horrid deed in every eye
25   That tears shall drown the wind. I have no spur
To prick the sides of my intent, but only
Vaulting ambition, which o'erleaps itself
And falls on th' other —

Enter Lady Macbeth.

                    How now? What news?
Lady. He has almost supped. Why have you left the
    chamber?
Macbeth. Hath he asked for me?
30   *Lady.*   Know you not he has?
Macbeth. We will proceed no further in this business.
He hath honored me of late, and I have bought
Golden opinions from all sorts of people,
Which would be worn now in their newest gloss,
Not cast aside so soon.
35   *Lady.*   Was the hope drunk
Wherein you dressed yourself? Hath it slept since?
And wakes it now to look so green and pale
At what it did so freely? From this time
Such I account thy love. Art thou afeared
40   To be the same in thine own act and valor
As thou art in desire? Wouldst thou have that
Which thou esteem'st the ornament of life,
And live a coward in thine own esteem?
Letting "I dare not" wait upon "I would,"
Like the poor cat i' th' adage.
45   *Macbeth.*   Prithee peace!
I dare do all that may become a man;
Who dares do more is none.
Lady.   What beast was't then
That made you break this enterprise to me?
When you durst do it, then you were a man;

---

32 *bought* acquired   37 *green* bilious   45 *cat i' th' adage* (who wants
the fish but doesn't want to get its paws wet)   48 *break* broach

And to be more than what you were, you would   50
Be so much more the man. Nor time nor place
Did then adhere, and yet you would make both.
They have made themselves, and that their fitness
      now
Does unmake you. I have given suck, and know
How tender 'tis to love the babe that milks me: 55
I would, while it was smiling in my face,
Have plucked my nipple from his boneless gums
And dashed the brains out, had I so sworn as you
Have done to this.

Macbeth.   If we should fail?

Lady.   We fail?
But screw your courage to the sticking place   60
And we'll not fail. When Duncan is asleep
(Whereto the rather shall his day's hard journey
Soundly invite him), his two chamberlains
Will I with wine and wassail so convince
That memory, the warder of the brain,   65
Shall be a fume, and the receipt of reason
A limbeck only. When in swinish sleep
Their drenchèd natures lie as in a death,
What cannot you and I perform upon
Th' unguarded Duncan? what not put upon   70
His spongy officers, who shall bear the guilt
Of our great quell?

Macbeth.   Bring forth men-children only;
For thy undaunted mettle should compose
Nothing but males. Will it not be received,
When we have marked with blood those sleepy two   75
Of his own chamber and used their very daggers,
That they have done't?

52 *adhere* lend themselves to the occasion 53 *that their fitness* their
very fitness 60 *sticking place* notch (holding the string of a crossbow
cranked taut for shooting) 64 *convince* overcome 66 *receipt* con-
tainer 67 *limbeck* cap of a still (to which the fumes rise) 72 *quell-*
killing 73 *mettle* vital substance

Lady.   Who dares receive it other,
As we shall make our griefs and clamor roar
Upon his death?

Macbeth.   I am settled and bend up
80   Each corporal agent to this terrible feat.
Away, and mock the time with fairest show;
False face must hide what the false heart doth
     know.   *Exit all.*

77 *other* otherwise   81 *mock* delude

ACT II, SCENE I

Enter Banquo and Fleance, with a torch before him.

Banquo. How goes the night, boy?
Fleance. The moon is down; I have not heard the
    clock.
Banquo. And she goes down at twelve.
Fleance.   I take't, 'tis later, sir.
Banquo. Hold, take my sword. There's husbandry in
    heaven;
  Their candles are all out. Take thee that too.   5
  A heavy summons lies like lead upon me,
  And yet I would not sleep. Merciful powers,
  Restrain in me the cursèd thoughts that nature
  Gives way to in repose.

Enter Macbeth, and a Servant with a torch.

                       Give me my sword!
  Who's there?   10
Macbeth. A friend.
Banquo. What, sir, not yet at rest? The King's abed.
  He hath been in unusual pleasure and
  Sent forth great largess to your offices.

II, i, 4 *husbandry* economy   6 *summons* signal to sleep   14 *largess to your offices* gratuities to your household departments

15   This diamond he greets your wife withal
    By the name of most kind hostess, and shut up
    In measureless content.

Macbeth.   Being unprepared,
    Our will became the servant to defect,
    Which else should free have wrought.

Banquo.   All's well.
20   I dreamt last night of the three weird sisters.
    To you they have showed some truth.

Macbeth.   I think not of them.
    Yet when we can entreat an hour to serve,
    We would spend it in some words upon that business,
    If you would grant the time.

Banquo.   At your kind'st leisure.
25 *Macbeth.* If you shall cleave to my consent, when 'tis,
    It shall make honor for you.

Banquo.   So I lose none
    In seeking to augment it, but still keep
    My bosom franchised and allegiance clear,
    I shall be counselled.

Macbeth.   Good repose the while.
30 *Banquo.* Thanks, sir. The like to you.

                        Exit Banquo and Fleance.

Macbeth. Go bid thy mistress, when my drink is ready,
    She strike upon the bell. Get thee to bed.

                            Exit Servant.

    Is this a dagger which I see before me,
    The handle toward my hand? Come, let me clutch thee!
35   I have thee not, and yet I see thee still.
    Art thou not, fatal vision, sensible
    To feeling as to sight? or art thou but
    A dagger of the mind, a false creation

---

16 *shut up* concluded 18 *will* good will *defect* deficient means 25 *cleave . . . when 'tis* favor my cause at the proper time 28 *franchised* free from guilt 29 *counselled* open to persuasion

Proceeding from the heat-oppressèd brain?
I see thee yet, in form as palpable   40
As this which now I draw.
Thou marshall'st me the way that I was going,
And such an instrument I was to use.
Mine eyes are made the fools o' th' other senses,
Or else worth all the rest. I see thee still,   45
And on thy blade and dudgeon gouts of blood,
Which was not so before. There's no such thing.
It is the bloody business which informs
Thus to mine eyes. Now o'er the one half-world
Nature seems dead, and wicked dreams abuse   50
The curtained sleep. Witchcraft celebrates
Pale Hecate's offerings; and withered murder,
Alarumed by his sentinel, the wolf,
Whose howl's his watch, thus with his stealthy
   pace,
With Tarquin's ravishing strides, towards his design   55
Moves like a ghost. Thou sure and firm-set earth,
Hear not my steps which way they walk, for fear
Thy very stones prate of my whereabout
And take the present horror from the time,
Which now suits with it. Whiles I threat, he lives;   60
Words to the heat of deeds too cold breath gives.
                                        A bell rings.

I go, and it is done. The bell invites me.
Hear it not, Duncan, for it is a knell
That summons thee to heaven, or to hell.   *Exit.*

---

46 *dudgeon* wooden hilt   *gouts* blobs   48 *informs* creates *impressions*
50 *abuse* deceive   52 *Hecate's offerings* worship of Hecate (goddess of
sorcery)   53 *Alarumed* given the signal   55 *Tarquin* Roman tyrant,
ravisher of Lucrece   59–60 *take . . . suits with it* delay, by prating,
the commission of the deed at this suitably horrible moment; or, reduce, by breaking the silence, the suitable horror of this moment

ACT II, SCENE II

Enter Lady Macbeth.

Lady. That which hath made them drunk hath made
    me bold;
    What hath quenched them hath given me fire. Hark!
    Peace!
    It was the owl that shrieked, the fatal bellman
    Which gives the stern'st good-night. He is about it.
5   The doors are open, and the surfeited grooms
    Do mock their charge with snores. I have drugged
    their possets,
    That death and nature do contend about them
    Whether they live or die.
Macbeth.   (*within*) Who's there? What, ho?
Lady. Alack, I am afraid they have awaked,
10   And 'tis not done! Th' attempt, and not the deed,
    Confounds us. Hark! I laid their daggers ready —
    He could not miss 'em. Had he not resembled
    My father as he slept, I had done't.

Enter Macbeth.

                        My husband!
Macbeth. I have done the deed. Didst thou not hear
    a noise?
15   *Lady.* I heard the owl scream and the crickets cry.
    Did not you speak?
Macbeth.   When?

II, ii, 3–4 *fatal bellman . . . good-night* i.e. like the night-watch cry to
felons scheduled for execution in the morning 6 *possets* bedtime
drinks

Lady.   Now.
Macbeth.   As I descended?
Lady. Ay.
Macbeth. Hark!
　Who lies i' th' second chamber?
Lady.   Donalbain.
Macbeth. This is a sorry sight.
Lady. A foolish thought, to say a sorry sight.   30
Macbeth. There's one did laugh in's sleep, and one
　　cried "Murder!"
　That they did wake each other. I stood and heard
　　them.
　But they did say their prayers and addressed them
　Again to sleep.
Lady.   There are two lodged together.
Macbeth. One cried "God bless us!" and "Amen!"
　　the other,
　As they had seen me with these hangman's hands,   25
　List'ning their fear. I could not say "Amen!"
　When they did say "God bless us!"
Lady.   Consider it not so deeply.
Macbeth. But wherefore could not I pronounce
　　"Amen"?
　I had most need of blessing, and "Amen"
　Stuck in my throat.
Lady.   These deeds must not be thought   30
　After these ways; so, it will make us mad.
Macbeth. Methought I heard a voice cry "Sleep no
　　more!
　Macbeth does murder sleep" — the innocent sleep,
　Sleep that knits up the ravelled sleave of care,
　The death of each day's life, sore labor's bath,   35
　Balm of hurt minds, great nature's second course,
　Chief nourisher in life's feast.
Lady.   What do you mean?

25 *hangman's hands* i.e. bloody, like an executioner's   34 *knits up . . . sleave* smooths out the tangled skein   36 *second course* i.e. sleep, after food

Macbeth. Still it cried "Sleep no more!" to all the
house;

"Glamis hath murdered sleep, and therefore Cawdor
40   Shall sleep no more, Macbeth shall sleep no more."
Lady. Who was it that thus cried? Why, worthy
Thane,

You do unbend your noble strength to think
So brainsickly of things. Go get some water
And wash this filthy witness from your hand.
45   Why did you bring these daggers from the place?
They must lie there: go carry them and smear
The sleepy grooms with blood.
Macbeth.   I'll go no more.
I am afraid to think what I have done;
Look on't again I dare not.
Lady.   Infirm of purpose!
50   Give me the daggers. The sleeping and the dead
Are but as pictures. 'Tis the eye of childhood
That fears a painted devil. If he do bleed,
I'll gild the faces of the grooms withal,
For it must seem their guilt.   *Exit. Knock within.*
Macbeth.   Whence is that knocking?
55   How is't with me when every noise appals me?
What hands are here? Ha! they pluck out mine eyes.
Will all great Neptune's ocean wash this blood
Clean from my hand? No, this my hand will rather
The multitudinous seas incarnadine,
60   Making the green one red.

Enter Lady Macbeth.

Lady. My hands are of your color, but I shame
To wear a heart so white. (*knock*) I hear a knocking
At the south entry. Retire we to our chamber.
A little water clears us of this deed.
65   How easy is it then! Your constancy

42 *unbend* relax 44 *witness* evidence 51 *as pictures* like pictures
(since without motion) 53 *gild* paint 59 *incarnadine* redden 60 *one*
uniformly

Hath left you unattended. (*knock*) Hark! more
 knocking.
Get on your nightgown, lest occasion call us
And show us to be watchers. Be not lost
So poorly in your thoughts.

Macbeth. To know my deed, 'twere best not know
 myself.   *Knock.* 70
 Wake Duncan with thy knocking! I would thou
 couldst.   *Exit both.*

>< ✺

ACT II, SCENE III

Enter a Porter. Knocking within.

Porter. Here's a knocking indeed! If a man were porter of hell gate, he should have old turning the key.
 (*knock*) Knock, knock, knock. Who's there, i' th'
 name of Belzebub? Here's a farmer that hanged
 himself on th' expectation of plenty. Come in time!   5
 Have napkins enow about you; here you'll sweat
 for't. (*knock*) Knock, knock. Who's there, in th'
 other devil's name? Faith, here's an equivocator, that
 could swear in both the scales against either scale;
 who committed treason enough for God's sake, yet   10
 could not equivocate to heaven. O come in, equivocator. (*knock*) Knock, knock, knock. Who's there?
 Faith, here's an English tailor come hither for stealing out of a French hose. Come in, tailor. Here you
 may roast your goose. (*knock*) Knock, knock. Never   15
 at quiet! What are you? — But this place is too
 cold for hell. I'll devil-porter it no further. I had

66 *unattended* deserted   67 *nightgown* dressing-gown   68 *watchers* i.e.
awake   69 *poorly* weakly   II, iii, 2 *old* much   4 *farmer* i.e. one who
has hoarded crops   5 *expectation of plenty* prospect of a crop surplus
(which will lower prices)   6 *enow* enough   8 *equivocator* (usually
considered an allusion to the Jesuits tried for political conspiracy)   14
French hose close-fitting breeches   15 *roast your goose* heat your
pressing-iron

thought to have let in some of all professions that
go the primrose way to th' everlasting bonfire.
20 (*knock*) Anon, anon! (*opens the way*) I pray you
remember the porter.

Enter Macduff and Lennox.

Macduff. Was it so late, friend, ere you went to bed,
That you do lie so late?

Porter. Faith, sir, we were carousing till the second
25 cock; and drink, sir, is a great provoker of three
things.

Macduff. What three things does drink especially provoke?

Porter. Marry, sir, nose-painting, sleep, and urine.
30 Lechery, sir, it provokes, and unprovokes: it provokes
the desire, but it takes away the performance. Therefore much drink may be said to be an equivocator
with lechery: it makes him, and it mars him; it sets
him on, and it takes him off; it persuades him, and
35 disheartens him; makes him stand to, and not stand
to; in conclusion, equivocates him in a sleep, and
giving him the lie, leaves him.

Macduff. I believe drink gave thee the lie last night.

Porter. That it did, sir, i' the very throat on me; but I
requited him for his lie; and, I think, being too
40 strong for him, though he took up my legs sometime, yet I made a shift to cast him.

Macduff. Is thy master stirring?

Enter Macbeth.

Our knocking has awaked him: here he comes.

Lennox. Good morrow, noble sir.

Macbeth.   Good morrow, both.

24–25 *second cock* second cock-crow (3 a.m.) 35 *stand to* stand his
guard 36 *gave thee the lie* called you a liar (i.e. unable to stand) 41
cast throw

Macduff. Is the King stirring, worthy Thane?

Macbeth.   Not yet.   45

Macduff. He did command me to call timely on him;
   I have almost slipped the hour.

Macbeth.   I'll bring you to him.

Macduff. I know this is a joyful trouble to you;
   But yet 'tis one.

Macbeth. The labor we delight in physics pain.   50
   This is the door.

Macduff.   I'll make so bold to call,
   For 'tis my limited service.   *Exit Macduff.*

Lennox. Goes the King hence today?

Macbeth   He does; he did appoint so.

Lennox. The night has been unruly. Where we lay,
   Our chimneys were blown down; and, as they say,   55
   Lamentings heard i' th' air, strange screams of
     death,
   And prophesying, with accents terrible,
   Of dire combustion and confused events
   New hatched to th' woeful time. The obscure bird
   Clamored the livelong night. Some say the earth   60
   Was feverous and did shake.

Macbeth.   'Twas a rough night.

Lennox. My young remembrance cannot parallel
   A fellow to it.

Enter Macduff.

Macduff. O horror, horror, horror! Tongue nor heart
   Cannot conceive nor name thee!   65

Macbeth and Lennox. What's the matter?

Macduff. Confusion now hath made his masterpiece:
   Most sacrilegious murder hath broke ope
   The Lord's anointed temple and stole thence
   The life o' th' building!

46 *timely* early   47 *slipped* let slip   50 *physics pain* cures trouble   52
limited appointed   58 *combustion* tumult   59 *obscure bird* i.e. the owl
67 *Confusion* destruction

70 *Macbeth.*   What is't you say? The life?
Lennox. Mean you his Majesty?
Macduff. Approach the chamber and destroy your
         sight
         With a new Gorgon. Do not bid me speak.
         See, and then speak yourselves.

                                 Exit Macbeth and Lennox.
                                         Awake, awake!
75   Ring the alarum bell! Murder and treason!
         Banquo and Donalbain! Malcolm, awake!
         Shake off this downy sleep, death's counterfeit,
         And look on death itself. Up, up, and see
         The great doom's image. Malcolm! Banquo!
80   As from your graves rise up and walk like sprites
         To countenance this horror. Ring the bell!

                                                 Bell rings

                          Enter Lady Macbeth.

Lady. What's the business,
         That such a hideous trumpet calls to parley
         The sleepers of the house? Speak, speak!
Macduff.   O gentle lady,
85   'Tis not for you to hear what I can speak:
         The repetition in a woman's ear
         Would murder as it fell.

                          Enter Banquo.

                                 O Banquo, Banquo,
         Our royal master's murdered!
Lady.   Woe, alas!
         What, in our house?
Banquo.   Too cruel anywhere.

---

73 *a new Gorgon* dragonlike creatures with wings and snakey hair
(like Medusa), capable of turning the beholder's eyes to stone 79
great doom's image a resemblance of the day of judgment 81 *countenance* appear in keeping with 86 *repetition* recital

Dear Duff, I prithee contradict thyself
And say it is not so.

Enter Macbeth, Lennox, and Ross.

Macbeth. Had I but died an hour before this chance,
    I had lived a blessèd time; for from this instant
    There's nothing serious in mortality:
    All is but toys. Renown and grace is dead,   95
    The wine of life is drawn, and the mere lees
    Is left this vault to brag of.

Enter Malcolm and Donalbain.

Donalbain. What is amiss?
Macbeth.   You are, and do not know't.
    The spring, the head, the fountain of your blood
    Is stopped, the very source of it is stopped.   100
Macduff. Your royal father's murdered.
Malcolm.   O, by whom?
Lennox. Those of his chamber, as it seemed, had
        done't.
    Their hands and faces were all badged with blood;
    So were their daggers, which unwiped we found
    Upon their pillows. They stared and were dis-
        tracted.   105
    No man's life was to be trusted with them.
Macbeth. O, yet I do repent me of my fury
    That I did kill them.
Macduff.   Wherefore did you so?
Macbeth. Who can be wise, amazed, temp'rate and
        furious,
    Loyal and neutral, in a moment? No man.   110
    The expedition of my violent love
    Outrun the pauser, reason. Here lay Duncan,

94 *serious in mortality* worthwhile in human life 95 *toys* trifles 96
lees dregs 97 *vault* wine-vault 103 *badged* marked 109 *amazed* confused 111 *expedition* haste

His silver skin laced with his golden blood;
And his gashed stabs looked like a breach in nature
115 For ruin's wasteful entrance: there, the murderers,
Steeped in the colors of their trade, their daggers
Unmannerly breeched with gore. Who could re-
    frain
That had a heart to love, and in that heart
Courage to make's love known?

Lady.   Help me hence, ho!

Macduff. Look to the lady.

Malcolm. (*aside to Donalbain*) Why do we hold our
120   tongues,
That most may claim this argument for ours?

Donalbain. (*to Malcolm*) What should be spoken
        here,
Where our fate, hid in an auger hole,
May rush and seize us? Let's away:
Our tears are not yet brewed.

125 *Malcolm.*   (*to Donalbain*) Nor our strong sorrow
Upon the foot of motion.

Banquo.   Look to the lady.
                    Lady Macbeth is carried out
And when we have our naked frailties hid,
That suffer in exposure, let us meet
And question this most bloody piece of work,
130 To know it further. Fears and scruples shake us.
In the great hand of God I stand, and thence
Against the undivulged pretense I fight
Of treasonous malice.

Macduff.   And so do I.

All.   So all.

Macbeth. Let's briefly put on manly readiness
And meet i' th' hall together.

135 *All.*   Well contented.
            Exit all but Malcolm and Donalbain.

117 *Unmannerly . . . gore* crudely wearing breeches of blood   *refrain*
restrain oneself   119 *look to* look after   121 *argument for ours* topic
as chiefly our concern   123 *auger hole* i.e. any tiny cranny   126 *Upon
the foot of motion* yet in motion   127 *frailties hid* bodies clothed   129
question discuss   130 *scruples* doubts   132 *undivulged pretense* secret
statagems

Malcolm. What will you do? Let's not consort with
    them.
  To show an unfelt sorrow is an office
  Which the false man does easy. I'll to England.
Donalbain. To Ireland I. Our separated fortune
  Shall keep us both the safer. Where we are,   140
  There's daggers in men's smiles; the near in blood,
  The nearer bloody.
Malcolm.   This murderous shaft that's shot
  Hath not yet lighted, and our safest way
  Is to avoid the aim. Therefore to horse,
  And let us not be dainty of leave-taking   145
  But shift away. There's warrant in that theft
  Which steals itself when there's no mercy left.
                            Exit both.

ACT II, SCENE IV

Enter Ross with an Old Man.

Old Man. Threescore and ten I can remember well;
  Within the volume of which time I have seen
  Hours dreadful and things strange, but this sore
    night
  Hath trifled former knowings.
Ross.   Ha, good father,
  Thou seest the heavens, as troubled with man's act,   5
  Threatens his bloody stage. By th' clock 'tis day,
  And yet dark night strangles the travelling lamp.
  Is't night's predominance, or the day's shame,

141 *near* nearer   146 *warrant* justification   II, iv, 4 *trifled former
knowings* made former experiences seem trifling   5 *man's act* the
human drama   7 *travelling lamp* i.e. of Phoebus, the sun   8 *predominance* supernatural ascendancy

That darkness does the face of earth entomb
When living light should kiss it?

10 *Old Man.*   'Tis unnatural,
Even like the deed that's done. On Tuesday last
A falcon, tow'ring in her pride of place,
Was by a mousing owl hawked at and killed.

Ross. And Duncan's horses (a thing most strange and
       certain),
15 Beauteous and swift, the minions of their race,
Turned wild in nature, broke their stalls, flung out,
Contending 'gainst obedience, as they would make
War with mankind.

Old Man.   'Tis said they eat each other.

Ross. They did so, to th' amazement of mine eyes
That looked upon't.

Enter Macduff.

20   Here comes the good Macduff.
How goes the world, sir, now?

Macduff.   Why, see you not?

Ross. Is't known who did this more than bloody deed?

Macduff. Those that Macbeth hath slain.

Ross.   Alas the day,
What good could they pretend?

Macduff.   They were suborned.
25 Malcolm and Donalbain, the King's two sons,
Are stol'n away and fled, which puts upon them
Suspicion of the deed.

Ross.   'Gainst nature still.
Thriftless ambition, that will raven up
Thine own live's means! Then 'tis most like
30 The sovereignty will fall upon Macbeth.

Macduff. He is already named, and gone to Scone
To be invested.

12 *tow'ring* soaring   13 *mousing* i.e. ordinarily preying on mice
hawked at swooped upon   14 *certain* significant   15 *minions* darlings
16 *flung out* lunged about   18 *eat* ate   24 *pretend* expect   *suborned*
bribed   28 *Thriftless* wasteful   *raven up* bolt, swallow   32 *invested*
crowned

Ross.   Where is Duncan's body?
Macduff. Carried to Colmekill,
  The sacred storehouse of his predecessors
  And guardian of their bones.
Ross.   Will you to Scone?   35
Macduff. No, cousin, I'll to Fife.
Ross.   Well, I will thither
Macduff. Well, may you see things well done there.
  Adieu, Lest our old robes sit easier than our new!
Ross. Farewell, father.
Old Man. God's benison go with you, and with those   40
  That would make good of bad, and friends of foes.
                                        Exit all.

40 *benison* blessing

ACT III, SCENE I

Enter Banquo.

Banquo. Thou hast it now — King, Cawdor, Glamis, all,
  As the weird women promised; and I fear
  Thou played'st most foully for't. Yet it was said
  It should not stand in thy posterity,
5 But that myself should be the root and father
  Of many kings. If there come truth from them
  (As upon thee, Macbeth, their speeches shine),
  Why, by the verities on thee made good,
  May they not be my oracles as well
10 And set me up in hope? But hush, no more!

    Sennet sounded. Enter Macbeth as King, Lady
    Macbeth, Lennox, Ross, Lords and Attendants.

Macbeth. Here's our chief guest.
Lady.   If he had been forgotten,
  It had been as a gap in our great feast,
  And all-thing unbecoming.
Macbeth. Tonight we hold a solemn supper, sir,
  And I'll request your presence.
15 *Banquo.*   Let your Highness

III, i, 3 *foully* cheatingly 4 *stand* continue as a legacy 7 *shine* are
brilliantly substantiated s.d. *Sennet* trumpet salute 13 *all-thing* altogether 14 *solemn* state

194

Command upon me, to the which my duties
Are with a most indissoluble tie
For ever knit.

Macbeth.   Ride you this afternoon?

Banquo. Ay, my good lord.

Macbeth. We should have else desired your good advice   20
(Which still hath been both grave and prosperous)
In this day's council; but we'll take tomorrow.
Is't far you ride?

Banquo. As far, my lord, as will fill up the time
'Twixt this and supper. Go not my horse the better,   25
I must become a borrower of the night
For a dark hour or twain.

Macbeth.   Fail not our feast.

Banquo. My lord, I will not.

Macbeth. We hear our bloody cousins are bestowed
In England and in Ireland, not confessing   30
Their cruel parricide, filling their hearers
With strange invention. But of that tomorrow,
When therewithal we shall have cause of state
Craving us jointly. Hie you to horse. Adieu,
Till you return at night. Goes Fleance with you?   35

Banquo. Ay, my good lord. Our time does call upon's.

Macbeth. I wish your horses swift and sure of foot,
And so I do commend you to their backs.
Farewell.   *Exit Banquo.*
Let every man be master of his time   40
Till seven at night. To make society
The sweeter welcome, we will keep ourself
Till supper time alone. While then, God be with
      you!   *Exit Lords and others.*

---

21 *still* always *prosperous* profitable 25 *Go not my horse the better*
i.e. unless my horse goes faster than anticipated 26 *borrower of* i.e.
borrower of time from 32 *invention* falsehoods 33–34 *cause* . .
jointly state business requiring our joint attention 43 *While* until

      Sirrah, a word with you. Attend those men

45   Our pleasure?

Servant. They are, my lord, without the palace gate.

Macbeth. Bring them before us.   *Exit Servant.*

      To be thus is nothing, but to be safely thus —

      Our fears in Banquo stick deep,

50   And in his royalty of nature reigns that

      Which would be feared. 'Tis much he dares;

      And to that dauntless temper of his mind

      He hath a wisdom that doth guide his valor

      To act in safety. There is none but he

55   Whose being I do fear; and under him

      My genius is rebuked, as it is said

      Mark Antony's was by Caesar. He chid the sisters

      When first they put the name of King upon me,

      And bade them speak to him. Then, prophetlike,

60   They hailed him father to a line of kings.

      Upon my head they placed a fruitless crown

      And put a barren sceptre in my gripe,

      Thence to be wrenched with an unlineal hand,

      No son of mine succeeding. If't be so,

65   For Banquo's issue have I filed my mind;

      For them the gracious Duncan have I murdered;

      Put rancors in the vessel of my peace

      Only for them, and mine eternal jewel

      Given to the common enemy of man

70   To make them kings — the seeds of Banquo kings.

      Rather than so, come, Fate, into the list,

      And champion me to th' utterance! Who's there?

Enter Servant and two Murderers.

Now go to the door and stay there till we call.

                       Exit Servant.

44 *Sirrah* form used in addressing inferiors *Attend* await 48 *but unless* 49 *in Banquo* about Banquo *stick deep* are deeply imbedded in me 51 *would be* deserves to be 56 *genius is rebuked* controlling spirit is daunted 62 *gripe* grasp 65 *filed* defiled 67 *rancors* bitter enmities 68 *jewel* soul 69 *common enemy of man* i.e. Satan 71 *list* lists, field of combat 72 *champion . . . utterance* engage with me to the death

Was it not yesterday we spoke together?
Murderers. It was, so please your Highness.
Macbeth.   Well then, now   75
    Have you considered of my speeches? Know
    That it was he, in the times past, which held you
    So under fortune, which you thought had been
    Our innocent self. This I made good to you
    In our last conference, passed in probation with you   80
    How you were borne in hand, how crossed; the in-
       struments;
    Who wrought with them; and all things else that
       might
    To half a soul and to a notion crazed
    Say "Thus did Banquo."
1. Murderer.   You made it known to us.
Macbeth. I did so; and went further, which is now   85
    Our point of second meeting. Do you find
    Your patience so predominant in your nature
    That you can let this go? Are you so gospelled
    To pray for this good man and for his issue,
    Whose heavy hand hath bowed you to the grave   90
    And beggared yours for ever?
1. Murderer.   We are men, my liege.
Macbeth. Ay, in the catalogue ye go for men,
    As hounds and greyhounds, mongrels, spaniels,
       curs,
    Shoughs, water-rugs, and demiwolves are clept
    All by the name of dogs. The valued file   95
    Distinguishes the swift, the slow, the subtle,
    The housekeeper, the hunter, every one
    According to the gift which bounteous nature
    Hath in him closed, whereby he does receive
    Particular addition, from the bill   100

78 *under fortune* out of favor with fortune   80 *passed in probation*
reviewed the evidence   81 *borne in hand* manipulated   *crossed*
thwarted   *instruments* agents   83 *half a soul* a halfwit   *notion* mind
86 *Our point of* the point of our   88 *gospelled* tamed by gospel precepts   94 *Shoughs* shaggy pet dogs   *water-rugs* long-haired water-dogs
clept named   95 *valued file* classification according to valuable traits
97 *housekeeper* watchdog   99 *closed* invested   100 *addition, from the
bill* distinction, contrary to the listing

That writes them all alike; and so of men.
Now, if you have a station in the file,
Not i' th' worst rank of manhood, say't;
And I will put that business in your bosoms

205   Whose execution takes your enemy off,
Grapples you to the heart and love of us,
Who wear our health but sickly in his life,
Which in his death were perfect.
2. *Murderer.*   I am one, my liege,
Whom the vile blows and buffets of the world

210   Have so incensed that I am reckless what
I do to spite the world.
1. *Murderer.*   And I another,
So weary with disasters, tugged with fortune,
That I would set my life on any chance
To mend it or be rid on't.
Macbeth.   Both of you
Know Banquo was your enemy.

215 *Murderers.*   True, my lord.
Macbeth. So is he mine, and in such bloody distance
That every minute of his being thrusts
Against my near'st of life; and though I could
With barefaced power sweep him from my sight

220   And bid my will avouch it, yet I must not,
For certain friends that are both his and mine,
Whose loves I may not drop, but wail his fall
Who I myself struck down. And thence it is
That I to your assistance do make love,

225   Masking the business from the common eye
For sundry weighty reasons.
2. *Murderer.*   We shall, my lord,
Perform what you command us.
1. *Murderer.*   Though our lives —
Macbeth. Your spirits shine through you. Within this
     hour at most
I will advise you where to plant yourselves,

104 *in your bosoms* in your trust   113 *set* risk   116 *distance* enmity
118 *near'st of life* vital parts   120 *avouch* justify   121 *For* because of
122 *wail* I must wail

Acquaint you with the perfect spy o' th' time   130
The moment on't, for't must be done tonight
And something from the palace (always thought
That I require a clearness); and with him,
To leave no rubs nor botches in the work,
Fleance his son, that keeps him company,   135
Whose absence is no less material to me
Than is his father's, must embrace the fate
Of that dark hour. Resolve yourselves apart;
I'll come to you anon.

Murderers.   We are resolved, my lord.

Macbeth. I'll call upon you straight. Abide within.   140
It is concluded. Banquo, thy soul's flight,
If it find heaven, must find it out tonight.   *Exit all.*

ACT III, SCENE II

Enter Macbeth's Lady and a Servant.

Lady. Is Banquo gone from court?

Servant. Ay, madam, but returns again tonight.

Lady. Say to the King I would attend his leisure
For a few words.

Servant.   Madame, I will.   *Exit.*

Lady.   Naught's had, all's spent,
Where our desire is got without content.   5
'Tis safer to be that which we destroy
Than by destruction dwell in doubtful joy.

Enter Macbeth.

How now, my lord? Why do you keep alone,

130 *with the perfect spy o' th' time* by means of a perfect look-out, or
with precise timing 132 *thought* borne in mind 133 *clearness* alibi
134 *rubs* defects

Of sorriest fancies your companions making,
Using those thoughts which should indeed have
10   died
With them they think on? Things without all
    remedy
Should be without regard. What's done is done.
Macbeth. We have scorched the snake, not killed it.
She'll close and be herself, whilst our poor malice
15 Remains in danger of her former tooth.
But let the frame of things disjoint, both the worlds
    suffer,
Ere we will eat our meal in fear, and sleep
In the affliction of these terrible dreams
That shake us nightly. Better be with the dead,
20 Whom we, to gain our peace, have sent to peace,
Than on the torture of the mind to lie
In restless ecstasy. Duncan is in his grave;
After life's fitful fever he sleeps well.
Treason has done his worst: nor steel nor poison,
25 Malice domestic, foreign levy, nothing,
Can touch him further.
Lady.   Come on.
Gentle my lord, sleek o'er your rugged looks;
Be bright and jovial among your guests tonight.
Macbeth. So shall I, love; and so, I pray, be you.
30 Let your remembrance apply to Banquo;
Present him eminence both with eye and tongue:
Unsafe the while, that we must lave
Our honors in these flattering streams
And make our faces vizards to our hearts,
Disguising what they are.
35 *Lady.*   You must leave this.
Macbeth. O, full of scorpions is my mind, dear wife!

III, ii, 9 *sorriest* most contemptible   11 *all remedy* any form of remedy
13 *scorched* slashed   14 *close* heal   *poor malice* feeble opposition   16
frame of things disjoint structure of the universe collapse   *both the
worlds* i.e. heaven and earth   21 *torture* rack   22 *ecstacy* frenzy   25
Malice domestic civil war   30 *remembrance* i.e. aware of the necessity
31 *Present him eminence* exalt him   32 *lave* dip   34 *vizards* masks

    Thou know'st that Banquo, and his Fleance, lives.

Lady. But in them Nature's copy's not eterne.

Macbeth. There's comfort yet; they are assailable.

    Then be thou jocund. Ere the bat hath flown   **40**

    His cloistered flight, ere to black Hecate's summons

    The shard-borne beetle with his drowsy hums

    Hath rung night's yawning peal, there shall be done

    A deed of dreadful note.

Lady.   What's to be done?

Macbeth. Be innocent of the knowledge, dearest

    chuck,   **45**

    Till thou applaud the deed. Come, seeling night,

    Scarf up the tender eye of pitiful day,

    And with thy bloody and invisible hand

    Cancel and tear to pieces that great bond

    Which keeps me pale. Light thickens, and the crow   **50**

    Makes wing to th' rooky wood.

    Good things of day begin to droop and drowse,

    Whiles night's black agents to their preys do

    rouse.

    Thou marvell'st at my words, but hold thee still;

    Things bad begun make strong themselves by ill.   **55**

    So prithee go with me.   *Exit both.*

ACT III, SCENE III

Enter three Murderers.

1. *Murderer.* But who did bid thee join with us?

3. *Murderer.*   Macbeth.

38 *Nature's copy* Nature's copyhold, lease on life   42 *shard-borne* borne on scaly wings   46 *seeling* sewing together the eyelids (from falconry)   47 *Scarf up* blindfold   49 *great bond* i.e. Banquo's lease on life (with suggestion also of the bond of human feeling)   51 *rooky* harboring rooks   III, iii, 2 *He needs not our mistrust* i.e. we need not mistrust this man

2. Murderer. He needs not our mistrust, since he
     delivers
  Our offices and what we have to do
  To the direction just.
1. Murderer.   Then stand with us.
5 The west yet glimmers with some streaks of day.
  Now spurs the lated traveller apace
  To gain the timely inn, and near approaches
  The subject of our watch.
3. Murderer.   Hark, I hear horses.
Banquo. (*within*) Give us a light there, ho!
2. Murderer.   Then 'tis he: the rest
10 That are within the note of expectation
  Already are i' th' court.
1. Murderer.   His horses go about.
3. Murderer. Almost a mile; but he does usually,
  So all men do, from hence to th' palace gate
  Make it their walk.

          Enter Banquo and Fleance, with a torch.

2. Murderer. A light, a light!
3. Murderer.   'Tis he.
15 *1. Murderer.*   Stand to't.
Banquo. It will be rain tonight.
1. Murderer.   Let it come down!
Banquo. O, treachery! Fly, good Fleance, fly, fly, fly!
                                 Exit Fleance.
    Thou mayst revenge — O slave!   *Banquo slain.*
3. Murderer. Who did strike out the light?
1. Murderer.   Was't not the way?
20 *3. Murderer.* There's but one down: the son is fled.
2. Murderer. We have lost best half of our affair.
1. Murderer. Well, let's away, and say how much is
     done.
                                 Exit all.

---

3 *offices* duties   6 *lated* belated   10 *within the note of expectation* on
the list of those expected (invited)   19 *Was't not the way* i.e. was it
not the right thing to do

꒰

ACT III, SCENE IV

*Banquet prepared. Enter Macbeth, Lady Macbeth,
Ross, Lennox, Lords, and Attendants.*

Macbeth. You know your own degrees — sit down:
  At first and last, the hearty welcome.
Lords. Thanks to your Majesty.
Macbeth. Ourself will mingle with society
  And play the humble host.   5
  Our hostess keeps her state, but in best time
  We will require her welcome.
Lady. Pronounce it for me, sir, to all our friends,
  For my heart speaks they are welcome.

Enter First Murderer.

Macbeth. See, they encounter thee with their hearts'
    thanks.   10
  Both sides are even. Here I'll sit i' th' midst.
  Be large in mirth; anon we'll drink a measure
  The table round.   *Goes to Murderer*
  There's blood upon thy face.
Murderer.   'Tis Banquo's then.
Macbeth. 'Tis better thee without than he within.   15
  Is he dispatched?
Murderer.   My lord, his throat is cut:
  That I did for him.
Macbeth.   Thou art the best o' th' cut-throats.
  Yet he's good that did the like for Fleance:
  If thou didst it, thou art the nonpareil.
Murderer. Most royal sir, Fleance is scaped.   20

III, iv, 1 *degrees* relative rank, order of precedence 4 *society* the
company 6 *keeps her state* remains seated in her chair of state 10
encounter greet

Macbeth. (*aside*) Then comes my fit again. I had else
    been perfect;
    Whole as the marble, founded as the rock,
    As broad and general as the casing air.
    But now I am cabined, cribbed, confined, bound in
25   To saucy doubts and fears. — But Banquo's safe?
Murderer. Ay, my good lord. Safe in a ditch he bides,
    With twenty trenchèd gashes on his head,
    The least a death to nature.
Macbeth.   Thanks for that. —
    (*aside*) There the grown serpent lies; the worm
    that's fled
30   Hath nature that in time will venom breed,
    No teeth for th' present. — Get thee gone. To-
    morrow
    We'll hear ourselves again.   *Exit Murderer.*
Lady.   My royal lord,
    You do not give the cheer. The feast is sold
    That is not often vouched, while 'tis a-making,
    'Tis given with welcome. To feed were best at
35   home;
    From thence, the sauce to meat is ceremony:
    Meeting were bare without it.

*Enter the Ghost of Banquo, and sits in
Macbeth's place.*

Macbeth.   Sweet remembrancer!
    Now good digestion wait on appetite,
    And health on both!
Lennox.   May't please your Highness sit.
Macbeth. Here had we now our country's honor
40   roofed

---

21 *perfect* sound of health   22 *founded* solidly based   23 *broad and
general* unconfined   *casing* enveloping   24 *cribbed* boxed in   25 *saucy*
insolent   27 *trenchèd* deep, trenchlike   29 *worm* serpent   32 *hear ourselves* confer   33 *cheer* tokens of convivial hospitality   *sold* i.e. not
freely given   34 *vouched* sworn   35 *To feed . . . home* i.e. mere eat-
ing is best done at home   36 *meat* food   37 *bare* barren, pointless
remembrancer prompter

Were the graced person of our Banquo present —
Who may I rather challenge for unkindness
Than pity for mischance!

Ross.   His absence, sir,
Lays blame upon his promise. Please't your Highness
To grace us with your royal company?   45

Macbeth. The table's full.

Lennox.   Here is a place reserved, sir.

Macbeth. Where?

Lennox. Here, my good lord. What is't that moves
your Highness?

Macbeth. Which of you have done this?

Lords.   What, my good lord?

Macbeth. Thou canst not say I did it. Never shake   50
Thy gory locks at me.

Ross. Gentlemen, rise. His Highness is not well.

Lady. Sit, worthy friends. My lord is often thus,
And hath been from his youth. Pray you keep seat.
The fit is momentary; upon a thought   55
He will again be well. If much you note him,
You shall offend him and extend his passion.
Feed, and regard him not. — Are you a man?

Macbeth. Ay, and a bold one, that dare look on that
Which might appal the devil.

Lady.   O proper stuff!   60
This is the very painting of your fear.
This is the air-drawn dagger which you said
Led you to Duncan. O, these flaws and starts
(Imposters to true fear) would well become
A woman's story at a winter's fire,   65
Authorized by her grandam. Shame itself!
Why do you make such faces? When all's done,
You look but on a stool.

---

42 *Who may . . . challenge* whom I hope I may reprove 57 *extend
his passion* prolong his seizure 62 *air-drawn* fashioned of air 63
flaws outbursts 64 *Imposters to true fear* i.e. because they are au-
thentic signs of false or unjustified fear 66 *Authorized* sanctioned

Macbeth.   Prithee see there!
Behold! Look! Lo! — How say you?
70 Why, what care I? If thou canst nod, speak too.
If charnel houses and our graves must send
Those that we bury back, our monuments
Shall be the maws of kites.   *Exit Ghost.*
Lady.   What, quite unmanned in folly?
Macbeth. If I stand here, I saw him.
Lady.   Fie, for shame!
Macbeth. Blood hath been shed ere now, i' th' olden
75   time,
Ere humane statute purged the gentle weal;
Ay, and since too, murders have been performed
Too terrible for the ear. The time has been
That, when the brains were out, the man would die,
80 And there an end. But now they rise again,
With twenty mortal murders on their crowns,
And push us from our stools. This is more strange
Than such a murder is.
Lady.   My worthy lord,
Your noble friends do lack you.
Macbeth.   I do forget.
85 Do not muse at me, my most worthy friends:
I have a strange infirmity, which is nothing
To those that know me. Come, love and health to
      all!
Then I'll sit down. Give me some wine, fill full.

                    Enter Ghost.

90 I drink to th' general joy o' th' whole table,
And to our dear friend Banquo, whom we miss.
Would he were here! To all, and him, we thirst,
And all to all.
Lords.   Our duties, and the pledge.

---

72 *monuments* i.e. our only tombs 73 *maws of kites* bellies of ravens
76 *purged the gentle weal* i.e. purged the state of savagery 81 *murders on their crowns* murderous gashes on their heads 92 *thirst* are
eager to drink 93 *all to all* let everyone drink to everyone

Macbeth. Avaunt, and quit my sight! Let the earth
    hide thee!
    Thy bones are marrowless, thy blood is cold;   95
    Thou hast no speculation in those eyes
    Which thou dost glare with!
Lady.   Think of this, good peers,
    But as a thing of custom. 'Tis no other.
    Only it spoils the pleasure of the time.
Macbeth. What man dare, I dare.   100
    Approach thou like the rugged Russian bear,
    The armed rhinoceros, or th' Hyrcan tiger;
    Take any shape but that, and my firm nerves
    Shall never tremble. Or be alive again
    And dare me to the desert with thy sword.   105
    If trembling I inhabit then, protest me
    The baby of a girl. Hence, horrible shadow!
    Unreal mock'ry, hence!   *Exit Ghost.*
                        Why, so; being gone,
    I am a man again. Pray you sit still.
Lady. You have displaced the mirth, broke the good
    meeting   110
    With most admired disorder.
Macbeth   Can such things be,
    And overcome us like a summer's cloud
    Without our special wonder? You make me strange
    Even to the disposition that I owe,
    When now I think you can behold such sights   115
    And keep the natural ruby of your cheeks
    When mine is blanched with fear.
Ross.   What sights, my lord?
Lady. I pray you speak not: he grows worse and
    worse;
    Question enrages him. At once, good night.

---

96 *speculation* intelligence, power of rational observation 102 *Hyrcan* from Hyrcania, in ancient times, a region near the Caspian Sea 105 *the desert* a solitary place 106 *If trembling I inhabit* if I tremble 107 *baby of a girl* a baby girl 111 *admired* wondered at 112 *overcome us* come over us 113–14 *You make . . . I owe* you oust me from my proper role as a brave man 117 *blanched* made pale

120   Stand not upon the order of your going,
       But go at once.
    Lennox.   Good night and better health
       Attend his Majesty.
    Lady.   A kind good night to all.
                                   Exit Lords.
    Macbeth. It will have blood, they say: blood will have
       blood.

       Stones have been known to move and trees to speak;
125   Augures and understood relations have
       By maggot-pies and choughs and rooks brought
       forth
       The secret'st man of blood. What is the night?
    Lady. Almost at odds with morning, which is which.
    Macbeth. How say'st thou, that Macduff denies his
       person
       At our great bidding?
130   *Lady.*   Did you send to him, sir?
    Macbeth. I hear it by the way; but I will send.
       There's not a one of them but in his house
       I keep a servant fee'd. I will tomorrow
       (And betimes I will) to the weird sisters.
135   More shall they speak, for now I am bent to know
       By the worst means the worst. For mine own good
       All causes shall give way. I am in blood
       Stepped in so far that, should I wade no more,
       Returning were as tedious as go o'er.
140   Strange things I have in head, that will to hand,
       Which must be acted ere they may be scanned.
    Lady. You lack the season of all natures, sleep.
    Macbeth. Come, we'll to sleep. My strange and self-
       abuse
       Is the initiate fear that wants hard use.
145   We are yet but young in deed.   *Exit both.*

125 *Augures* auguries — signs, omens   *relations* utterances   126 *maggot-pies* magpies   *choughs* jackdaws (capable of "utterances," as are magpies and rooks)   131 *by the way* casually   133 *fee'd* paid to spy 134 *betimes* speedily   135 *bent* inclined, determined   141 *ere they may be scanned* i.e. without being closely studied   142 *season* seasoning, preservative   143 *self-abuse* delusion   144 *initiate fear* beginner's fear *wants hard use* lacks toughening practice

❧

ACT III, SCENE V

Thunder. Enter the three Witches, meeting Hecate.

1. *Witch.* Why, how now, Hecate? You look angerly.
Hecate. Have I not reason, beldams as you are,
   Saucy and overbold? How did you dare
   To trade and traffic with Macbeth
   In riddles and affairs of death;   5
   And I, the mistress of your charms,
   The close contriver of all harms,
   Was never called to bear my part
   Or show the glory of our art?
   And, which is worse, all you have done   10
   Hath been but for a wayward son,
   Spiteful and wrathful, who, as others do,
   Loves for his own ends, not for you.
   But make amends now: get you gone
   And at the pit of Acheron   15
   Meet me i' th' morning. Thither he
   Will come to know his destiny.
   Your vessels and your spells provide,
   Your charms and everything beside.
   I am for th' air. This night I'll spend   20
   Unto a dismal and a fatal end.
   Great business must be wrought ere noon.
   Upon the corner of the moon
   There hangs a vap'rous drop profound;
   I'll catch it ere it come to ground: 25
   And that, distilled by magic sleights,
   Shall raise such artificial sprites

III, v, 2 *beldams* old crones   7 *close* secret   15 *Acheron* a river of
Hades   24 *profound* weighty   26 *sleights* devices   27 *artificial sprites*
spirits created by magic arts

As by the strength of their illusion
Shall draw him on to his confusion.
30 He shall spurn fate, scorn death, and bear
His hopes 'bove wisdom, grace, and fear:
And you all know security
Is mortals' chiefest enemy.
                    Music, and a song.
Hark! I am called. My little spirit, see,
35 Sits in a foggy cloud and stays for me.   *Exit.*

Singing within, "Come away, come away," etc.

1. Witch. Come, let's make haste: she'll soon be
back again.   *Exit all.*

⚜

ACT III, SCENE VI

Enter Lennox and another Lord.

Lennox. My former speeches have but hit your
      thoughts,
   Which can interpret farther. Only I say
   Things have been strangely borne. The gracious
      Duncan
   Was pitied of Macbeth. Marry, he was dead!
5   And the right valiant Banquo walked too late;
   Whom, you may say (if't please you) Fleance killed,
   For Fleance fled. Men must not walk too late.
   Who cannot want the thought how monstrous
   It was for Malcolm and for Donalbain
10   To kill their gracious father? Damnèd fact,
   How it did grieve Macbeth! Did he not straight,

32 *security* over-confidence   III, vi, 1 *My former speeches* what I have
just said   *hit* matched   2 *interpret farther* draw further conclusions
8 *cannot want the thought* can avoid thinking   10 *fact* deed

In pious rage, the two delinquents tear
That were the slaves of drink and thralls of sleep?
Was not that nobly done? Ay, and wisely too,
For 'twould have angered any heart alive   15
To hear the men deny't. So that I say
He has borne all things well; and I do think
That, had he Duncan's sons under his key
(As, an't please heaven, he shall not), they should
      find
What 'twere to kill a father. So should Fleance.   20
But peace! for from broad words, and 'cause he
      failed
His presence at the tyrant's feast, I hear
Macduff lives in disgrace. Sir, can you tell
Where he bestows himself?

Lord.   The son of Duncan,
From whom this tyrant holds the due of birth,   25
Lives in the English court, and is received
Of the most pious Edward with such grace
That the malevolence of fortune nothing
Takes from his high respect. Thither Macduff
Is gone to pray the holy King upon his aid   30
To wake Northumberland and warlike Siward;
That by the help of these (with Him above
To ratify the work) we may again
Give to our tables meat, sleep to our nights,
Free from our feasts and banquets bloody knives,   35
Do faithful homage and receive free honors —
All which we pine for now. And this report
Hath so exasperate the King that he
Prepares for some attempt of war.

Lennox.   Sent he to Macduff?

---

13 *thralls* slaves   17 *borne* carried off   19 *an't* if it   21 *from broad
words* through plain speaking   25 *due of birth* birthright   29 *his high
respect* high respect for him   30 *upon his aid* upon Malcolm's behalf
31 *wake* arouse   *Northumberland* English county bordering Scotland
36 *free* untainted

40 *Lord.* He did; and with an absolute "Sir, not I,"
        The cloudy messenger turns me his back
        And hums, as who should say, "You'll rue the time
        That clogs me with this answer."

    Lennox.   And that well might
        Advise him to a caution t' hold what distance
45   His wisdom can provide. Some holy angel
        Fly to the court of England and unfold
        His message ere he come, that a swift blessing
        May soon return to this our suffering country
        Under a hand accursed!

    Lord.   I'll send my prayers with him.
                                              Exit both.

41 *cloudy* angry 43 *clogs* encumbers 44–45 *Advise him . . . can provide* warn him to keep at as safe a distance as he can devise

ACT IV, SCENE I

Thunder. Enter the three Witches.

1. *Witch.* Thrice the brinded cat hath mewed.
2. *Witch.* Thrice, and once the hedge-pig whined.
3. *Witch.* Harpier cries. — 'Tis time, 'tis time!
1. *Witch.* Round about the cauldron go;
   In the poisoned entrails throw.   5
   Toad, that under cold stone
   Days and nights has thirty-one
   Swelt'red venom, sleeping got,
   Boil thou first i' th' charmèd pot.
All. Double, double, toil and trouble,   10
   Fire burn, and cauldron bubble.
2. *Witch.* Cool it with a baboon's blood,
   In the cauldron boil and bake;
   Eye of newt, and toe of frog,
   Wool of bat, and tongue of dog,   15
   Adder's fork, and blindworm's sting,
   Lizard's leg, and howlet's wing —
   For a charm of pow'rful trouble
   Like a hell-broth boil and bubble.
All. Double, double, toil and trouble,   20
   Fire burn, and cauldron bubble.
3. *Witch.* Scale of dragon, tooth of wolf,

IV, i, 1 *brinded* brindled, striped 3 *Harpier* name of familiar spirit, suggestive of harpy, frightful flying creatures of Greek mythology with huge beaks and claws 8 *Swelt'red venom, sleeping got* exuded venom formed while sleeping 12 *fenny* swamp 16 *blindworm* a lizard, popularly supposed poisonous

213

Witch's mummy, maw and gulf
Of the ravined salt-sea shark,
25   Root of hemlock digged i' th' dark,
Liver of blaspheming Jew,
Gall of goat, and slips of yew
Silvered in the moon's eclipse,
Nose of Turk, and Tartar's lips,
30   Finger of birth-strangled babe
Ditch-delivered by a drab
Make the gruel thick and slab.
Add thereto a tiger's chaudron
For th' ingredience of our cauldron.
35 *All.* Double, double, toil and trouble,
Fire, burn, and cauldron bubble.
2. Witch. Cool it with a baboon's blood,
Then the charm is firm and good.

Enter Hecate and the other three Witches.

Hecate. O, well done! I commend your pains,
40   And every one shall share i' th' gains.
And now about the cauldron sing
Like elves and fairies in a ring,
Enchanting all that you put in.

Music and a song, "Black spirits," etc.

Exit Hecate and singers.
2. Witch. Cool it with a baboon's blood,
45   Something wicked this way comes.
Open locks,
Whoever knocks!

Enter Macbeth.

Macbeth. How now, you secret, black, and midnight
hags,

23 *maw and gulf* stomach and gullet   24 *ravined* insatiable   31 *drab*
harlot   32 *slab* sticky   33 *chaudron* guts

What is't you do?

All.   A deed without a name.

Macbeth. I conjure you by that which you profess,   50
Howe'er you come to know it, answer me.
Though you untie the winds and let them fight
Against the churches, though the yesty waves
Confound and swallow navigation up,
Though bladed corn be lodged and trees blown
  down,   55
Though castles topple on their warders' heads,
Though palaces and pyramids do slope
Their heads to their foundations, though the trea-
  sure
Of nature's germens tumble all together
Even till destruction sicken, answer me   60
To what I ask you.

1. Witch.   Speak.

2. Witch.   Demand.

3. Witch.   We'll answer.

1. Witch. Say if th' hadst rather hear it from our
  mouths
Or from our masters.

Macbeth.   Call 'em. Let me see 'em.

1. Witch. Pour in sow's blood, that hath eaten
Her nine farrow; grease that's sweaten   65
From the murderer's gibbet throw
Into the flame.

All.   Come, high or low,
Thyself and office deftly show!

Thunder. First Apparition, an Armed Head.

Macbeth. Tell me, thou unknown power —

1. Witch.   He knows thy thought:
Hear his speech, but say thou naught.   70

53 *yesty* yeasty, foamy 54 *Confound* destroy 55 *bladed corn be
lodged* ripe grain be beaten to earth 57 *slope* incline 59 *nature's
germens* seeds of creation 60 *sicken* shall surfeit 65 *nine farrow* litter
of nine 68 *office* function

1. Apparition. Macbeth, Macbeth, Macbeth, beware
        Macduff!
    Beware the Thane of Fife! Dismiss me. — Enough.
                                                    He descends.
Macbeth. Whate'er thou art, for thy good caution
        thanks:
    Thou hast harped my fear aright. But one word
        more —
75 *1. Witch.* He will not be commanded. Here's another,
        More potent than the first.

            Thunder. Second Apparition, a Bloody Child.

2. Apparition. Macbeth, Macbeth, Macbeth —
Macbeth. Had I three ears, I'ld hear thee.
2. Apparition. Be bloody, bold, and resolute! Laugh
        to scorn
80 The pow'r of man, for none of woman born
    Shall harm Macbeth.   *Descends.*
Macbeth. Then live, Macduff, — what need I fear of
        thee?
    But yet I'll make assurance double sure
    And take a bond of fate. Thou shalt not live;
85 That I may tell pale-hearted fear it lies
    And sleep in spite of thunder.

    *Thunder. Third Apparition, a Child Crowned, with
                a tree in his hand.*

                                    What is this
    That rises like the issue of a king
    And wears upon his baby-brow the round
    And top of sovereignty?
All.   Listen, but speak not to't.
    3. Apparition. Be lion-mettled, proud, and take no
90   care

---

74 *harped* hit the tune of   84 *take a bond of* secure a guarantee from
88 *round* crown

Who chafes, who frets, or where conspirers are!
Macbeth shall never vanquished be until
Great Birnam Wood to high Dunsinane Hill
Shall come against him   *Descends.*
Macbeth.   That will never be.
Who can impress the forest, bid the tree   95
Unfix his earth-bound root? Sweet bodements,
    good!
Rebellious dead rise never till the Wood
Of Birnam rise, and our high-placed Macbeth
Shall live the lease of nature, pay his breath
To time and mortal custom. Yet my heart   100
Throbs to know one thing. Tell me, if your art
Can tell so much: Shall Banquo's issue ever
Reign in this kingdom?
All.   Seek to know no more.
Macbeth. I will be satisfied. Deny me this,
And an eternal curse fall on you! Let me know.   105
Why sinks that cauldron? and what noise is this?
                                        Hautboys.
1. Witch. Show!
2. Witch. Show!
3. Witch. Show!
All. Show his eyes, and grieve his heart!   110
Come like shadows, so depart!

        A show of eight Kings and Banquo, last King
            with a glass in his hand.

Macbeth. Thou art too like the spirit of Banquo.
    Down!
Thy crown does sear mine eyeballs. And thy hair,
Thou other gold-bound brow, is like the first.
A third is like the former. Filthy hags,   115
Why do you show me this? A fourth? Start, eyes!

95 *impress* conscript 96 *bodements* prophecies 99 *lease of nature*
i.e. the full lifespan 100 *mortal custom* normal death 102 *issue* offspring 106 *noise* music 116 *Start* budge

What, will the line stretch out to th' crack of doom?
Another yet? A seventh? I'll see no more.
And yet the eighth appears, who bears a glass
120   Which shows me many more; and some I see
That twofold balls and treble sceptres carry.
Horrible sight! Now I see 'tis true;
For the blood-boltered Banquo smiles upon me
And points at them for his. What? Is this so?
125 1. *Witch.* Ay, sir, all this is so. But why
Stands Macbeth thus amazedly?
Come, sisters, cheer we up his sprites
And show the best of our delights.
I'll charm the air to give a sound
130   While you perform your antic round,
That this great king may kindly say
Our duties did his welcome pay.
                    Music. The Witches dance, and vanish.
Macbeth. Where are they? Gone? Let this pernicious
          hour
     Stand aye accursèd in the calendar!
     Come in without there!

                    Enter Lennox.

135 *Lennox.*   What's your Grace's will?
Macbeth. Saw you the weird sisters?
Lennox.   No, my lord.
Macbeth. Came they not by you?
Lennox.   No indeed, my lord.
Macbeth. Infected be the air whereon they ride,
     And damned all those that trust them! I did hear
140   The galloping of horse. Who was't came by?
Lennox. 'Tis two or three, my lord, that bring you
          word
     Macduff is fled to England.

---

121 *twofold balls and treble sceptres* (English coronation insignia)
123 *blood-boltered* matted with blood 127 *sprites* spirits 130 *antic round* grotesque circular dance 144 *anticipat'st* forestall

Macbeth.   Fled to England?

Lennox. Ay, my good lord.

Macbeth. (aside) Time, thou anticipat'st my dread
    exploits.
    The flighty purpose never is o'ertook   145
    Unless the deed go with it. From this moment
    The very firstlings of my heart shall be
    The firstlings of my hand. And even now,
    To crown my thoughts with acts, be it thought and
      done:
    The castle of Macduff I will surprise,   150
    Seize upon Fife, give to th' edge o' th' sword
    His wife, his babes, and all unfortunate souls
    That trace him in his line. No boasting like a fool;
    This deed I'll do before this purpose cool.
    But no more sights! — Where are these gentle-
      men?   155
    Come, bring me where they are.   Exit both.

ACT IV, SCENE II

Enter Macduff's Wife, her Son, and Ross.

Wife. What had he done to make him fly the land?

Ross. You must have patience, madam.

Wife.   He had none.
    His flight was madness. When our actions do not,
    Our fears do make us traitors.

Ross.   You know not
    Whether it was his wisdom or his fear.   5

Wife. Wisdom? To leave his wife, to leave his babes,

145 *flighty* fleeting 147–48 *firstlings . . . my hand* i.e. I shall act at
the moment I feel the first impulse 153 *trace* follow *line* family line
IV, ii, 2 *patience* self-control 4 *traitors* i.e. traitors to ourselves

His mansion and his titles in a place
From whence himself does fly? He loves us not,
He wants the natural touch. For the poor wren
10 (The most diminutive of birds) will fight,
Her young ones in her nest, against the owl.
All is the fear and nothing is the love,
As little is the wisdom, where the flight
So runs against all reason.

Ross.   My dearest coz,
15 I pray you school yourself. But for your husband,
He is noble, wise, judicious, and best knows
The fits o' th' season. I dare not speak much further,
But cruel are the times when we are traitors
And do not know ourselves; when we hold rumor
20 From what we fear, yet know not what we fear
But float upon a wild and violent sea
Each way and none. I take my leave of you.
Shall not be long but I'll be here again.
Things at the worst will cease, or else climb upward
25 To what they were before. — My pretty cousin,
Blessing upon you!

Wife. Fathered he is, and yet he's fatherless.

Ross. I am so much a fool, should I stay longer
It would be my disgrace and your discomfort.
I take my leave at once.   *Exit.*

30 *Wife.*   Sirrah, your father's dead;
And what will you do now? How will you live?

Son. As birds do, mother.

Wife.   What, with worms and flies?

Son. With what I get, I mean; and so do they.

Wife. Poor bird! thou'dst never fear the net nor lime,
35 The pitfall nor the gin.

Son. Why should I, mother? Poor birds they are not
set for.

---

9 *wants* lacks 14 *coz* cousin, kinswoman 17 *fits o' th' season* present
disorders 19 *know ourselves* know ourselves to be so 19–20 *hold
rumor . . . we fear* are credulous in accordance with our fears 24
will cease i.e. must cease descending 29 *would be my* would be to my
(i.e. his weeping) 34 *lime* birdlime 35 *gin* trap

My father is not dead for all your saying.

Wife. Yes, he is dead. How wilt thou do for a father?

Son. Nay, how will you do for a husband?

Wife. Why, I can buy me twenty at any market.   40

Son. Then you'll buy 'em to sell again.

Wife. Thou speak'st with all thy wit; and yet, i' faith,
   With wit enough for thee.

Son. Was my father a traitor, mother?

Wife. Ay, that he was!   45

Son. What is a traitor?

Wife. Why, one that swears and lies.

Son. And be all traitors that do so?

Wife. Every one that does so is a traitor and must be
   hanged.

Son. And must they all be hanged that swear and lie?   50

Wife. Every one.

Son. Who must hang them?

Wife. Why, the honest men.

Son. Then the liars and swearers are fools, for there
   are liars and swearers enow to beat the honest men   55
   and hang up them.

Wife. Now God help thee, poor monkey! But how
   wilt thou do for a father?

Son. If he were dead, you'ld weep for him. If you
   would not, it were a good sign that I should quickly   60
   have a new father.

Wife. Poor prattler, how thou talk'st!

Enter a Messenger.

Messenger. Bless you, fair dame! I am not to you
   known,
   Though in your state of honor I am perfect.
   I doubt some danger does approach you nearly.   65
   If you will take a homely man's advice,

---

41 *sell* betray 42–43 *Thou speak'st . . . for thee* i.e. you use all the
intelligence you have, and it is quite enough 55 *enow* enough 64 *in
your state . . . perfect* I am informed of your noble identity 65 *doubt*
fear 66 *homely* plain

Be not found here. Hence with your little ones!
To fright you thus methinks I am too savage;
To do worse to you were fell cruelty,
Which is too nigh your person. Heaven preserve
70   you!
I dare abide no longer.   *Exit.*
Wife.   Whither should I fly?
I have done no harm. But I remember now
I am in this earthly world, where to do harm
Is often laudable, to do good sometime
75 Accounted dangerous folly. Why then, alas,
Do I put up that womanly defense
To say I have done no harm? — What are these
     faces?

                         Enter Murderers.

Murderer. Where is your husband?
Wife. I hope in no place so unsanctified
     Where such as thou mayst find him.
80 *Murderer.*   He's a traitor.
Son. Thou liest, thou shag-eared villain!
Murderer.   What, you egg! *Stabs him.*
     Young fry of treachery!
Son.   He has killed me, mother.
     Run away, I pray you!   *Dies.*
Exit Wife, crying "Murder!" Pursued by Murderers.

<hr>

69–70 *To do worse . . . your person* i.e. not to frighten you were to
do worse, expose you to that fierce cruelty which is impending 81
shag-earned i.e. with shaggy hair falling about the ears 82 *fry* spawn

✌

ACT IV, SCENE III

Enter Malcolm and Macduff.

Malcolm. Let us seek out some desolate shade, and
    there
  Weep our sad bosoms empty.
Macduff.   Let us rather
  Hold fast the mortal sword and, like good men,
  Bestride our downfall'n birthdom. Each new morn
  New widows howl, new orphans cry, new sorrows   5
  Strike heaven on the face, that it resounds
  As if it felt with Scotland and yelled out
  Like syllable of dolor.
Malcolm.   What I believe, I'll wail;
  What know, believe; and what I can redress,
  As I shall find the time to friend, I will.   10
  What you have spoke, it may be so perchance.
  This tyrant, whose sole name blisters our tongues,
  Was once thought honest; you have loved him well;
  He hath not touched you yet. I am young; but
    something
  You may deserve of him through me, and wisdom   15
  To offer up a weak, poor, innocent lamb
  T" appease an angry god.
Macduff. I am not treacherous.
Malcolm.   But Macbeth is.
  A good and virtuous nature may recoil
  In an imperial charge. But I shall crave your pardon.   20

IV, iii, 3 *mortal* deadly   4 *Bestride* i.e. stand over protectively *birthdom* place of birth   8 *Like syllable of dolor* a similar cry of pain   10
time to friend time propitious   12 *sole name* very name   14 *young* i.e.
young and inexperienced   15 *wisdom* i.e. it may be wise   19–20 *recoil
. . . imperial charge* reverse itself under royal pressure

That which you are, my thoughts cannot transpose:
Angels are bright still though the brightest fell;
Though all things foul would wear the brows of
        grace,
Yet grace must still look so.
Macduff.   I have lost my hopes.
Malcolm. Perchance even there where I did find my
25   doubts.
Why in that rawness left you wife and child,
Those precious motives, those strong knots of love
Without leave-taking? I pray you,
Let not my jealousies be your dishonors,
30   But mine own safeties. You may be rightly just
Whatever I shall think.
Macduff.   Bleed, bleed, poor country
Great tyranny, lay thou thy basis sure,
For goodness dare not check thee, wear thou thy
        wrongs,
The title is affeered! Fare thee well, lord.
35   I would not be the villain that thou think'st
For the whole space that's in the tyrant's grasp
And the rich East to boot.
Malcolm.   Be not offended.
I speak not as in absolute fear of you.
I think our country sinks beneath the yoke,
40   It weeps, it bleeds, and each new day a gash
Is added to her wounds. I think withal
There would be hands uplifted in my right;
And here from gracious England have I offer
Of goodly thousands. But, for all this,
45   When I shall tread upon the tyrant's head
Or wear it on my sword, yet my poor country
Shall have more vices than it had before,
More suffer, and more sundry ways than ever,
By him that shall succeed.

21 *transpose* alter   22 *the brightest* i.e. Lucifer   26 *rawness* unpro
tected state   29 *jealousies* suspicions   32 *basis* foundation   34 *affeered*
confirmed by law   38 *absolute* complete   41 *withal* furthermore

Macduff.   What should he be?

Malcolm. It is myself I mean, in whom I know   50
  All the particulars of vice so grafted
  That, when they shall be opened, black Macbeth
  Will seem as pure as snow, and the poor state
  Esteem him as a lamb, being compared
  With my confineless harms.

Macduff.   Not in the legions   55
  Of horrid hell can come a devil more damned
  In evils to top Macbeth.

Malcolm.   I grant him bloody,
  Luxurious, avaricious, false, deceitful,
  Sudden, malicious, smacking of every sin
  That has a name. But there's no bottom, none,   60
  In my voluptuousness. Your wives, your daughters,
  Your matrons, and your maids could not fill up
  The cistern of my lust; and my desire
  All continent impediments would o'erbear
  That did oppose my will. Better Macbeth   65
  Than such an one to reign.

Macduff.   Boundless intemperance
  In nature is a tyranny. It hath been
  Th' untimely emptying of the happy throne
  And fall of many kings. But fear not yet
  To take upon you what is yours. You may   70
  Convey your pleasures in a spacious plenty
  And yet seem cold — the time you may so hood-
      wink.
  We have willing dames enough. There cannot be
  That vulture in you to devour so many
  As will to greatness dedicate themselves,   75
  Finding it so inclined.

Malcolm.   With this there grows
  In my most ill-composed affection such

51 *particulars* varieties *grafted* implanted 52 *opened* revealed 55
confineless harms unlimited vices 58 *Luxurious* lecherous 59 *Sudden*
violent 64 *continent* containing, restraining 67 *In nature* in one's
nature 71 *Convey* obtain by stealth 77 *ill-composed affection* disordered disposition

A stanchless avarice that, were I King,
I should cut off the nobles for their lands,
80 Desire his jewels, and this other's house,
And my more-having would be as a sauce
To make me hunger more, that I should forge
Quarrels unjust against the good and loyal,
Destroying them for wealth.

Macduff.   This avarice
85 Sticks deeper, grows with more pernicious root
Than summer-seeming lust, and it hath been
The sword of our slain kings. Yet do not fear.
Scotland hath foisons to fill up your will
Of your mere own. All these are portable,
90 With other graces weighed.

Malcolm. But I have none. The king-becoming graces,
As justice, verity, temp'rance, stableness,
Bounty, perseverance, mercy, lowliness,
Devotion, patience, courage, fortitude,
95 I have no relish of them, but abound
In the division of each several crime,
Acting it many ways. Nay, had I pow'r, I should
Pour the sweet milk of concord into hell,
Uproar the universal peace, confound
All unity on earth.

100 *Macduff.*   O Scotland, Scotland!

Malcolm. If such a one be fit to govern, speak.
I am as I have spoken.

Macduff.   Fit to govern?
No, not to live! O nation miserable,
With an untitled tyrant bloody-sceptred,
105 When shalt thou see thy wholesome days again,
Since that the truest issue of thy throne
By his own interdiction stands accursed

78 *stanchless* insatiable 82 *forge* fabricate 86 *summer-seeming* i.e.
seasonal, transitory 87 *sword of our slain* cause of death of our 88–
89 *foisons . . . mere own* riches of your own enough to satisfy you
89 *portable* bearable 93 *lowliness* humility 95 *relish* trace 96 *division* subdivisions 99 *Uproar* blast 107 *interdiction* curse

And does blaspheme his breed? Thy royal father
Was a most sainted king; the queen that bore thee,
Oft'ner upon her knees than on her feet,   110
Died every day she lived. Fare thee well.
These evils thou repeat'st upon thyself
Hath banished me from Scotland. O my breast,
Thy hope ends here!

Malcolm.   Macduff, this noble passion,
Child of integrity, hath from my soul   115
Wiped the black scruples, reconciled my thoughts
To thy good truth and honor. Devilish Macbeth
By many of these trains hath sought to win me
Into his power; and modest wisdom plucks me
From over-credulous haste; but God above   120
Deal between thee and me, for even now
I put myself to thy direction and
Unspeak mine own detraction, here abjure
The taints and blames I laid upon myself
For strangers to my nature. I am yet   125
Unknown to woman, never was forsworn,
Scarcely have coveted what was mine own,
At no time broke my faith, would not betray
The devil to his fellow, and delight
No less in truth than life. My first false speaking   130
Was this upon myself. What I am truly,
Is thine and my poor country's to command;
Whither indeed, before thy here-approach,
Old Siward with ten thousand warlike men
Already at a point was setting forth.   135
Now we'll together; and the chance of goodness
Be like our warranted quarrel! Why are you silent?

Macduff. Such welcome and unwelcome things at once
'Tis hard to reconcile.

---

111 *Died* i.e. turned away from this life 116 *scruples* doubts 118
trains plots 119 *modest* cautious *plucks* holds 125 *For* as 131
upon against 135 *at a point* armed 136–37 *the chance . . . warranted quarrel* i.e. let the chance of success equal the justice of our cause

Enter a Doctor.

Malcolm. Well, more anon. Comes the King forth, I
140   pray you?
   Doctor. Ay, sir. There are a crew of wretched souls
     That stay his cure. Their malady convinces
     The great assay of art; but at his touch,
     Such sanctity hath heaven given his hand,
     They presently amend.
145 *Malcolm.*   Thank you, doctor.
                                     Exit Doctor.
   Macduff. What's the disease he means?
   Malcolm.   'Tis called the evil.
     A most miraculous work in this good King,
     Which often since my here-remain in England
     I have seen him do: how he solicits heaven
150   Himself best knows, but strangely visited people,
     All swol'n and ulcerous, pitiful to the eye,
     The mere despair of surgery, he cures,
     Hanging a golden stamp about their necks,
     Put on with holy prayers; and 'tis spoken,
155   To the succeeding royalty he leaves
     The healing benediction. With this strange virtue,
     He hath a heavenly gift of prophecy,
     And sundry blessings hang about his throne
     That speak him full of grace.

Enter Ross.

   Macduff.   See who comes here.
160 *Malcolm.* My countryman; but yet I know him not.
   Macduff. My ever gentle cousin, welcome hither.
   Malcolm. I know him now. Good God betimes re-
     move

---

140 *anon* soon 142 *stay* await *convinces* baffles 143 *assay of art*
resources of medical science 146 *evil* scrofula (king's evil) 150
strangely visited unusually afflicted 152 *mere* utter 153 *stamp* coin
162 *betimes* quickly

    The means that makes us strangers!

Ross.   Sir, amen.

Macduff. Stands Scotland where it did?

Ross.   Alas, poor country,
    Almost afraid to know itself. It cannot   165
    Be called our mother but our grave, where nothing
    But who knows nothing is once seen to smile;
    Where sighs and groans, and shrieks that rent the
        air,
    Are made, not marked; where violent sorrow seems
    A modern ecstasy. The dead man's knell   170
    Is there scarce asked for who, and good men's lives
    Expire before the flowers in their caps,
    Dying or ere they sicken.

Macduff.   O, relation
    Too nice, and yet too true!

Malcolm.   What's the newest grief?

Ross. That of an hour's age doth hiss the speaker;   175
    Each minute teems a new one.

Macduff.   How does my wife?

Ross. Why, well.

Macduff.   And all my children?

Ross.   Well too.

Macduff. The tyrant has not battered at their peace?

Ross. No, they were well at peace when I did leave
    'em.

Macduff. Be not a niggard of your speech. How goes't? 180

Ross. When I came hither to transport the tidings
    Which I have heavily borne, there ran a rumor
    Of many worthy fellows that were out,
    Which was to my belief witnessed the rather
    For that I saw the tyrant's power afoot.   185
    Now is the time of help. Your eye in Scotland
    Would create soldiers, make our women fight
    To doff their dire distresses.

---

166 *nothing* no one 169 *marked* noticed 170 *modern ectasy* commonplace emotion 171 *Is there . . . for who* scarely calls forth an inquiry about identity 174 *nice* precise 175 *hiss the speaker* causes the speaker to be hissed (for stale repetition) 176 *teems* brings forth 182 *heavily borne* sadly carried 183 *out* up in arms

Malcolm.   Be't their comfort
We are coming thither. Gracious England hath
190   Lent us good Siward and ten thousand men,
An older and a better soldier none
That Christendom gives out.

Ross.   Would I could answer
This comfort with the like. But I have words
That would be howled out in the desert air,
Where hearing should not latch them.

195 *Macduff.*   What concern they,
The general cause or is it a fee-grief
Due to some single breast?

Ross.   No mind that's honest
But in it shares some woe, though the main part
Pertains to you alone.

Macduff.   If it be mine,
200   Keep it not from me, quickly let me have it.

Ross. Let not your ears despise my tongue for ever,
Which shall possess them with the heaviest sound
That ever yet they heard.

Macduff.   Humh! I guess at it.

Ross. Your castle is surprised, your wife and babes
205   Savagely slaughtered. To relate the manner
Were, on the quarry of these murdered deer,
To add the death of you.

Malcolm.   Merciful heaven!
What, man! Ne'er pull your hat upon your brows.
Give sorrow words. The grief that does not speak
210   Whispers the o'erfraught heart and bids it break.

Macduff. My children too?

Ross.   Wife, children, servants, all
That could be found.

Macduff.   And I must be from thence?
My wife killed too?

Ross.   I have said.

195 *latch* catch hold of   196 *fee-grief* i.e. a grief possessed in private
197 *Due* belonging   204 *surprised* attacked   206 *quarry* heap of game

Malcolm.   Be comforted.
  Let's make us med'cines of our great revenge
  To cure this deadly grief.   215
Macduff. He has no children. All my pretty ones?
  Did you say all? O hell-kite! All?
  What, all my pretty chickens and their dam
  At one fell swoop?
Malcolm. Dispute it like a man.
Macduff.   I shall do so;   220
  But I must also feel it as a man.
  I cannot but remember such things were
  That were most precious to me. Did heaven look on
  And would not take their part? Sinful Macduff,
  They were all struck for thee! Naught that I am,   225
  Not for their own demerits but for mine
  Fell slaughter on their souls. Heaven rest them now!
Malcolm. Be this the whetstone of your sword. Let
    grief
  Convert to anger; blunt not the heart, enrage it.
Macduff. O, I could play the woman with mine eyes   230
  And braggart with my tongue. But, gentle heavens,
  Cut short all intermission. Front to front
  Bring thou this fiend of Scotland and myself.
  Within my sword's length set him. If he scape,
  Heaven forgive him too!
Malcolm.   This tune goes manly.   235
  Come, go we to the King. Our power is ready;
  Our lack is nothing but our leave. Macbeth
  Is ripe for shaking, and the pow'rs above
  Put on their instruments. Receive what cheer you
    may.
  The night is long that never finds the day.   240

                            Exit all.

---

210 *Whispers* whispers to   220 *Dispute* revenge   225 *Naught* wicked
232 *intermission* interval   *Front to front* face to face   236 *power*
army   237 *Our luck . . . our leave* i.e. nothing remains but to say
farewell   239 *Put on their instruments* urge on their agents

ACT V, SCENE I

Enter a Doctor of Physic and a Waiting Gentlewoman.

   Doctor. I have two nights watched with you, but can perceive no truth in your report. When was it she last walked?

5   *Gentlewoman.* Since his Majesty went into the field I have seen her rise from her bed, throw her nightgown upon her, unlock her closet, take forth paper, fold it, write upon't, read it, afterwards seal it, and again return to bed; yet all this while in a most fast sleep.

10   *Doctor.* A great perturbation in nature, to receive at once the benefit of sleep and do the effects of watching! In this slumb'ry agitation, besides her walking and other actual performances, what (at any time) have you heard her say?

15   *Gentlewoman.* That, sir, which I will not report after her.

   Doctor. You may to me, and 'tis most meet you should.

   Gentlewoman. Neither to you nor any one, having no
20 witness to confirm my speech.

Enter Lady Macbeth, with a taper.

V, 1, 6 *closet* a chest, or desk 11–12 *do the effects of watching* act as
if awake 17 *meet* fitting

Lo you, here she comes! This is her very guise, and,
upon my life, fast asleep! Observe her; stand close.

Doctor. How came she by that light?

Gentlewoman. Why, it stood by her. She has light by
-her continually. 'Tis her command.   25

Doctor. You see her eyes are open.

Gentlewoman. Ay, but their sense are shut.

Doctor. What is it she does now? Look how she rubs
her hands.

Gentlewoman. It is an accustomed action with her,   30
to seem thus washing her hands. I have known her
continue in this a quarter of an hour.

Lady. Yet here's a spot.

Doctor. Hark, she speaks. I will set down what comes
from her, to satisfy my remembrance the more   35
strongly.

Lady. Out, damnèd spot! Out, I say! One — two —
why then 'tis time to do't. Hell is murky. Fie, my
lord, fie! a soldier and afeard? What need we fear
who knows it, when none can call our pow'r to ac-   40
compt? Yet who would have thought the old man
to have had so much blood in him?

Doctor. Do you mark that?

Lady. The Thane of Fife had a wife. Where is she
now? What, will these hands ne'er be clean? No   45
more o' that, my lord, no more o' that! You mar all
with this starting.

Doctor. Go to, go to! You have known what you should
not.

Gentlewoman. She has spoke what she should not, I   50
am sure of that. Heaven knows what she has known.

Lady. Here's the smell of the blood still. All the per-
fumes of Arabia will not sweeten this little hand.
Oh, oh, oh!

---

22 *close* concealed   27 *sense* powers of sensation   40 *call our pow'r to
accompt* call to account anyone so powerful as we   47 *starting* startled
movements

55 *Doctor.* What a sigh is there! The heart is sorely
      charged.

Gentlewoman. I would not have such a heart in my
      bosom for the dignity of the whole body.

Doctor. Well, well, well.

60 *Gentlewoman.* Pray God it be, sir.

Doctor. This disease is beyond my practice. Yet I have
      known those which have walked in their sleep who
      have died holily in their beds.

Lady. Wash your hands, put on your nightgown, look
65   not so pale! I tell you yet again, Banquo's buried.
      He cannot come out on's grave.

Doctor. Even so?

Lady. To bed, to bed! There's knocking at the gate.
      Come, come, come, come, give me your hand!
70   What's done cannot be undone. To bed, to bed,
      to bed!   *Exit.*

Doctor. Will she go now to bed?

Gentlewoman. Directly.

Doctor. Foul whisp'rings are abroad. Unnatural deeds
75   Do breed unnatural troubles. Infected minds
      To their deaf pillows will discharge their secrets.
      More needs she the divine than the physician.
      God, God forgive us all! Look after her;
      Remove from her the means of all annoyance,
80   And still keep eyes upon her. So good night.
      My mind she has mated, and amazed my sight.
      I think, but dare not speak.

Gentlewoman.   Good night, good doctor.
                                                 Exit both

---

56 *charged* laden   61 *practice* professional competence   79 *annoyance*
self-injury   81 *mated* bemused

⤳

ACT V, SCENE II

Drum and Colors. Enter Menteith, Caithness, Angus,
Lennox, Soldiers.

Menteith. The English pow'r is near, led on by Mal-
 colm,
 His uncle Siward, and the good Macduff.
 Revenges burn in them; for their dear causes
 Would to the bleeding and the grim alarm
 Excite the mortified man.
Angus.   Near Birnam Wood   5
 Shall we well meet them; that way are they coming.
Caithness. Who knows if Donalbain be with his
 brother?
Lennox. For certain, sir, he is not. I have a file
 Of all the gentry. There is Siward's son   10
 And many unrough youths that even now
 Protest their first of manhood.
Menteith.   What does the tyrant?
Caithness. Great Dunsinane he strongly fortifies.
 Some say he's mad; others, that lesser hate him,
 Do call it valiant fury; but for certain   15
 He cannot buckle his distempered cause
 Within the belt of rule.
Angus.   Now does he feel
 His secret murders sticking on his hands.
 Now minutely revolts upbraid his faith-breach.
 Those he commands move only in command,   20
 Nothing in love. Now does he feel his title
 Hang loose about him, like a giant's robe
 Upon a dwarfish thief.

V, ii, 4 *bleeding* blood of battle   5 *Excite* incite   *mortified* dead   6
well surely   9 *file* list   11 *unrough* unbearded   12 *Protest* assert   16
distempered disease-swollen   17 *rule* reason   19 *minutely* every minute
revolts rebellions

Menteith.   Who then shall blame
His pestered senses to recoil and start,
25 When all that is within him does condemn
Itself for being there?
Caithness.   Well, march we on
To give obedience where 'tis truly owed.
Meet we the med'cine of the sickly weal;
And with him pour we in our country's purge
Each drop of us.
30 *Lennox.*   Or so much as it needs
To dew the sovereign flower and drown the weeds.
Make we our march towards Birnam.

                                    Exit all, marching.

⁂

ACT V, SCENE III

Enter Macbeth, Doctor, and Attendants.

Macbeth. Bring me no more reports. Let them fly all!
Till Birnam Wood remove to Dunsinane,
I cannot taint with fear. What's the boy Malcolm?
Was he not born of woman? The spirits that know
5 All mortal consequences have pronounced me thus:
"Fear not, Macbeth. No man that's born of woman
Shall e'er have power upon thee." Then fly, false
   thanes,
And mingle with the English epicures.
The mind I sway by and the heart I bear
10 Shall never sag with doubt nor shake with fear.

Enter Servant.

24 *pestered* tormented   28 *med'cine* cure (i.e. Malcolm)   *weal* com-
monwealth   31 *dew* water   V, iii, 3 *taint* become tainted   5 *consequences* sequence of events   8 *English epicures* i.e. as compared with
the austerely living Scots   9 *sway* direct myself

    The devil damn thee black, thou cream-faced loon!
    Where got'st thou that goose look?
Servant. There is ten thousand —
Macbeth.   Geese, villain?
Servant.   Soldiers, sir.
Macbeth. Go prick thy face and over-red thy fear,
    Thou lily-livered boy. What soldiers, patch?   15
    Death of thy soul! those linen cheeks of thine
    Are counsellors to fear. What soldiers, whey-face?
Servant. The English force, so please you.
Macbeth. Take thy face hence.   *Exit Servant.*
                 Seyton! — I am sick at heart,
    When I behold — Seyton, I say! — This push   20
    Will cheer me ever, or disseat me now.
    I have lived long enough. My way of life
    Is fall'n into the sear, the yellow leaf,
    And that which should accompany old age,
    As honor, love, obedience, troops of friends,   25
    I must not look to have; but, in their stead,
    Curses not loud but deep, mouth-honor, breath,
    Which the poor heart would fain deny, and dare
       not.
    Seyton!

Enter Seyton.

Seyton. What's your gracious pleasure?
Macbeth.   What news more?   30
Seyton. All is confirmed, my lord, which was reported.
Macbeth. I'll fight till from my bones my flesh be
    hacked. Give me my armor.
Seyton.   'Tis not needed yet.
Macbeth. I'll put it on.
    Send out moe horses, skirr the country round,   35

---

11 *loon* lout 14 *over-red thy fear* i.e. paint red your fearful pal-
lor 15 *patch* fool 20 *push* struggle 23 *sear* dry, withered 35 *moe*
more *skirr* scour

Hang those that talk of fear. Give me mine armor.
How does your patient, doctor?

Doctor.   Not so sick, my lord,
As she is troubled with thick-coming fancies
That keep her from her rest.

Macbeth.   Cure her of that!
40   Canst thou not minister to a mind diseased,
Pluck from the memory a rooted sorrow,
Raze out the written troubles of the brain,
And with some sweet oblivious antidote
Cleanse the stuffed bosom of that perilous stuff
45   Which weighs upon the heart?

Doctor.   Therein the patient
Must minister to himself.

Macbeth. Throw physic to the dogs, I'll none of it!
Come, put mine armor on. Give me my staff.
Seyton, send out. — Doctor, the thanes fly from
me. —
50   Come, sir, dispatch. — If thou couldst, doctor, cast
The water of my land, find her disease,
And purge it to a sound and pristine health,
I would applaud thee to the very echo,
That should applaud again. — Pull't off, I say. —
55   What rhubarb, senna, or what purgative drug
Would scour these English hence? Hear'st thou of
them?

Doctor. Ay, my good lord. Your royal preparation
Makes us hear something.

Macbeth.   Bring it after me!
I will not be afraid of death and bane
60   Till Birnam Forest come to Dunsinane.

Exit all but the Doctor.

Doctor. Were I from Dunsinane away and clear,
Profit again should hardly draw me here.   *Exit.*

---

42 *Raze* erase   43 *oblivious antidote* opiate, medicine of forgetfulness
44 *stuffed* choked up   47 *physic* medicine   50 *dispatch* hasten   50-51
cast . . . water analyze the urine   58 *it* i.e. the remainder of the
armor   59 *bane* destruction

✄

ACT V, SCENE IV

*Drum and Colors. Enter Malcolm, Siward, Macduff,
Siward's Son, Menteith, Caithness, Angus,
Lennox, Ross, and Soldiers, marching.*

Malcolm. Cousins, I hope the days are near at hand
   That chambers will be safe.
Menteith.   We doubt it nothing.
Siward. What wood is this before us?
Menteith.   The Wood of Birnam.
Malcolm. Let every soldier hew him down a bough
   And bear't before him. Thereby shall we shadow   5
   The numbers of our host and make discovery
   Err in report of us.
Soldiers.   It shall be done.
Siward. We learn no other but the confident tyrant
   Keeps still in Dunsinane and will endure
   Our setting down before't.
Malcolm.   'Tis his main hope,   10
   For where there is advantage to be given
   Both more and less have given him the revolt,
   And none serve with him but constrainèd things
   Whose hearts are absent too.
Macduff.   Let our just censures
   Attend the true event, and put we on   15
   Industrious soldiership.
Siward.   The time approaches
   That will with due decision make us know
   What we shall say we have and what we owe.
   Thoughts speculative their unsure hopes relate,
   But certain issue strokes must arbitrate —   20
   Towards which advance the war.

                       Exit all, marching.

V, iv, 2 *That chambers* when sleeping-chambers *nothing* not at all
6 *discovery* i.e. reports by scouts 11 *advantage* opportunity 12 *more
and less* high and low 14 *just censures* impartial judgment 15 *Attend*
await *put we on* let us put on 20 *certain issue* the definite outcome
arbitrate decide 21 *war* army

ACT V, SCENE V

Enter Macbeth, Seyton, and Soldiers, with Drum and Colors.

Macbeth. Hang out our banners on the outward walls.
    The cry is still, "They come!" Our castle's strength
    Will laugh a siege to scorn. Here let them lie
    Till famine and the ague eat them up.
5   Were they not forced with those that should be ours,
    We might have met them dareful, beard to beard,
    And beat them backward home.

                    A cry within of women.
                    What is that noise?
Seyton. It is the cry of women, my good lord.   *Exit.*
Macbeth. I have almost forgot the taste of fears.
10   The time has been my senses would have cooled
    To hear a night-shriek, and my fell of hair
    Would at a dismal treatise rouse and stir
    As life were in't. I have supped full with horrors.
    Direness, familiar to my slaughterous thoughts,
    Cannot once start me.

Enter Seyton.

15   Wherefore was that cry?
Seyton. The Queen, my lord, is dead.
Macbeth. She should have died hereafter:
    There would have been a time for such a word.
    Tomorrow, and tomorrow, and tomorrow
20   Creeps in this petty pace from day to day

V, v, 5 *forced* reinforced 11 *fell* pelt 12 *treatise* story 14 *Direness* horror 15 *start me* make me start

To the last syllable of recorded time,
And all our yesterdays have lighted fools
The way to dusty death. Out, out, brief candle!
Life's but a walking shadow, a poor player
That struts and frets his hour upon the stage   25
And then is heard no more. It is a tale
Told by an idiot, full of sound and fury,
Signifying nothing.

Enter a Messenger.

Thou com'st to use thy tongue: thy story quickly!
Messenger. Gracious my lord,   30
  I should report that which I say I saw,
  But know not how to do't.
Macbeth.   Well, say, sir.
Messenger. As I did stand my watch upon the hill,
  I looked toward Birnam, and anon methought
  The wood began to move.
Macbeth.   Liar and slave!   35
Messenger. Let me endure your wrath if't be not so.
  Within this three mile may you see it coming.
  I say, a moving grove.
Macbeth.   If thou speak'st false,
  Upon the next tree shalt thou hang alive
  Till famine cling thee. If thy speech be sooth,   40
  I care not if thou dost for me as much.
  I pull in resolution, and begin
  To doubt th' equivocation of the fiend,
  That lies like truth. "Fear not, till Birnam Wood
  Do come to Dunsinane!" and now a wood   45
  Comes toward Dunsinane. Arm, arm, and out!
  If this which he avouches does appear,
  There is nor flying hence nor tarrying here.
  I' gin to be aweary of the sun,

31 *say* i.e. affirm   40 *cling* shrivel   *sooth* truth   42 *pull in* curb, check
43 *doubt* suspect   *equivocation* double-talk   47 *avouches* affirms   52
harness armor

50   And wish th' estate o' th' world were now undone.
      Ring the alarum bell! Blow wind, come wrack,
      At least we'll die with harness on our back.

                                              Exit all.

                            ❧

                    ACT V, SCENE VI

      Drum and Colors. Enter Malcolm, Siward, Macduff,
              and their Army, with boughs.

      Malcolm. Now near enough. Your leavy screens throw
            down
      And show like those you are. You, worthy uncle,
5   Shall with my cousin, your right noble son,
      Lead our first battle. Worthy Macduff and we
      Shall take upon's what else remains to do,
      According to our order.
      Siward.   Fare you well.
      Do we but find the tyrant's power tonight,
      Let us be beaten if we cannot fight.
      Macduff. Make all our trumpets speak, give them all
            breath,
10   Those clamorous harbingers of blood and death.

                                              Exit all.

V, vi, 4 *battle* battalion   6 *order* battle-plan   7 *power* forces

ACT V, SCENE VII

Enter Macbeth.

Macbeth. They have tied me to a stake. I cannot fly,
But bearlike I must fight the course. What's he
That was not born of woman? Such a one
Am I to fear, or none.

Enter Young Siward.

Young Siward. What is thy name?
Macbeth.   Thou'lt be afraid to hear it.   5
Young Siward. No, though thou call'st thyself a hotter name
Than any is in hell.
Macbeth.   My name's Macbeth.
Young Siward. The devil himself could not pronounce a title
More hateful to mine ear.
Macbeth.   No, nor more fearful.
Young Siward. Thou liest, abhorrèd tyrant! With my sword   10
I'll prove the lie thou speak'st.
                    Fight, and Young Siward slain.
Macbeth.   Thou wast born of woman.
But swords I smile at, weapons laugh to scorn,
Brandished by man that's of a woman born.   *Exit.*

Alarums. Enter Macduff.

Macduff. That way the noise is. Tyrant, show thy face!

V, vii, 2 *course* attack (like a bear tied to a stake and baited by dogs or men)

15   If thou beest slain and with no stroke of mine,
       My wife and children's ghosts will haunt me still.
       I cannot strike at wretched kerns, whose arms
       Are hired to bear their staves. Either thou, Mac-
          beth,
       Or else my sword with an unbattered edge
20   I sheathe again undeeded. There thou shouldst be:
       By this great clatter one of greatest note
       Seems bruited. Let me find him, Fortune,
       And more I beg not!   *Exit. Alarums.*

           Enter Malcolm and Siward.

  Siward. This way, my lord. The castle's gently
       rend'red:
25   The tyrant's people on both sides do fight,
       The noble thanes do bravely in the war,
       The day almost itself professes yours
       And little is to do.
  Malcolm.   We have met with foes
       That strike beside us.
  Siward.   Enter, sir, the castle.
                      Exit both. Alarum.

ACT V, SCENE VIII

Enter Macbeth.

  Macbeth. Why should I play the Roman fool and die
    On mine own sword? Whiles I see lives, the gashes
    Do better upon them.

17 *kerns* soldiers of meanest rank 18 *staves* spears 20 *undeeded* not
glorified by deeds 22 *bruited* reported 24 *rend'red* surrendered 27
itself professes declares itself 29 *beside us* at our side, or without trying to hit us V, viii, 2 *lives* living bodies

Enter Macduff

Macduff.   Turn, hellhound, turn!
Macbeth. Of all men else I have avoided thee.
   But get thee back! My soul is too much charged   5
   With blood of thine already.
Macduff.   I have no words;
   My voice is in my sword, thou bloodier villain
   Than terms can give thee out!   *Fight. Alarum.*
Macbeth.   Thou losest labor.
   As easy mayst thou the intrenchant air
   With thy keen sword impress as make me bleed.   10
   Let fall thy blade on vulnerable crests.
   I bear a charmèd life, which must not yield
   To one of woman born.
Macduff.   Despair thy charm,
   And let the angel whom thou still hast served
   Tell thee, Macduff was from his mother's womb   15
   Untimely ripped.
Macbeth. Accursèd be that tongue that tells me so,
   For it hath cowed my better part of man!
   And be these juggling fiends no more believed,
   That palter with us in a double sense,   20
   That keep the word of promise to our ear
   And break it to our hope. I'll not fight with thee.
Macduff. Then yield thee, coward,
   And live to be the show and gaze o' th' time.
   We'll have thee, as our rarer monsters are,   25
   Painted upon a pole, and underwrit
   "Here may you see the tyrant."
Macbeth.   I will not yield,
   To kiss the ground before young Malcolm's feet
   And to be baited with the rabble's curse.
   Though Birnam Wood be come to Dunsinane,   30
   And thou opposed, being of no woman born,

---

5 *charged* burdened   9 *intrenchant* incapable of being trenched
(gashed)   13 *Despair* despair of   14 *angel* i.e. of the host of Lucifer
18 *better part of man* most manly side   20 *palter* quibble   24 *gaze*
sight   25 *monsters* freaks   26 *Painted upon a pole* pictured on a show-
man's banner

Yet I will try the last. Before my body
I throw my warlike shield. Lay on, Macduff.
And damned be him that first cries "Hold, enough!"
                                    Exit all fighting. Alarums.
Reenter fighting, and Macbeth slain. Exit Macduff.
Retreat and flourish. Enter, with Drum and Colors,
     Malcolm, Siward, Ross, Thanes, and Soldiers.

Malcolm. I would the friends we miss were safe ar-
35   rived.
Siward. Some must go off; and yet, by these I see,
     So great a day as this is cheaply bought.
Malcolm. Macduff is missing, and your noble son.
Ross. Your son, my lord, has paid a soldier's debt.
40   He only lived but till he was a man,
     The which no sooner had his prowess confirmed
     In the unshrinking station where he fought
     But like a man he died.
Siward.   Then he is dead?
Ross. Ay, and brought off the field. Your cause of
     sorrow
45   Must not be measured by his worth, for then
     It hath no end.
Siward.   Had he his hurts before?
Ross. Ay, on the front.
Siward.   Why then, God's soldier be he.
     Had I as many sons as I have hairs,
     I would not wish them to a fairer death:
     And so his knell is knolled.
50 *Malcolm.*   He's worth more sorrow,
     And that I'll spend for him.
Siward.   He's worth no more.
     They say he parted well and paid his score,
     And so, God be with him. Here comes newer com-
     fort.

---

36 *go off* perish *these* i.e. these here assembled 42 *unshrinking station* place from which he did not retreat 52 *score* reckoning

Enter Macduff, with Macbeth's head.

Macduff. Hail, King, for so thou art. Behold where
    stands
  Th' usurper's cursèd head. The time is free.   55
  I see thee compassed with thy kingdom's pearl,
  That speak my salutation in their minds,
  Whose voices I desire aloud with mine —
  Hail, King of Scotland!
All.   Hail, King of Scotland! *Flourish.*
Malcolm. We shall not spend a large expense of time   60
  Before we reckon with your several loves
  And make us even with you. My Thanes and kins-
    men,
  Henceforth be Earls, the first that ever Scotland
  In such an honor named. What's more to do
  Which would be planted newly with the time —   65
  As calling home our exiled friends abroad
  That fled the snares of watchful tyranny,
  Producing forth the cruel ministers
  Of this dead butcher and his fiend-like queen,
  Who (as 'tis thought) by self and violent hands   70
  Took off her life — this, and what needful else
  That calls upon us, by the grace of Grace
  We will perform in measure, time, and place.
  So thanks to all at once and to each one,
  Whom we invite to see us crowned at Scone.   75
                    Flourish. Exit all.

---

55 *free* released from tyranny 56 *compassed* surrounded 61 *reckon*
come to an accounting 62 *make us even with you* repay you 65
would be planted newly with the time i.e. should be done at the outset
of this new era 68 *minsters* agents 70 *self and violent* her own
violent 73 *in measure* with decorum *time, and place* at the proper
time and place

The Tragedy of
KING LEAR

William Shakespeare

Edited by Alfred Harbage

Note on the text: This edition follows the folio of
1623 (thought to be based on a carelessly copied
version of Shakespeare's rough draft and on a later
official playhouse manuscript), as edited for the
Pelican Shakespeare series in 1958. Footnotes are
from the Pelican Shakespeare edition.

NAMES OF THE ACTORS

Lear, King of Britain
King of France
Duke of Burgundy
Duke of Cornwall
Duke of Albany
Earl of Kent
Earl of Gloucester
Edgar, son to Gloucester
Edmund, bastard son to Gloucester
Curan, a courtier
Old Man, tenant to Gloucester
Doctor
Lear's Fool
Oswald, steward to Goneril
A Captain under Edmund's command
Gentlemen
A Herald
Servants to Cornwall
Goneril ⎫
Regan ⎬ daughters to Lear
Cordelia ⎭
Knights attending on Lear, Officers, Messengers,
 Soldiers, Attendants

SCENE
Britain

ACT I, SCENE I

Enter Kent, Gloucester, and Edmund.

Kent. I thought the King had more affected the Duke
    of Albany than Cornwall.

Gloucester. It did always seem so to us; but now, in
    the division of the kingdom, it appears not which
    of the dukes he values most, for equalities are so   5
    weighed that curiosity in neither can make
    choice of either's moiety.

Kent. Is not this your son, my lord?

Gloucester. His breeding, sir, hath been at my charge.
    I have so often blushed to acknowledge him that   10
    now I am brazed to't.

Kent. I cannot conceive you.

Gloucester. Sir, this young fellow's mother could;
    whereupon she grew round-wombed, and had in-
    deed, sir, a son for her cradle ere she had a husband   15
    for her bed. Do you smell a fault?

Kent. I cannot wish the fault undone, the issue of it
    being so proper.

Gloucester. But I have a son, sir, by order of law,
    some year elder than this who yet is no dearer in   20

I, i, 1 *affected* warmly regarded 2 *Albany* i.e. Scotland (once ruled
by "Albanacte") 5-6 *equalities . . . weighed* i.e. the portions weigh
so equally 6-7 *curiosity . . . moiety* careful analysis by neither can
make him prefer the other's portion 9 *breeding* rearing 11 *brazed*
brazened 12 *conceive* understand (with pun following) 18 *proper*
handsome

251

my account: though this knave came something
saucily to the world before he was sent for, yet was
his mother fair, there was good sport at his making, and the whoreson must be acknowledged. Do
25   you know this noble gentleman, Edmund?

Edmund. No, my lord.

Gloucester. My Lord of Kent. Remember him hereafter as my honorable friend.

Edmund. My services to your lordship.

30 *Kent.* I must love you, and sue to know you better.

Edmund. Sir, I shall study deserving.

Gloucester. He hath been out nine years, and away
he shall again.   *Sound a sennet.*
The King is coming.

*Enter one bearing a coronet, then King Lear, then the
Dukes of Cornwall and Albany, next Goneril,
Regan, Cordelia, and Attendants.*

35 *Lear.* Attend the lords of France and Burgundy,
Gloucester.

Gloucester. I shall, my lord.   *Exit with Edmund.*

Lear. Meantime we shall express our darker purpose.
Give me the map there. Know that we have divided
40   In three our kingdom; and 'tis our fast intent
To shake all cares and business from our age,
Conferring them on younger strengths while we
Unburdened crawl toward death. Our son of Corn-
wall,
And you our no less loving son of Albany,
45   We have this hour a constant will to publish
Our daughters' several dowers, that future strife

21 *account* estimation 22 *saucily* (1) impertinently (2) bawdily 24
whoreson (affectionate abuse, but literally applicable, like "knave"
above) 32 *out* away (for training, or in military service) 33 s.d. *sennet* trumpet flourish (heralding a procession) 38 *darker purpose* more
secret intention (to require declarations of affection) 40 *fast* firm
45 *constant . . . publish* fixed intention to announce 46 *several* individual

    May be prevented now. The princes, France and
        Burgundy,
    Great rivals in our youngest daughter's love,
    Long in our court have made their amorous so-
        journ,
    And here are to be answered. Tell me, my daugh-
        ters   50
    (Since now we will divest us both of rule,
    Interest of territory, cares of state),
    Which of you shall we say doth love us most,
    That we our largest bounty may extend
    Where nature doth with merit challenge. Goneril,   55
    Our eldest-born, speak first.
Goneril. Sir, I love you more than word can wield the
        matter;
    Dearer than eyesight, space, and liberty;
    Beyond what can be valuèd, rich or rare;
    No less than life, with grace, health, beauty,
        honor;   60
    As much as child e'er loved, or father found;
    A love that makes breath poor, and speech unable.
    Beyond all manner of so much I love you.
Cordelia. (*aside*) What shall Cordelia speak? Love,
        and be silent.
Lear. Of all these bounds, even from this line to this,   65
    With shadowy forests and with champains riched,
    With plenteous rivers and wide-skirted meads,
    We make thee lady. To thine and Albany's issues
    Be this perpetual. — What says our second daugh-
        ter,
    Our dearest Regan, wife of Cornwall?   70
Regan. I am made of that self mettle as my sister,

---

49 *amorous sojourn* i.e. visit of courtship   52 *Interest* legal possession
55 *nature . . . challenge* natural affection matches other merits   57
wield handle   58 *space* scope (for the exercise of "liberty")   62
breath voice   *unable* inadequate   66 *champains riched* plains enriched
67 *wide-skirted* far-spreading   68 *issues* descendants   69 *perpetual* in
perpetuity

And prize me at her worth. In my true heart
I find she names my very deed of love;
Only she comes too short, that I profess
75 Myself an enemy to all other joys
Which the most precious square of sense possesses,
And find I am alone felicitate
In your dear Highness' love.

Cordelia.   (aside) Then poor Cordelia;
And yet not so, since I am sure my love's
80 More ponderous than my tongue.

Lear. To thee and thine hereditary ever
Remain this ample third of our fair kingdom,
No less in space, validity, and pleasure
Than that conferred on Goneril. — Now, our joy,
85 Although our last and least; to whose young love
The vines of France and milk of Burgundy
Strive to be interest; what can you say to draw
A third more opulent than your sisters? Speak.

Cordelia. Nothing, my lord.

90 Lear. Nothing?

Cordelia. Nothing.

Lear. Nothing will come of nothing. Speak again.

Cordelia. Unhappy that I am, I cannot heave
My heart into my mouth. I love your Majesty
95 According to my bond, no more nor less.

Lear. How, how, Cordelia? Mend your speech a little,
Lest you may mar your fortunes.

Cordelia.   Good my lord,
You have begot me, bred me, loved me. I
Return those duties back as are right fit,
100 Obey you, love you, and most honor you.
Why have my sisters husbands if they say

---

72 *prize . . . worth* value me at her value   73 *my very deed of* the
true fact of my   76 *Which . . . possesses* which the most precise
measurement by the senses holds to be most precious   77 *felicitate*
made happy   80 *ponderous* weighty   83 *validity* value   *pleasure* pleasing qualities   85 *least* smallest, youngest   86 *vines* vineyards   *milk*
pasture-lands   87 *interest* concerned as interested parties   95 *bond*
obligation   99 *Return . . . fit* I.e. am fittingly dutiful in return

    They love you all? Haply, when I shall wed,
    That lord whose hand must take my plight shall
      carry
    Half my love with him, half my care and duty.   105
    Sure I shall never marry like my sisters,
    To love my father all.
Lear. But goes thy heart with this?
Cordelia.   Ay, my good lord.
Lear. So young, and so untender?
Cordelia. So young, my lord, and true.   110
Lear. Let it be so, thy truth then be thy dower!
    For, by the sacred radiance of the sun,
    The mysteries of Hecate and the night,
    By all the operation of the orbs
    From whom we do exist and cease to be,   115
    Here I disclaim all my paternal care,
    Propinquity and property of blood,
    And as a stranger to my heart and me
    Hold thee from this for ever. The barbarous Scy-
      thian,
    Or he that makes his generation messes   120
    To gorge his appetite, shall to my bosom
    Be as well neighbored, pitied, and relieved,
    As thou my sometime daughter.
Kent.   Good my liege —
Lear. Peace, Kent!
    Come not between the dragon and his wrath.   125
    I loved her most, and thought to set my rest
    On her kind nursery. — Hence and avoid my
      sight! —
    So be my grave my peace as here I give

103 *plight* pledge, troth-plight 113 *Hecate* infernal goddess, patroness
of witches 114 *operation . . . orbs* astrological influences 117 *Pro-*
pinquity relationship *property* i.e. common property, something
shared 119 *Scythian* proverbially barbarous 120 *makes . . . messes*
makes meals of his offspring 123 *sometime* former 125 *his* its 126
set my rest (1) risk my stake (a term in the card game primero) (2)
rely for my repose 127 *nursery* nursing, care 128 *So . . . peace as*
let me rest peacefully in my grave only as

Her father's heart from her! Call France. Who stirs!
130 Call Burgundy. Cornwall and Albany,
     With my two daughters' dowers digest the third;
     Let pride, which she calls plainness, marry her.
     I do invest you jointly with my power,
     Preeminence, and all the large effects
135 That troop with majesty. Ourself, by monthly
         course,
     With reservation of an hundred knights,
     By you to be sustained, shall our abode
     Make with you by due turn. Only we shall retain
     The name, and all th' addition to a king. The sway,
140 Revenue, execution of the rest,
     Belovèd sons, be yours; which to confirm,
     This coronet part between you.

Kent.   Royal Lear,
     Whom I have ever honored as my king,
     Loved as my father, as my master followed,
145 As my great patron thought on in my prayers —

Lear. The bow is bent and drawn; make from the
         shaft.

Kent. Let it fall rather, though the fork invade
     The region of my heart. Be Kent unmannerly
     When Lear is mad. What wouldst thou do, old
         man?
150 Think'st thou that duty shall have dread to speak
     When power to flattery bows? To plainness honor's
         bound
     When majesty falls to folly. Reserve thy state,
     And in thy best consideration check
     This hideous rashness. Answer my life my judg-
         ment,

---

134 *effects* tokens   135 *Ourself* I (royal plural)   139 *th' addition*
honors and prerogatives   142 *coronet* symbol of rule, not necessarily
the royal crown   146 *make* make away   147 *fall* strike   *fork* two-
pronged head   152 *Reserve thy state* retain your kingly authority   153
best consideration most careful deliberation   154 *Answer my life* i.e.
I'll stake my life on

Thy youngest daughter does not love thee least,   155
Nor are those empty-hearted whose low sounds
Reverb no hollowness.
Lear.   Kent, on thy life, no more!
Kent. My life I never held but as a pawn
To wage against thine enemies; ne'er fear to lose it,
Thy safety being motive.
Lear.   Out of my sight!   160
Kent. See better, Lear, and let me still remain
The true blank of thine eye.
Lear. Now by Apollo —
Kent.   Now by Apollo, King,
Thou swear'st thy gods in vain.
Lear.   O vassal! Miscreant!
                              Grasping his sword.
                                                                 165
Albany, Cornwall. Dear sir, forbear!
Kent. Kill thy physician, and thy fee bestow
Upon the foul disease. Revoke thy gift,
Or, whilst I can vent clamor from my throat,
I'll tell thee thou dost evil.
Lear.   Hear me, recreant,
On thine allegiance, hear me!   170
That thou hast sought to make us break our vows,
Which we durst never yet, and with strained pride
To come betwixt our sentence and our power,
Which nor our nature nor our place can bear,
Our potency made good, take thy reward.   175
Five days we do allot thee for provision
To shield thee from disasters of the world,
And on the sixth to turn thy hated back
Upon our kingdom. If, on the tenth day following,
Thy banished trunk be found in our dominions,   180

---

157 *Reverb no hollowness* i.e. do not reverberate (like a drum) as a
result of hollowness 158 *pawn* stake 159 *wage* wager, pit 160 *motive* the moving cause 161 *still* always 162 *blank* center of the target
(to guide your aim truly) 164 *Miscreant* (1) rascal (2) infidel 169
recreant traitor 171 *That* in that, since 172 *strained* excessive 173
To come . . . power i.e. to oppose my power to sentence 175 *Our
. . . good* if my power is to be demonstrated as real 177 *disasters*
accidents 180 *trunk* body

The moment is thy death. Away. By Jupiter,
This shall not be revoked.

Kent. Fare thee well, King. Sith thus thou wilt appear,
Freedom lives hence, and banishment is here.

185   (*to Cordelia*) The gods to their dear shelter take
thee, maid,
That justly think'st and hast most rightly said.

(*to Regan and Goneril*) And your large speeches
may your deeds approve,
That good effects may spring from words of love.

Thus Kent, O princes, bids you all adieu;

190   He'll shape his old course in a country new.   *Exit*

*Flourish. Enter Gloucester, with France and
Burgundy; Attendants.*

Gloucester. Here's France and Burgundy, my noble
lord.

Lear. My Lord of Burgundy,
We first address toward you, who with this king
Hath rivalled for our daughter. What in the least

195   Will you require in present dower with her,
Or cease your quest of love?

Burgundy.   Most royal Majesty,
I crave no more than hath your Highness offered
Nor will you tender less.

Lear.   Right noble Burgundy,
When she was dear to us, we did hold her so;

200   But now her price is fallen. Sir, there she stands.
If aught within that little seeming substance,
Or all of it, with our displeasure pieced
And nothing more, may fitly like your Grace,
She's there, and she is yours.

Burgundy.   I know no answer

---

183 *Sith* since   187 *approve* confirm   188 *effects* consequences   190
shape . . . course keep to his customary ways (of honesty)   201
seeming substance i.e. nothing, mere shell   202 *pieced* joined

Lear. Will you, with those infirmities she owes,   205
    Unfriended, new adopted to our hate,
    Dow'red with our curse, and strangered with our
      oath,
    Take her, or leave her?
Burgundy.   Pardon me, royal sir.
    Election makes not up on such conditions.
Lear. Then leave her, sir, for by the pow'r that made   210
     me
    I tell you all her wealth. (*to France*) For you, great
      King,
    I would not from your love make such a stray
    To match you where I hate; therefore beseech you
    T' avert your liking a more worthier way
    Than on a wretch whom nature is ashamed   215
    Almost t' acknowledge hers.
France.   This is most strange,
    That she whom even but now was your best object,
    The argument of your praise, balm of your age,
    The best, the dearest, should in this trice of time
    Commit a thing so monstrous to dismantle   220
    So many folds of favor. Sure her offense
    Must be of such unnatural degree
    That monsters it, or your fore-vouched affection
    Fall'n into taint; which to believe of her
    Must be a faith that reason without miracle   225
    Should never plant in me.
Cordelia.   I yet beseech your Majesty,
    If for I want that glib and oily art
    To speak and purpose not since what I well intend
    I'll do't before I speak, that you make known

---

205 *owes* owns 207 *strangered with* made alien by 209 *Election . . .
conditions* no choice is possible on such terms 212 *make . . . stray*
stray so far as 214 *avert* turn 217 *best* favorite 218 *argument*
theme 220 *to dismantle* so to strip off 223 *That monsters it* as makes
it monstrous (i.e. abnormal, freakish) *fore-vouched* previously sworn
224 *taint* decay (with the implication that the affection, and the oath
attesting it, were tainted in the first place) 225 *reason . . . miracle*
i.e. rational, unaided by miraculous, means of persuasion 228 *purpose not* i.e. without intending to act in accordance with my words

230   It is no vicious blot, murder, or foulness,
      No unchaste action or dishonorèd step,
      That hath deprived me of your grace and favor;
      But even for want of that for which I am richer —
      A still-soliciting eye, and such a tongue
235   That I am glad I have not, though not to have it
      Hath lost me in your liking.

Lear.   Better thou
      Hadst not been born than not t' have pleased me
        better.

France. Is it but this? A tardiness in nature
      Which often leaves the history unspoke
240   That it intends to do. My Lord of Burgundy,
      What say you to the lady? Love's not love
      When it is mingled with regards that stands
      Aloof from th' entire point. Will you have her?
      She is herself a dowry.

Burgundy.   Royal King,
245   Give but that portion which yourself proposed,
      And here I take Cordelia by the hand,
      Duchess of Burgundy.

Lear. Nothing. I have sworn. I am firm.

Burgundy. I am sorry then you have so lost a father
      That you must lose a husband.

250   *Cordelia.*   Peace be with Burgundy
      Since that respects of fortune are his love,
      I shall not be his wife.

France. Fairest Cordelia, that art most rich being
        poor,
      Most choice forsaken, and most loved despised,
255   Thee and thy virtues here I seize upon.
      Be it lawful I take up what's cast away.
      Gods, gods! 'Tis strange that from their cold'st
        neglect

---

234 *still-soliciting* always-begging 238 *tardiness in nature* natural
reticence 239 *history unspoke* actions unannounced 242–43 *mingled
. . . point* i.e. mixed with irrelevant considerations 251 *respects*
considerations

My love should kindle to inflamed respect.
Thy dow'rless daughter, King, thrown to my
  chance,
Is queen of us, of ours, and our fair France.   260
Not all the dukes of wat'rish Burgundy
Can buy this unprized precious maid of me.
Bid them farewell, Cordelia, though unkind.
Thou losest here, a better where to find.

Lear. Thou hast her, France; let her be thine, for we   265
Have no such daughter, nor shall ever see
That face of hers again. Therefore be gone
Without our grace, our love, our benison.
Come, noble Burgundy.

> *Flourish. Exit Lear, Burgundy, Cornwall, Albany,*
> *Gloucester, and Attendants.*

France. Bid farewell to your sisters.   270

Cordelia. The jewels of our father, with washed eyes
Cordelia leaves you. I know you what you are;
And, like a sister, am most loath to call
Your faults as they are named. Love well our father.
To your professèd bosoms I commit him;   275
But yet, alas, stood I within his grace,
I would prefer him to a better place.
So farewell to you both.

Regan. Prescribe not us our duty.

Goneril.   Let your study
Be to content your lord, who hath received you   280
At fortune's alms. You have obedience scanted,
And well are worth the want that you have wanted.

Cordelia. Time shall unfold what plighted cunning
  hides,

---

258 *inflamed respect* ardent regard   261 *wat'rish* watery, weak   262
unprized unvalued   264 *here* this place   *where* other place   268 *benison* blessing   271 *jewels* i.e. things held precious   *washed* tear-washed
273 *like a sister* i.e. with sisterly loyalty   274 *as . . . named* by their
true names   275 *professèd* i.e. love-professing   277 *prefer* promote
281 *alms* small offerings   282 *worth . . . wanted* i.e. deserving no
affection since you have shown no affection   283 *plighted* pleated, enfolded

Who covers faults, at last with shame derides.
Well may you prosper.

285 *France.*   Come, my fair Cordelia.

Exit France and Cordelia.

Goneril. Sister, it is not little I have to say of what
most nearly appertains to us both. I think our father will hence tonight.

Regan. That's most certain, and with you; next month
290   with us.

Goneril. You see how full of changes his age is. The
observation we have made of it hath not been
little. He always loved our sister most, and with
what poor judgment he hath now cast her off ap-
295   pears too grossly.

Regan. 'Tis the infirmity of his age; yet he hath ever
but slenderly known himself.

Goneril. The best and soundest of his time hath been
but rash; then must we look from his age to re-
300   ceive not alone the imperfections of long-ingraffed
condition, but therewithal the unruly waywardness
that infirm and choleric years bring with them.

Regan. Such unconstant starts are we like to have
from him as this of Kent's banishment.

305 *Goneril.* There is further compliment of leave-taking
between France and him. Pray you let us hit together; if our father carry authority with such disposition as he bears, this last surrender of his will
but offend us.

310 *Regan.* We shall further think of it.

Goneril. We must do something, and i' th' heat.

Exit both

---

284 *Who . . . derides* i.e. time at first conceals faults, then exposes
them to shame 295 *grossly* crudely conspicuous 297 *known himself*
i.e. been aware of what he truly is 298 *of his time* period of his past
life 300 *long-ingraffed* ingrown, chronic 301 *therewithal* along with
that 303 *unconstant starts* impulses moves 305 *compliment* formality
306 *hit* agree 308 *surrender* i.e. yielding up of authority *offend* harm
311 *i' th' heat* i.e. while the iron is hot

ACT I, SCENE II

Enter Bastard (Edmund), solus, with a letter.

Edmund. Thou, Nature, art my goddess; to thy law
My services are bound. Wherefore should I
Stand in the plague of custom, and permit
The curiosity of nations to deprive me,
For that I am some twelve or fourteen moonshines   5
Lag of a brother? Why bastard? Wherefore base,
When my dimensions are as well compact,
My mind as generous, and my shape as true,
As honest madam's issue? Why brand they us
With base? with baseness? Bastardy base? Base?   10
Who, in the lusty stealth of nature, take
More composition and fierce quality
Than doth, within a dull, stale, tirèd bed,
Go to th' creating a whole tribe of fops
Got 'tween asleep and wake? Well then,   15
Legitimate Edgar, I must have your land.
Our father's love is to the bastard Edmund
As to th' legitimate. Fine word, "legitimate."
Well, my legitimate, if this letter speed,
And my invention thrive, Edmund the base   20
Shall top th' legitimate. I grow, I prosper.
Now, gods, stand up for bastards.

Enter Gloucester.

Gloucester. Kent banished thus? and France in choler
parted?

I, ii, 1 *Nature* i.e. the material and mechanistic as distinct from the
spiritual and heaven-ordained 3 *Stand . . . custom* submit to the
affliction of convention 4 *curiosity* nice distinctions 5 *For that* because *moonshines* months 6 *Lag of* behind (in age) 7 *compact*
fitted, matched 8 *generous* befitting the high-born 9 *honest* chaste
11 *lusty . . . nature* secrecy of natural lust 12 *composition* complete-
ness of constitution, robustness *fierce* mettlesome, thoroughbred 14
fops fools 15 *Got* begotten 20 *invention thrive* plot succeed

And the King gone tonight? prescribèd his pow'r?
25 Confined to exhibition? All this done
    Upon the gad? Edmund, how now? What news?
Edmund. So please your lordship, none.
Gloucester. Why so earnestly seek you to put up that
    letter?
Edmund. I know no news, my lord.
30 *Gloucester.* What paper were you reading?
Edmund. Nothing, my lord.
Gloucester. No? What needed then that terrible dis-
    patch of it into your pocket? The quality of nothing
    hath not such need to hide itself. Let's see. Come,
35 if it be nothing, I shall not need spectacles.
Edmund. I beseech you, sir, pardon me. It is a letter
    from my brother that I have not all o'er-read; and
    for so much as I have perused, I find it not fit for
    your o'erlooking.
40 *Gloucester.* Give me the letter, sir.
Edmund. I shall offend, either to detain or give it.
    The contents, as in part I understand them, are to
    blame.
Gloucester. Let's see, let's see.
45 *Edmund.* I hope, for my brother's justification, he
    wrote this but as an essay or taste of my virtue.
Gloucester. (*reads*) "This policy and reverence of age
    makes the world bitter to the best of our times;
    keeps our fortunes from us till our oldness cannot
50 relish them. I begin to find an idle and fond bond-
    age in the oppression of aged tyranny, who sways,
    not as it hath power, but as it is suffered. Come to
    me, that of this I may speak more. If our father
    would sleep till I waked him, you should enjoy

---

24 *prescribèd* limited 25 *exhibition* an allowance, a pension 26 *gad*
spur 28 *put up* put away 39 *o'erlooking* examination 42–43 *to
blame* blameworthy 46 *essay* trial *taste* test 47 *policy and reverence* policy of reverencing 48 *the best of our times* our best years
50 *idle, fond* foolish (synonyms) 51 *who sways* which rules 52 *suf-
fered* allowed

half his revenue for ever, and live the beloved of   55
your brother,

                                    EDGAR."

Hum! Conspiracy? "Sleep till I waked him, you
should enjoy half his revenue." My son Edgar! Had
he a hand to write this? A heart and brain to breed   60
it in? When came you to this? Who brought it?

Edmund. It was not brought me, my lord; there's
the cunning of it. I found it thrown in at the casement of my closet.

Gloucester. You know the character to be your broth-   65
er's?

Edmund. If the matter were good, my lord, I durst
swear it were his; but in respect of that, I would
fain think it were not.

Gloucester. It is his.   70

Edmund. It is his hand, my lord; but I hope his heart
is not in the contents.

Gloucester. Has he never before sounded you in this
business?

Edmund. Never, my lord. But I have heard him oft   75
maintain it to be fit that, sons at perfect age, and
fathers declined, the father should be as ward to
the son, and the son manage his revenue.

Gloucester. O villain, villain! His very opinion in the
letter. Abhorred villain, unnatural, detested, brutish   80
villain; worse than brutish! Go, sirrah, seek him.
I'll apprehend him. Abominable villain! Where is
he?

Edmund. I do not well know, my lord. If it shall
please you to suspend your indignation against my   85
brother till you can derive from him better testi-

---

55 *revenue* income   61 *to this* upon this   63–64 *casement* window   64
closet room   65 *character* handwriting   67 *matter* contents   68 *in
respect of that* i.e. considering what those contents are   69 *fain* prefer
to   73 *sounded you* sounded you out   76 *perfect age* prime of life
81 *sirrah* sir (familiar, or contemptuous, form)

mony of his intent, you should run a certain course;
where, if you violently proceed against him, mistak-
ing his purpose, it would make a great gap in your
90   own honor and shake in pieces the heart of his
obedience. I dare pawn down my life for him that
he hath writ this to feel my affection to your honor,
and to no other pretense of danger.

Gloucester. Think you so?

95 *Edmund.* If your honor judge it meet, I will place
you where you shall hear us confer of this and by an
auricular assurance have your satisfaction, and that
without any further delay than this very evening.

Gloucester. He cannot be such a monster.

100 *Edmund.* Nor is not, sure.

Gloucester. To his father, that so tenderly and entirely loves him. Heaven and earth! Edmund, seek
him out; wind me into him, I pray you; frame the
business after your own wisdom. I would unstate
105   myself to be in a due resolution.

Edmund. I will seek him, sir, presently; convey the
business as I shall find means, and acquaint you
withal.

Gloucester. These late eclipses in the sun and moon
110   portend no good to us. Though the wisdom of nature can reason it thus and thus, yet nature finds
itself scourged by the sequent effects. Love cools,
friendship falls off, brothers divide. In cities, mutinies; in countries, discord; in palaces, treason; and
115   the bond cracked 'twixt son and father. This villain
of mine comes under the prediction, there's son

---

87 *run . . . course* i.e. know where you are going   92 *feel* feel out,
test   *affection* attachment, loyalty   93 *pretense of danger* dangerous
intention   95 *judge it meet* consider it fitting   96–97 *by . . . assurance* i.e. by the proof of your own ears   103 *wind me* worm   *frame*
plan   104–5 *unstate . . . resolution* i.e. give everything to know for
certain   106 *presently* at once   *convey* conduct   108 *withal* therewith
109 *late* recent   110–11 *wisdom of nature* natural lore, science   111–12
can . . . effects i.e. can supply explanations, yet punitive upheavals
in nature (such as earthquakes) follow   112 *scourged* whipped   *sequent* following   113–14 *mutinies* rebellions   116 *comes . . . prediction* i.e. is included among these ill-omened things

against father; the King falls from bias of nature,
there's father against child. We have seen the best
of our time. Machinations, hollowness, treachery,
and all ruinous disorders follow us disquietly to   120
our graves. Find out this villain, Edmund, it shall
lose thee nothing; do it carefully. And the noble and
true-hearted Kent banished; his offense, honesty.
'Tis strange.   *Exit.*

Edmund. This is the excellent foppery of the world, 125
that when we are sick in fortune, often the surfeits
of our own behavior, we make guilty of our disasters
the sun, the moon, and stars; as if we were villains
on necessity; fools by heavenly compulsion; knaves,
thieves, and treachers by spherical predominance;   130
drunkards, liars, and adulterers by an enforced obedience of planetary influence; and all that we are
evil in, by a divine thrusting on. An admirable eva-
sion of whoremaster man, to lay his goatish disposition on the charge of a star. My father com-   135
pounded with my mother under the Dragon's Tail,
and my nativity was under Ursa Major, so that it
follows I am rough and lecherous. Fut! I should
have been that I am, had the maidenliest star in
the firmament twinkled on my bastardizing. Ed-   140
gar —

Enter Edgar.

and pat he comes, like the catastrophe of the old
comedy. My cue is villainous melancholy, with a

---

117 *bias of nature* natural tendency 122 *lose thee nothing* i.e. you
will not lose by it 125 *foppery* foolishness 126 *we are sick* . . .
surfeits i.e. our fortunes grow sickly, often from the excesses 130
treachers traitors *spherical predominance* i.e. ascendancy, or rule,
of a particular sphere 134 *goatish* lecherous 135–36 *compounded*
(1) came to terms (2) created 136, 137 *Dragon's Tail, Ursa Major*
constellations, cited because of the suggestiveness of their names 137
nativity birthday 142 *catastrophe* conclusion

sigh like Tom o' Bedlam. — O, these eclipses do
145 portend these divisions. Fa, sol, la, mi.

Edgar. How now, brother Edmund; what serious con-
templation are you in?

Edmund. I am thinking, brother, of a prediction I
read this other day, what should follow these
150 eclipses.

Edgar. Do you busy yourself with that?

Edmund. I promise you, the effects he writes of succeed unhappily: as of unnaturalness between the
child and the parent; death, dearth, dissolutions of
155 ancient amities; divisions in state, menaces and
maledictions against king and nobles; needless diffidences, banishment of friends, dissipation of cohorts, nuptial breaches, and I know not what.

Edgar. How long have you been a sectary astronomi-
160 cal?

Edmund. Come, come, when saw you my father last?

Edgar. The night gone by.

Edmund. Spake you with him?

Edgar. Ay, two hours together.

165 *Edmund.* Parted you in good terms? Found you no
displeasure in him by word nor countenance?

Edgar. None at all.

Edmund. Bethink yourself wherein you may have offended him; and at my entreaty forbear his presence
170 until some little time hath qualified the heat of his
displeasure, which at this instant so rageth in him
that with the mischief of your person it would
scarcely allay.

Edgar. Some villain hath done me wrong.

175 *Edmund.* That's my fear. I pray you have a continent

---

144 *Tom o' Bedlam* a type of beggar, mad or pretending to be, so
named from the London madhouse, Bethlehem or "Bedlam" Hospital
152–53 *succeed unhappily* unluckily follow 153 *unnaturalness* unkindness, enmity 156–57 *diffidences* instances of distrust 157–58 *dissipation of cohorts* melting away of supporters 159–60 *sectary astro-
nomical* of the astrological sect 166 *countenance* expression, look
170 *qualified* moderated 172 *mischief* injury 173 *allay* be appeased
175–76 *continent forbearance* cautious inaccessibility

forbearance till the speed of his rage goes slower;
and, as I say, retire with me to my lodging, from
whence I will fitly bring you to hear my lord speak.
Pray ye, go; there's my key. If you do stir abroad, go
armed.   180

Edgar. Armed, brother?

Edmund. Brother, I advise you to the best. Go armed.
I am no honest man if there be any good meaning
toward you. I have told you what I have seen and
heard; but faintly, nothing like the image and hor-   185
ror of it. Pray you, away.

Edgar. Shall I hear from you anon?

Edmund. I do serve you in this business.

                                 Exit Edgar.

A credulous father, and a brother noble,
Whose nature is so far from doing harms   190
That he suspects none; on whose foolish honesty
My practices ride easy. I see the business.
Let me, if not by birth, have lands by wit;
All with me's meet that I can fashion fit.   *Exit.*

❧

ACT I, SCENE III

Enter Goneril and Steward (Oswald).

Goneril. Did my father strike my gentleman for chid-
    ing of his fool?

Oswald. Ay, madam.

Goneril. By day and night, he wrongs me! Every hour
He flashes into one gross crime or other
That sets us all at odds. I'll not endure it.   5
His knights grow riotous, and himself upbraids us

178 *fitly* conveniently   185–86 *image and horror* horrible true picture
187 *anon* soon   192 *practices* plots   193 *wit* intelligence   194 *meet*
proper, acceptable   *fashion fit* i.e. rig up, shape to the purpose   I, iii,
3 *day and night* an oath   4 *crime* offense   6 *riotous* boisterous

On every trifle. When he returns from hunting,
I will not speak with him. Say I am sick.
If you come slack of former services,

10   You shall do well; the fault of it I'll answer.

                                        Horns within.

Oswald. He's coming, madam; I hear him.
Goneril. Put on what weary negligence you please,
You and your fellows. I'd have it come to question.
If he distaste it, let him to my sister

15   Whose mind and mine I know in that are one,
Not to be overruled. Idle old man,
That still would manage those authorities
That he hath given away. Now, by my life,
Old fools are babes again, and must be used

20   With checks as flatteries, when they are seen abused.
Remember what I have said.
Oswald.   Well, madam.
Goneril. And let his knights have colder looks among
    you.
What grows of it, no matter; advise your fellows so.
I would breed from hence occasions, and I shall,

25   That I may speak. I'll write straight to my sister
To hold my course. Prepare for dinner.   *Exit both.*

ACT I, SCENE IV

Enter Kent (disguised).

Kent. If but as well I other accents borrow
That can my speech defuse, my good intent

9 *come . . . services* i.e. serve him less well than formerly   10 *answer*
answer for   13 *question* i.e. open issue, a thing discussed   14 *distaste*
dislike   16 *Idle* foolish   20 *checks . . . abused* restraints in place of
cajolery when they (the old men) are seen to be deceived (about their
true state)   24–25 *breed . . . speak* i.e. make an issue of it so that
I may speak   I, iv, 2 *defuse* disorder, disguise

May carry through itself to that full issue
For which I razed my likeness. Now, banished Kent,
If thou canst serve where thou dost stand con-
    demned,   5
So may it come, thy master whom thou lov'st
Shall find thee full of labors.

Horns within. Enter Lear, Knight, and Attendants.

Lear. Let me not stay a jot for dinner; go get it ready.
    (*Exit an Attendant.*) How now, what art thou?
Kent. A man, sir.   10
Lear. What dost thou profess? What wouldst thou
    with us?
Kent. I do profess to be no less than I seem, to serve
    him truly that will put me in trust, to love him that
    is honest, to converse with him that is wise and   15
    says little, to fear judgment, to fight when I cannot
    choose, and to eat no fish.
Lear. What art thou?
Kent. A very honest-hearted fellow, and as poor as the
    King.   20
Lear. If thou be'st as poor for a subject as he's for a
    king, thou art poor enough. What wouldst thou?
Kent. Service.
Lear. Who wouldst thou serve?
Kent. You.   25
Lear. Dost thou know me, fellow?
Kent. No, sir, but you have that in your countenance
    which I would fain call master.
Lear. What's that?
Kent. Authority.   30
Lear. What services canst thou do?

---

3 *full issue* perfect result   4 *razed my likeness* erased my natural appearance   8 *stay* wait   11 *profess* do, work at (with pun following)
12 *profess* claim   15 *converse* associate   16 *judgment* i.e. God's judgment   17 *eat no fish* be a Protestant (anachronism), or avoid unmanly diet   28 *fain* like to

Kent. I can keep honest counsel, ride, run, mar a
curious tale in telling it and deliver a plain message
bluntly. That which ordinary men are fit for I am
35   qualified in, and the best of me is diligence.

Lear. How old art thou?

Kent. Not so young, sir, to love a woman for singing,
nor so old to dote on her for anything. I have years
on my back forty-eight.

40 *Lear.* Follow me; thou shalt serve me. If I like thee no
worse after dinner, I will not part from thee yet.
Dinner, ho, dinner! Where's my knave? my fool? Go
you and call my fool hither.   *Exit an Attendant.*

Enter Steward (Oswald).

You, you, sirrah, where's my daughter?

45 *Oswald.* So please you ——   *Exit.*

Lear. What says the fellow there? Call the clotpoll
back. (*Exit Knight.*) Where's my fool? Ho, I think
the world's asleep.

Enter Knight.

How now? Where's that mongrel?

50 *Knight.* He says, my lord, your daughter is not well.

Lear. Why came not the slave back to me when I
called him?

Knight. Sir, he answered me in the roundest manner,
he would not.

55 *Lear.* He would not?

Knight. My lord, I know not what the matter is; but
to my judgment your Highness is not entertained
with that ceremonious affection as you were wont.
There's a great abatement of kindness appears as

32 *keep honest counsel* keep counsel honestly, i.e. respect confidences
curious elaborate, embroidered (as contrasted with "plain") 42
knave boy 46 *clotpoll* clodpoll, dolt 57 *entertained* rendered hospitality

well in the general dependants as in the Duke him-   60
self also and your daughter.

Lear. Ha? Say'st thou so?

Knight. I beseech you pardon me, my lord, if I be mis-
taken; for my duty cannot be silent when I think
your Highness wronged.   65

Lear. Thou but rememb'rest me of mine own conception. I have perceived a most faint neglect of late,
which I have rather blamed as mine own jealous
curiosity than as a very pretense and purpose of
unkindness. I will look further into't. But where's   70
my fool? I have not seen him this two days.

Knight. Since my young lady's going into France, sir,
the fool hath much pined away.

Lear. No more of that; I have noted it well. Go you
and tell my daughter I would speak with her.   75

                                        Exit Knight.

Go you, call hither my fool.   *Exit an Attendant.*

Enter Steward (Oswald).

O, you, sir, you! Come you hither, sir. Who am I,
sir?

Oswald. My lady's father.

Lear. "My lady's father"? My lord's knave, you whore- 80
son dog, you slave, you cur!

Oswald. I am none of these, my lord; I beseech your
pardon.

Lear. Do you bandy looks with me, you rascal?

                                          Strikes him.

Oswald. I'll not be strucken, my lord.   85

Kent. Nor tripped neither, you base football player.

                                       Trips up his heels.

Lear. I thank thee, fellow. Thou serv'st me, and I'll
love thee.

66 *rememb'rest* remind   68–69 *jealous curiosity* i.e. suspicious concern
about trifles   69 *very pretense* true intention   84 *bandy* volley, exchange   85 *strucken* struck   86 *football* an impromptu street and field
game, held in low esteem

Kent. Come, sir, arise, away. I'll teach you differences.
90 Away, away. If you will measure your lubber's
length again, tarry; but away. Go to! Have you wisdom? So.   *Pushes him out.*
Lear. Now, my friendly knave, I thank thee. There's
earnest of thy service.   *Gives money.*

Enter Fool.

95 *Fool.* Let me hire him too. Here's my coxcomb.
                            Offers Kent his cap.
Lear. How now, my pretty knave? How dost thou?
Fool. Sirrah, you were best take my coxcomb.
Kent. Why, fool?
Fool. Why? For taking one's part that's out of favor.
100 Nay, an thou canst not smile as the wind sits,
thou'lt catch cold shortly. There, take my coxcomb.
Why, this fellow has banished two on's daughters,
and did the third a blessing against his will. If thou
follow him, thou must needs wear my coxcomb. —
105 How now, nuncle? Would I had two coxcombs and
two daughters.
Lear. Why, my boy?
Fool. If I gave them all my living, I'ld keep my coxcombs myself. There's mine; beg another of thy
110 daughters.
Lear. Take heed, sirrah — the whip.
Fool. Truth's a dog must to kennel; he must be
whipped out, when the Lady Brach may stand by th'
fire and stink.
115 *Lear.* A pestilent gall to me.
Fool. Sirrah, I'll teach thee a speech.
Lear. Do.

89 *differences* distinctions in rank   91–92 *Go to! . . . wisdom* i.e. Get
along! Do you know what's good for you?   94 *earnest* part payment
95 *coxcomb* cap of the professional fool, topped with an imitation
comb   100 *smile . . . sits* i.e. adapt yourself to prevailing forces   102
banished i.e. provided the means for them to become alien to him
105 *nuncle* mine uncle   113 *Brach* hound bitch   115 *gall* sore, source
of irritation

Fool. Mark it, nuncle.

Have more than thou showest,   120

Speak less than thou knowest,

Lend less than thou owest,

Ride more than thou goest,

Learn more than thou trowest,

Set less than thou throwest;   125

Leave thy drink and thy whore,

And keep in-a-door,

And thou shalt have more

Than two tens to a score.

Kent. This is nothing, fool.   130

Fool. Then 'tis like the breath of an unfee'd lawyer
—you gave me nothing for't. Can you make no
use of nothing, nuncle?

Lear. Why, no, boy. Nothing can be made out of
nothing.   135

Fool. (to Kent) Prithee tell him, so much the rent of
his land comes to; he will not believe a fool.

Lear. A bitter fool.

Fool. Dost thou know the difference, my boy, between
a bitter fool and a sweet one?   140

Lear. No, lad; teach me.

Fool.   That lord that counselled thee

To give away thy land,

Come place him here by me —

Do thou for him stand.   145

The sweet and bitter fool

Will presently appear;

The one in motley here,

The other found out there.

122 *owest* borrow, or own, keep 123 *goest* walk 124 *Learn* hear, listen to *trowest* believe 125 *Set* . . . *throwest* stake less than you
throw for (i.e. play for odds) 128–29 *have . . . score* i.e. do better
than break even 131 *breath* voice, counsel (reliable only when paid
for) 136–37 *rent . . . land* nothing, since he has no land 140 *bitter, sweet* satirical, nonsatirical 145 *Do . . . stand* the Fool thus
identifying Lear as his own foolish counselor 149 *found out* revealed
(Lear is the "born" fool as distinct from himself, the fool in motley,
a characteristic multicolored garment habitually worn by jesters)

150 *Lear.* Dost thou call me fool, boy?

Fool. All thy other titles thou hast given away; that
      thou wast born with.

Kent. This is not altogether fool, my lord.

Fool. No, faith; lords and great men will not let me.
155   If I had a monopoly out, they would have part on't.
      And ladies too, they will not let me have all the
      fool to myself; they'll be snatching. Nuncle, give
      me an egg, and I'll give thee two crowns.

Lear. What two crowns shall they be?

160 *Fool.* Why, after I have cut the egg i' th' middle and
      eat up the meat, the two crowns of the egg. When
      thou clovest thy crown i' th' middle and gav'st
      away both parts, thou bor'st thine ass on thy back
      o'er the dirt. Thou hadst little wit in thy bald
165   crown when thou gav'st thy golden one away. If I
      speak like myself in this, let him be whipped that
      first finds it so.

      (*sings*) Fools had ne'er less grace in a year,
                  For wise men are grown foppish.
170   And know not how their wits to wear,
                  Their manners are so apish.

Lear. When were you wont to be so full of songs,
      sirrah?

Fool. I have used it, nuncle, e'er since thou mad'st
175   thy daughters thy mothers; for when thou gav'st
      them the rod, and put'st down thine own breeches,
      (*sings*) Then they for sudden joy did weep,
                  And I for sorrow sung,
                  That such a king should play bo-peep
180   And go the fools among.

---

154 *let me* i.e. be all fool, since they seek a share of folly   157 *snatch-
ing* like greedy courtiers seeking shares in royal patents of monopoly
163–64 *bor'st . . . dirt* thus foolishly reversing normal behavior   166
like myself i.e. like a fool   166–67 *let . . . so* i.e. let him be whipped,
(as a fool) who mistakes this truth as my typical folly   168 *grace . . .
year* favor at any time   170 *their wits to wear* i.e. to use their intelligence   174 *used* practiced   179 *play bo-peep* i.e. act like a child

Prithee, nuncle, keep a schoolmaster that can teach
thy fool to lie. I would fain learn to lie.

Lear. An you lie, sirrah, we'll have you whipped.

Fool. I marvel what kin thou and thy daughters are.
They'll have me whipped for speaking true; thou'lt   185
have me whipped for lying; and sometimes I am
whipped for holding my peace. I had rather be any
kind o' thing than a fool, and yet I would not be
thee, nuncle: thou hast pared thy wit o' both sides
and left nothing i' th' middle. Here comes one o'   190
the parings.

Enter Goneril.

Lear. How now, daughter? What makes that frontlet
on? You are too much of late i' th' frown.

Fool. Thou wast a pretty fellow when thou hadst no   195
need to care for her frowning. Now thou art an O
without a figure. I am better than thou art now: I
am a fool, thou art nothing. (*to Goneril*) Yes, for-
sooth, I will hold my tongue. So your face bids me,
though you say nothing. Mum, mum,

>   He that keeps nor crust nor crum,   200
>   Weary of all, shall want some. —

(*points at Lear*) That's a shealed peascod.

Goneril. Not only, sir, this your all-licensed fool,
But other of your insolent retinue
Do hourly carp and quarrel, breaking forth   205
In rank and not-to-be-endurèd riots. Sir,
I had thought by making this well known unto you
To have found a safe redress, but now grow fearful,
By what yourself too late have spoke and done,

183 *An* if   189-90 *pared . . . middle* i.e. completely disposed of your
wits (in disposing of your power)   192 *frontlet* band worn across the
brow; hence, frown   195-96 *O . . . figure* cipher without a digit to
give it value   200 *crum* soft bread within the crust   201 *want* need
202 *shealed* shelled, empty   *peascod* pea-pod   203 *all-licensed* all-
privileged   205 *carp* complain   208 *safe* sure

210   That you protect this course, and put it on
       By your allowance; which if you should, the fault
       Would not 'scape censure, nor the redresses sleep,
       Which, in the tender of a wholesome weal,
       Might in their working do you that offense,
215   Which else were shame, that then necessity
       Will call discreet proceeding.

Fool. For you know, nuncle,
           The hedge-sparrow fed the cuckoo so long
           That it's had it head bit off by it young.
220   So out went the candle, and we were left darkling.

Lear. Are you our daughter?

Goneril. I would you would make use of your good
           wisdom
           (Whereof I know you are fraught) and put away
225   These dispositions which of late transport you
           From what you rightly are.

Fool. May not an ass know when the cart draws the
           horse?
           Whoop, Jug, I love thee!

Lear. Does any here know me? This is not Lear.
           Does Lear walk thus? Speak thus? Where are his
230   eyes?
           Either his notion weakens, his discernings
           Are lethargied — Ha! Waking? 'Tis not so.
           Who is it that can tell me who I am?

Fool. Lear's shadow.

Lear. I would learn that; for, by the marks of sover-
235   eignty,

---

210 *put it on* instigate it   211 *allowance* approval   212 *redresses sleep*
correction lie dormant   213 *tender of* care for   *weal* state   214–16
Might . . . proceeding in their operation might be considered humili-
ating to you but, under the circumstances, are merely prudent   218
cuckoo an image suggesting illegitimacy as well as voraciousness, since
the cuckoo lays its eggs in the nests of other birds   219 *it* its   220
darkling in the dark (like the dead hedge-sparrow and the threatened
Lear)   223 *fraught* freighted, laden   225 *dispositions* moods   228 *Jug*
Joan (evidently part of some catch-phrase)   231 *notion* understanding
232 *Ha! Waking* i.e. so I am really awake (presumably accompanied
by the "business" of pinching himself)   235 *marks of sovereignty* evi-
dences that I am King (and hence the father of the princesses)

　Knowledge, and reason, I should be false persuaded
　I had daughters.
Fool. Which they will make an obedient father.
Lear. Your name, fair gentlewoman?
Goneril. This admiration, sir, is much o' th' savor　　　240
　Of other your new pranks. I do beseech you
　To understand my purposes aright.
　As you are old and reverend, should be wise.
　Here do you keep a hundred knights and squires,
　Men so disordered, so deboshed, and bold　　　245
　That this our court, infected with their manners,
　Shows like a riotous inn. Epicurism and lust
　Makes it more like a tavern or a brothel
　Than a graced palace. The shame itself doth speak
　For instant remedy. Be then desired　　　250
　By her that else will take the thing she begs
　A little to disquantity your train,
　And the remainders that shall still depend
　To be such men as may besort your age,
　Which know themselves, and you.
Lear.　　　　　　　　　　　　Darkness and devils!　　255
　Saddle my horses; call my train together.
　Degenerate bastard, I'll not trouble thee:
　Yet have I left a daughter.
Goneril. You strike my people, and your disordered
　　rabble
　Make servants of their betters.　　　260

Enter Albany.

Lear. Woe that too late repents. — O, sir, are you
　　come?
　Is it your will? Speak, sir. — Prepare my horses.

240 *admiration* air of wonderment   245 *deboshed* debauched   247 *Epicurism* a school of thought given to the pursuit of pleasure and sensuous gratification   249 *graced* honored   *shame* disgrace   252 *disquantity your train* reduce the size of your retinue   253 *depend* be attached   254 *besort* befit   255 *Which know* i.e. who are aware of the status of

Ingratitude! thou marble-hearted fiend,
More hideous when thou show'st thee in a child
Than the sea-monster.

265 *Albany.*   Pray, sir, be patient.

Lear. Detested kite, thou liest.
My train are men of choice and rarest parts,
That all particulars of duty know
And in the most exact regard support

270 The worships of their name. O most small fault,
How ugly didst thou in Cordelia show!
Which, like an engine, wrenched my frame of na-
ture
From the fixed place; drew from my heart all love
And added to the gall. O Lear, Lear, Lear!

275 Beat at this gate that let thy folly in

                                   Strikes his head.

And thy dear judgment out. Go, go, my people.

Albany. My lord, I am guiltless, as I am ignorant
Of what hath moved you.

Lear.   It may be so, my lord.
Hear, Nature, hear; dear goddess, hear:

280 Suspend thy purpose if thou didst intend
To make this creature fruitful.
Into her womb convey sterility,
Dry up in her the organs of increase,
And from her derogate body never spring

285 A babe to honor her. If she must teem,
Create her child of spleen, that it may live
And be a thwart disnatured torment to her.
Let it stamp wrinkles in her brow of youth,
With cadent tears fret channels in her cheeks,

290 Turn all her mother's pains and benefits

---

266 *Detested kite* detestable bird of prey   267 *parts* accomplishments
269 *exact regard* careful attention, punctiliousness   270 *worships* honor
272 *engine* destructive contrivance of war   272-73 *wrenched . . .
place* distorted my normal self   274 *gall* bitterness   284 *derogate* de-
graded   285 *teem* increase   286 *spleen* ill-humor, spitefulness   287
thwart disnatured perverse, unnatural   289 *cadent* falling   *fret* wear
290 *pains and benefits* care and offerings

    To laughter and contempt, that she may feel
    How sharper than a serpent's tooth it is
    To have a thankless child. Away, away!   *Exit.*
Albany. Now, gods that we adore, whereof comes this?
Goneril. Never afflict yourself to know more of it,   295
    But let his disposition have that scope
    As dotage gives it.

Enter Lear.

Lear. What, fifty of my followers at a clap?
    Within a fortnight?
Albany.   What's the matter, sir?
Lear. I'll tell thee. *(to Goneril)* Life and death, I am
    ashamed   300
    That thou hast power to shake my manhood thus!
    That these hot tears, which break from me perforce,
    Should make thee worth them. Blasts and fogs
      upon thee!
    Th' untented woundings of a father's curse
    Pierce every sense about thee! Old fond eyes,   305
    Beweep this cause again I'll pluck ye out
    And cast you, with the waters that you loose,
    To temper clay. Yea, is it come to this?
    Ha! Let it be so. I have another daughter,
    Who I am sure is kind and comfortable.   310
    When she shall hear this of thee, with her nails
    She'll flay thy wolvish visage. Thou shalt find
    That I'll resume the shape which thou dost think
    I have cast off for ever.
                Exit Lear with Kent and Attendants.
Goneril.   Do you mark that?

---

296 *disposition* mood 302 *perforce* by force, against my will 304
untented untentable, too deep for treatment by a probe 305 *sense
about* faculty possessed by *fond* foolish 306 *Beweep this cause* if
you weep over this matter 307 *loose* let loose 308 *temper* soften
310 *comfortable* ready to comfort 313 *shape* i.e. role of authority

315 *Albany.* I cannot be so partial, Goneril,
          To the great love I bear you —
       Goneril. Pray you, content. — What, Oswald, ho!
          (*to Fool*) You, sir, more knave than fool, after your
              master!
       Fool. Nuncle Lear, nuncle Lear, tarry. Take the fool
320   with thee.

                    A fox, when one has caught her,
                    And such a daughter,
                    Should sure to the slaughter,
                    If my cap would buy a halter.
325   So the fool follows after.   *Exit.*

       Goneril. This man hath had good counsel — a hun-
              dred knights!
          'Tis politic and safe to let him keep
          At point a hundred knights — yes, that on every
              dream,
          Each buzz, each fancy, each complaint, dislike,
330   He may enguard his dotage with their pow'rs
          And hold our lives in mercy. — Oswald, I say!
       Albany. Well, you may fear too far.
       Goneril.   Safer than trust too far.
          Let me still take away the harms I fear,
          Not fear still to be taken. I know his heart.
335   What he hath uttered I have writ my sister.
          If she sustain him and his hundred knights,
          When I have showed th' unfitness —

                       Enter Steward (Oswald).

                                                How now, Oswald?
          What, have you writ that letter to my sister?

       315–16 *partial . . . To* made partial . . . by   319 *the fool* i.e. both
       your fool and your folly   323 *slaughter* hanging and quartering   324,
       325 *halter, after* (pronounced "hauter," "auter")   326 *good counsel*
       i.e. from such company (ironic)   327 *politic* prudent   328 *At point* in
       arms   329 *buzz* murmur   331 *in mercy* at his mercy   333 *still . . .
       harms* always eliminates the sources of injury   334 *still . . . taken*
       always to be overtaken (by them)

Oswald. Ay, madam.

Goneril. Take you some company, and away to horse.   340
    Inform her full of my particular fear,
    And thereto add such reasons of your own
    As may compact it more. Get you gone,
    And hasten your return. (*Exit Oswald.*) No, no, my
      lord,
    This milky gentleness and course of yours,   345
    Though I condemn not, yet under pardon,
    You are much more ataskèd for want of wisdom
    Than praised for harmful mildness.

Albany. How far your eyes may pierce I cannot tell;
    Striving to better, oft we mar what's well.   350

Goneril. Nay then —

Albany. Well, well; th' event.   *Exit all.*

ACT I, SCENE V

Enter Lear, Kent, and Fool.

Lear. Go you before to Gloucester with these letters.
    Acquaint my daughter no further with anything you
    know than comes from her demand out of the letter.
    If your diligence be not speedy, I shall be there afore
    you.   5

340 *some company* an escort 341 *particular* own 343 *compact it
more* substantiate it further 345 *milky . . . course* mildly gentle way
347 *ataskèd* censured, taken to task 348 *harmful mildness* mildness
that proves harmful 352 *th' event* the outcome, i.e. we shall see what
happens I, v, 3 *demand out of* i.e. questioning provoked by reading

Kent. I will not sleep, my lord, till I have delivered
    your letter.   *Exit.*

Fool. If a man's brains were in's heels, were't not in
    danger of kibes?

10 *Lear.* Ay, boy.

Fool. Then I prithee be merry. Thy wit shall not go
    slipshod.

Lear. Ha, ha, ha.

Fool. Shalt see thy other daughter will use thee kindly;
15   for though she's as like this as a crab's like an apple,
    yet I can tell what I can tell.

Lear. What canst tell, boy?

Fool. She will taste as like this as a crab does to a
    crab. Thou canst tell why one's nose stands i' th'
20   middle on's face?

Lear. No.

Fool. Why, to keep one's eyes of either side 's nose,
    that what a man cannot smell out he may spy into.

Lear. I did her wrong.

25 *Fool.* Canst tell how an oyster makes his shell?

Lear. No.

Fool. Nor I neither; but I can tell why a snail has a
    house.

Lear. Why?

30 *Fool.* Why, to put 's head in; not to give it away to
    his daughters, and leave his horns without a case.

Lear. I will forget my nature. So kind a father! — Be
    my horses ready?

Fool. Thy asses are gone about 'em. The reason why
35   the seven stars are no moe than seven is a pretty
    reason.

---

9 *kibes* chilblains 11–12 *wit . . . slipshod* intelligence (brain) shall
not go slippered (because of "kibes") 14 *Shalt* thou shalt *kindly*
after her kind, i.e. in the same way as this daughter 15 *crab* crab-
apple 24 *her* i.e. Cordelia (the first of the remarkable intimations of
Lear's inner thoughts in this scene) 31 *horns* i.e. snail's horns (with
pun on cuckold's horns; the legitimacy of Goneril and Regan being,
figuratively, suspect throughout) *case* covering 32 *nature* i.e. fatherly
instincts 35 *moe* more

Lear. Because they are not eight.

Fool. Yes indeed. Thou wouldst make a good fool.

Lear. To take 't again perforce — Monster ingratitude!   40

Fool. If thou wert my fool, nuncle, I'ld have thee
beaten for being old before thy time.

Lear. How's that?

Fool. Thou shouldst not have been old till thou hadst
been wise.   45

Lear. O, let me not be mad, not mad, sweet heaven!
Keep me in temper; I would not be mad!

Enter a Gentleman.

How now, are the horses ready?

Gentleman. Ready, my lord.

Lear. Come, boy.   50

Fool. She that's a maid now, and laughs at my depar-
ture,
Shall not be a maid long, unless things be cut
shorter.   *Exit all.*

---

39 *perforce* by force   47 *in temper* properly balanced   51-54 *She . . .
shorter* (a bawdy gag addressed to the audience, calculated to embar-
rass the maids who joined in the laughter)

ACT II, SCENE I

Enter Bastard (Edmund) and Curan severally.

Edmund. Save thee, Curan.

Curan. And you, sir. I have been with your father,
and given him notice that the Duke of Cornwall
and Regan his Duchess will be here with him this
5   night.

Edmund. How comes that?

Curan. Nay, I know not. You have heard of the news
abroad — I mean the whispered ones, for they are
yet but ear-kissing arguments?

10   *Edmund.* Not I. Pray you, what are they?

Curan. Have you heard of no likely wars toward,
'twixt the Dukes of Cornwall and Albany?

Edmund. Not a word.

Curan. You may do, then, in time. Fare you well, sir.
                                                              Exit.

Edmund. The Duke be here tonight? The better
15   best!

This weaves itself perforce into my business.

My father hath set guard to take my brother,

And I have one thing of a queasy question

II, i, 1 *Save* God save   9 *ear-kissing arguments* whispered topics   11
likely probable   *toward* impending   15 *better best* (hyperbole)   16
perforce of necessity or of its own accord   18 *of . . . question* deli-
cately balanced as to outcome, touch-and-go

Which I must act. Briefness and fortune, work!
Brother, a word: descend. Brother, I say!   20

Enter Edgar.

My father watches. O sir, fly this place.
Intelligence is given where you are hid.
You have now the good advantage of the night.
Have you not spoken 'gainst the Duke of Cornwall?
He's coming hither; now i' th' night, i' th' haste,   25
And Regan with him. Have you nothing said
Upon his party 'gainst the Duke of Albany?
Advise yourself.

Edgar.   I am sure on't, not a word.

Edmund. I hear my father coming. Pardon me:
In cunning I must draw my sword upon you.   30
Draw, seem to defend yourself; now quit you
      well. —
Yield! Come before my father! Light ho, here! —
Fly, brother. — Torches, torches! — So farewell.
                                        Exit Edgar.
Some blood drawn on me would beget opinion
Of my more fierce endeavor. (*wounds his arm*) I   35
      have seen drunkards
Do more than this in sport. — Father, father!
Stop, stop! No help?

Enter Gloucester, and Servants with torches.

Gloucester. Now, Edmund, where's the villain?
Edmund. Here stood he in the dark, his sharp sword
      out,
Mumbling of wicked charms, conjuring the moon   40
To stand auspicious mistress.

19 *Briefness and fortune* decisive speed and good luck   27 *Upon his
party 'gainst* i.e. reflecting upon his feud against   28 *Advise yourself*
take thought   *on't* of it   30 *In cunning* i.e. as a ruse   31 *quit you*
acquit yourself

Gloucester.   But where is he?

Edmund. Look, sir, I bleed.

Gloucester.   Where is the villain, Edmund?

Edmund. Fled this way, sir, when by no means he
   could —

Gloucester. Pursue him, ho! Go after.

                                      Exit some Servants

45   By no means what?

Edmund. Persuade me to the murder of your lord-
   ship;
   But that I told him the revenging gods
   'Gainst parricides did all the thunder bend;
   Spoke with how manifold and strong a bond
50   The child was bound to th' father — sir, in fine,
   Seeing how loathly opposite I stood
   To his unnatural purpose, in fell motion
   With his preparèd sword he charges home
   My unprovided body, latched mine arm;
55   And when he saw my best alarumed spirits
   Bold in the quarrel's right, roused to th' encounter,
   Or whether gasted by the noise I made,
   Full suddenly he fled.

Gloucester.   Let him fly far.
   Not in this land shall he remain uncaught;
60   And found — dispatch. The noble Duke my master,
   My worthy arch and patron, comes tonight:
   By his authority I will proclaim it
   That he which finds him shall deserve our thanks,
   Bringing the murderous coward to the stake;
65   He that conceals him, death.

Edmund. When I dissuaded him from his intent
   And found him pight to do it, with curst speech
   I threatened to discover him. He replied,
   "Thou unpossessing bastard; dost thou think,

---

48 *bend* aim   50 *in fine* finally   51 *loathly opposite* in loathing opposition   52 *fell* deadly   54 *unprovided* undefended   *latched* lanced,
pierced   55 *best alarumed* fully aroused   56 *Bold . . . right* confident
in the justice of the cause   57 *gasted* struck aghast   60 *dispatch* equivalent to "death" or "finis"   61 *arch* superior   67 *pight* determined,
set   *curst* angry   68 *discover* expose

If I would stand against thee, would the reposal   70
Of any trust, virtue, or worth in thee
Make thy words faithed? No. What I should deny
(As this I would, ay, though thou didst produce
My very character) I'ld turn it all
To thy suggestion, plot, and damnèd practice;   75
And thou must make a dullard of the world,
If they not thought the profits of my death
Were very pregnant and potential spirits
To make thee seek it."

Gloucester.   O strange and fast'ned villain!
Would he deny his letter, said he? I never got him.   80
                              Tucket within.

Hark, the Duke's trumpets. I know not why he
    comes.
All ports I'll bar; the villain shall not 'scape;
The Duke must grant me that. Besides, his picture
I will send far and near, that all the kingdom
May have due note of him; and of my land,   85
Loyal and natural boy, I'll work the means
To make thee capable.

Enter Cornwall, Regan, and Attendants.

Cornwall. How now, my noble friend? Since I came
    hither (Which I can call but now) I have heard
    strange news.   90
Regan. If it be true, all vengeance comes too short
    Which can pursue th' offender. How dost, my lord?
Gloucester. O madam, my old heart is cracked, it's
    cracked.

69 *unpossessing* having no claim, landless 70 *reposal* placing 72
falthed believed 74 *character* written testimony 75 *suggestion* insti-
gation *practice* devices 76 *make . . . world* i.e. consider everyone
stupid 77 *not thought* did not think 78 *pregnant . . . spirits* teem-
ing and powerful spirits, i.e. the devils which "possess" him 79
fast'ned confirmed 80 *got* begot s.d. *Tucket* (personal signature in
trumpet notes) 87 *capable* i.e. legitimate, able to inherit 89 *call* i.e.
say was

95 *Regan.* What, did my father's godson seek your life?
    He whom my father named, your Edgar?
Gloucester. O lady, lady, shame would have it hid.
Regan. Was he not companion with the riotous
    knights
    That tended upon my father?
100 *Gloucester.* I know not, madam. 'Tis too bad, too bad.
Edmund. Yes, madam, he was of that consort.
Regan. No marvel then though he were ill affected.
    'Tis they have put him on the old man's death,
    To have th' expense and waste of his revenues.
105   I have this present evening from my sister
    Been well informed of them, and with such cautions
    That, if they come to sojourn at my house,
    I'll not be there.
Cornwall.   Nor I, assure thee, Regan.
    Edmund, I hear that you have shown your father
    A childlike office.
110 *Edmund.*   It was my duty, sir.
Gloucester. He did bewray his practice, and received
    This hurt you see, striving to apprehend him.
Cornwall. Is he pursued?
Gloucester.   Ay, my good lord.
Cornwall. If he be taken, he shall never more
115   Be feared of doing harm. Make your own purpose,
    How in my strength you please. For you, Edmund,
    Whose virtue and obedience doth this instant
    So much commend itself, you shall be ours.
    Natures of such deep trust we shall much need;
    You we first seize on.
120 *Edmund.*   I shall serve you, sir,
    Truly, however else.
Gloucester.   For him I thank your Grace.
Cornwall. You know not why we came to visit you?

101 *consort* company, set   102 *affected* disposed   103 *put* set   104 *expense and waste* wasteful expenditure   110 *childlike* filial   111 *bewray his practice* expose his plot   115 *of doing* lest he do   115–16 *Make . . . please* i.e. accomplish your purpose, making free use of my powers   117 *virtue and obedience* virtuous obedience

Regan. Thus out of season, threading dark-eyed night.
Occasions, noble Gloucester, of some prize,
Wherein we must have use of your advice.   125
Our father he hath writ, so hath our sister,
Of differences, which I best thought it fit
To answer from our home. The several messengers
From hence attend dispatch. Our good old friend,
Lay comforts to your bosom, and bestow   130
Your needful counsel to our businesses,
Which craves the instant use.
Gloucester.   I serve you, madam.
Your Graces are right welcome. *Exit all. Flourish.*

ACT II, SCENE II

Enter Kent and Steward (Oswald), severally.

Oswald. Good dawning to thee, friend. Art of this
house?
Kent. Ay.
Oswald. Where may we set our horses?   5
Kent. I' th' mire.
Oswald. Prithee, if thou lov'st me, tell me.
Kent. I love thee not.

124 *prize* price, importance 127 *differences* quarrels *which* refers,
indefinitely, to the whole situation 128 *answer . . . home* cope with
away from home (where she need not receive Lear) 129 *attend dis-*
patch i.e. await settlement of the business 130 *Lay . . . bosom* be
consoled (about your own trouble) 131 *needful* needed 132 *craves*
. . . use requires immediate transaction, or use of your counsel II, ii,
1 *dawning* (perhaps indicating that it is too early for "good morning")
1–2 *Art . . . house* i.e. do you belong to this household?

Oswald. Why then, I care not for thee.

Kent. If I had thee in Lipsbury Pinfold, I would make
10   thee care for me.

Oswald. Why dost thou use me thus? I know thee not.

Kent. Fellow, I know thee.

Oswald. What dost thou know me for?

Kent. A knave, a rascal, an eater of broken meats; a
15   base, proud, shallow, beggarly, three-suited, hun-
      dred-pound, filthy worsted-stocking knave; a lily-
      livered, action-taking, whoreson, glass-gazing,
      superserviceable, finical rogue; one-trunk-inheriting
      slave; one that wouldst be a bawd in way of good
20   service, and art nothing but the composition of a
      knave, beggar, coward, pander, and the son and heir
      of a mongrel bitch; one whom I will beat into
      clamorous whining if thou deny'st the least syllable
      of thy addition.

25 *Oswald.* Why, what a monstrous fellow art thou, thus
      to rail on one that is neither known of thee nor
      knows thee!

Kent. What a brazen-faced varlet art thou to deny thou
      knowest me! Is it two days ago since I tripped up
30   thy heels and beat thee before the King? (*draws his
      sword*) Draw, you rogue, for though it be night,
      yet the moon shines. I'll make a sop o' th' moon-
      shine of you. You whoreson cullionly barbermonger,
      draw!

35 *Oswald.* Away, I have nothing to do with thee.

Kent. Draw, you rascal. You come with letters against
      the King, and take Vanity the puppet's part against

9 *Lipsbury Pinfold* i.e. between the teeth (cant term: "pen in the region of the lips")   14 *broken meats* scraps   15 *three-suited* with three
suits (the wardrobe allowed serving-men)   15–16 *hundred-pound* the
minimal estate for anyone aspiring to gentility   16 *worsted-stocking*
(serving-men's attire)   17 *action-taking* i.e. cowardly (resorting to
law instead of fighting)   17, 18 *glass-gazing, superserviceable, finical*
i.e. conceited, toadying, foppish   18 *inheriting* possessing   19–20 *a
bawd . . . service* i.e. a pander, if pleasing your employer required it
20 *composition* composite   24 *addition* titles   32–33 *sop o' th' moonshine* i.e. something that sops moonshine through its perforations
33 *cullionly barbermonger* vile fop (i.e. always dealing with hair-
dressers)   37 *Vanity the puppet* i.e. Goneril (here equated with a
stock figure in morality plays, now dwindled into puppet shows)

the royalty of her father. Draw, you rogue, or I'll so
carbonado your shanks. Draw, you rascal. Come
your ways!   40

Oswald. Help, ho! Murder! Help!

Kent. Strike, you slave! Stand, rogue! Stand, you neat
slave! Strike!   *Beats him.*

Oswald. Help, ho! Murder, murder!

*Enter Bastard (Edmund, with his rapier drawn),
Cornwall, Regan, Gloucester, Servants.*

Edmund. How now? What's the matter? Part!   45

Kent. With you, goodman boy, if you please! Come,
I'll flesh ye; come on, young master.

Gloucester. Weapons? Arms? What's the matter here?

Cornwall. Keep peace, upon your lives.
He dies that strikes again. What is the matter?   50

Regan. The messengers from our sister and the King.

Cornwall. What is your difference? Speak.

Oswald. I am scarce in breath, my lord.

Kent. No marvel, you have so bestirred your valor.
You cowardly rascal, nature disclaims in thee. A   55
tailor made thee.

Cornwall. Thou art a strange fellow. A tailor make a
man?

Kent. A tailor, sir. A stonecutter or a painter could
not have made him so ill, though they had been   60
but two years o' th' trade.

Cornwall. Speak yet, how grew your quarrel?

Oswald. This ancient ruffian, sir, whose life I have
spared at suit of his gray beard —

Kent. Thou whoreson zed, thou unnecessary letter! 65

39 *carbonado* dice (like a steak)   40 *your ways* get along   42 *neat*
primping   46 *goodman boy* doubly contemptuous, since peasants were
addressed as "goodmen"   47 *flesh ye* give you your first taste of blood
54 *bestirred* exercised   55 *disclaims* claims no part   59 *stonecutter*
sculptor   64 *At suit of* on the plea of, moved to mercy by   65 *zed* z
(last and least useful of letters)

My lord, if you will give me leave, I will tread this
unbolted villain into mortar and daub the wall of a
jakes with him. Spare my gray beard? You wagtail.
Cornwall. Peace, sirrah!
70   You beastly knave, know you no reverence?
Kent. Yes, sir, but anger hath a privilege.
Cornwall. Why art thou angry?
Kent. That such a slave as this should wear a sword,
     Who wears no honesty. Such smiling rogues as
        these
75   Like rats oft bite the holy cords atwain
     Which are too intrinse t' unloose; smooth every
        passion
     That in the natures of their lords rebel,
     Being oil to fire, snow to the colder moods;
     Renege, affirm, and turn their halcyon beaks
80   With every gale and vary of their masters,
     Knowing naught, like dogs, but following.
     A plague upon your epileptic visage!
     Smile you my speeches, as I were a fool?
     Goose, if I had you upon Sarum Plain,
85   I'ld drive ye cackling home to Camelot.
Cornwall. What, art thou mad, old fellow?
Gloucester. How fell you out? Say that.
Kent. No contraries hold more antipathy
     Than I and such a knave.

---

67 *unbolted* unsifted, crude   68 *jakes* privy or outhouse   *wagtail* any
of several birds whose tail-feathers wag or bob, suggesting obsequious-
ness or effeminacy   70 *beastly* beastlike, irrational   75 *holy cords*
sacred bonds (between parents and children, husbands and wives, man
and God)   76 *intrinse* intrinsic, inextricable   *smooth* flatter, cater to
77 *rebel* i.e. against reason and moral restraint   78 *Being . . . moods*
i.e. feeders of intemperance   79 *Renege* deny   *halcyon beaks* king-
fisher beaks (supposedly serving as weathervanes when the birds were
hung up by their necks)   80 *gale and vary* varying wind   82 *epileptic*
contorted in a grin   83 *Smile you* smile you at, mock you   84 *Sarum
Plain* Salisbury Plain (said to have been associated with geese, but
the allusion remains cryptic)   85 *Camelot* legendary seat of King
Arthur, variously sited at Winchester, near Cadbury, in Wales, etc.
88 *contraries* opposites

Cornwall. Why dost thou call him knave? What is his
    fault?   90
Kent. His countenance likes me not.
Cornwall. No more perchance does mine, nor his, nor
    hers.
Kent. Sir, 'tis my occupation to be plain:
    I have seen better faces in my time
    Than stands on any shoulder that I see   95
    Before me at this instant.
Cornwall.   This is some fellow
    Who, having been praised for bluntness, doth affect
    A saucy roughness, and constrains the garb
    Quite from his nature. He cannot flatter, he;
    An honest mind and plain — he must speak truth.   100
    An they will take it, so; if not, he's plain.
    These kind of knaves I know which in this plain-
        ness
    Harbor more craft and more corrupter ends
    Than twenty silly-ducking observants
    That stretch their duties nicely.   105
Kent. Sir, in good faith, in sincere verity,
    Under th' allowance of your great aspect,
    Whose influence, like the wreath of radiant fire
    On flick'ring Phoebus' front —
Cornwall.   What mean'st by this?
Kent. To go out of my dialect, which you discom-   110
    mend so much. I know, sir, I am no flatterer. He
    that beguiled you in a plain accent was a plain
    knave, which, for my part, I will not be, though I
    should win your displeasure to entreat me to't.
Cornwall. What was th' offense you gave him?   115

98–99 *constrains . . . nature* distorts the plain fashion from its true
nature, caricatures it   104 *silly-ducking observants* ludicrously bowing
form-servers   105 *nicely* fussily   107 *allowance* approval   *aspect* (1)
appearance (2) heavenly position   108 *influence* astrological force
109 *Phoebus' front* sun's forehead (i.e. face)   110 *go . . . dialect*
depart from my way of speaking   111 *He* (the type of plain-speaker
Cornwall has condemned)   113–14 *though . . . to't* though I should
persuade your disapproving self to beg me to do so

Oswald. I never gave him any.
　　　It pleased the King his master very late
　　　To strike at me, upon his misconstruction;
　　　When he, compact, and flattering his displeasure,
120　Tripped me behind; being down, insulted, railed,
　　　And put upon him such a deal of man
　　　That worthied him, got praises of the King
　　　For him attempting who was self-subdued;
　　　And, in the fleshment of this dread exploit,
　　　Drew on me here again.
125 *Kent.*　　　　　　　None of these rogues and cowards
　　　But Ajax is their fool.
Cornwall.　　　　　　　Fetch forth the stocks!
　　　You stubborn ancient knave, you reverent braggart,
　　　We'll teach you.
Kent.　　　　　Sir, I am too old to learn.
　　　Call not your stocks for me, I serve the King —
130　On whose employment I was sent to you;
　　　You shall do small respect, show too bold malice
　　　Against the grace and person of my master,
　　　Stocking his messenger.
Cornwall. Fetch forth the stocks. As I have life and
　　　honor,
135　There shall he sit till noon.
Regan. Till noon? Till night, my lord, and all night
　　　too.
Kent. Why, madam, if I were your father's dog,
　　　You should not use me so.
Regan.　　　　　　　Sir, being his knave, I will.
Cornwall. This is a fellow of the selfsame color
140　Our sister speaks of. Come, bring away the stocks.
　　　　　　　　　　　　　　　　　Stocks brought out.

117 *very late* quite recently 118 *misconstruction* misunderstanding
119 *compact* in league with 121 *And put . . . man* i.e. affected such
excessive manliness 122 *worthied* enhanced his worth 123 *For him
. . . self-subdued* for assailing him (Oswald) who chose not to resist
124 *fleshment of* bloodthirstiness induced by 125–26 *None . . . fool*
i.e. the Ajax type, stupidly belligerent, is the favorite butt of cowardly
rogues like Oswald 127 *Stubborn* rude *reverent* aged 131 *malice*
ill will 132 *grace* royal honor 139 *color* kind 140 *away* along

Gloucester. Let me beseech your Grace not to do so.
　His fault is much, and the good King his master
　Will check him for't. Your purposed low correction
　Is such as basest and contemnèd'st wretches
　For pilf'rings and most common trespasses   145
　Are punished with.
　The King his master needs must take it ill
　That he, so slightly valued in his messenger,
　Should have him thus restrained.
Cornwall.   I'll answer that.
Regan. My sister may receive it much more worse,   150
　To have her gentleman abused, assaulted,
　For following her affairs. Put in his legs.
　　　　　　　　　　　　　Kent is put in the stocks.
Cornwall. Come, my lord, away!
　　　　　　　　　Exit all but Gloucester and Kent.
Gloucester. I am sorry for thee, friend. 'Tis the Duke's
　pleasure,
　Whose disposition all the world well knows   155
　Will not be rubbed nor stopped. I'll entreat for
　thee.
Kent. Pray do not, sir. I have watched and travelled
　hard.
　Some time I shall sleep out, the rest I'll whistle.
　A good man's fortune may grow out at heels.
　Give you good morrow.   160
Gloucester. The Duke 's to blame in this. 'Twill be ill
　taken.   *Exit.*
Kent. Good King, that must approve the common
　saw,
　Thou out of heaven's benediction com'st
　To the warm sun.

143 *check* rebuke *purposed* intended 144 *contemnèd'st* most harshly
sentenced 148 *slightly valued in* i.e. little respected in the person of
149 *answer* answer for 155 *disposition* inclination 156 *rubbed* deflected (bowling term) used in the Elizabethan sport of duck pins
157 *watched* gone sleepless 159 *A good . . . heels* i.e. it is no disgrace to decline in fortune 160 *Give you* God give 161 *taken* received
162 *approve* demonstrate the truth of *saw* saying, proverb 163–64
Thou . . . sun proverb, meaning from better to worse, i.e. from
heavenly shelter to earthly exposure—"the heat of the day"

165   Approach, thou beacon to this under globe,
      That by thy comfortable beams I may
      Peruse this letter. Nothing almost sees miracles
      But misery. I know 'tis from Cordelia,
      Who hath most fortunately been informed
170   Of my obscurèd course. And shall find time
      From this enormous state, seeking to give
      Losses their remedies. — All weary and o'erwatched,
      Take vantage, heavy eyes, not to behold
      This shameful lodging. Fortune, good night;
175   Smile once more, turn thy wheel.   *Sleeps.*

ACT II, SCENE III

Enter Edgar.

Edgar. I heard myself proclaimed,
      And by the happy hollow of a tree
      Escaped the hunt. No port is free, no place
      That guard and most unusual vigilance
5   Does not attend my taking. Whiles I may 'scape,
      I will preserve myself; and am bethought
      To take the basest and most poorest shape
      That ever penury, in contempt of man,
      Brought near to beast: my face I'll grime with filth,
10   Blanket my loins, elf all my hairs in knots,
      And with presented nakedness outface
      The winds and persecutions of the sky.

165 *beacon . . . globe* i.e. the sun (here viewed as benign) 167–68
Nothing . . . misery i.e. miraculous aid is seldom seen except by the
miserable 170 *obscurèd* disguised 170–72 *And . . . remedies* (in-
coherent: perhaps corrupt, or perhaps snatches read from the letter)
171 *enormous state* monstrous situation 172 *Losses* reverses 173
vantage i.e. advantage of sleep 174 *lodging* (in the stocks) 175 *wheel*
Fortune's wheel was represented as vertical. Kent is at its bottom
II, iii, 2 *happy hollow* i.e. lucky hiding-place 5 *attend my taking*
contemplate my capture 6 *bethought* in mind 10 *elf* tangle (into
"elf-locks") 11 *presented* a show of

The country gives me proof and precedent
Of Bedlam beggars, who, with roaring voices,
Strike in their numbed and mortified bare arms   15
Pins, wooden pricks, nails, sprigs of rosemary;
And with this horrible object, from low farms,
Poor pelting villages, sheepcotes, and mills,
Sometimes with lunatic bans, sometime with prayers,
Enforce their charity. Poor Turlygod, poor Tom,   20
That's something yet: Edgar I nothing am.   *Exit.*

ACT II, SCENE IV

Enter Lear, Fool, and Gentleman.

Lear. 'Tis strange that they should so depart from
        home,
    And not send back my messenger.
Gentleman.   As I learned,
    The night before there was no purpose in them
    Of this remove.
Kent.   Hail to thee, noble master.
Lear. Ha!   5
    Mak'st thou this shame thy pastime?
Kent.   No, my lord.
Fool. Ha, ha, he wears cruel garters. Horses are tied
    by the heads, dogs and bears by th' neck, monkeys
    by th' loins, and men by th' legs. When a man's

13 *proof* example 15 *Strike* stick *mortified* deadened to pain 16
pricks skewers 17 *object* picture 18 *pelting* paltry 19 *bans* curses
20 *Turlygod* (unidentified, but evidently another name for a Tom
o' Bedlam) II, iv, 4 *purpose* intention 5 *remove* removal 7 *cruel*
painful (with pun on "crewel," a yarn used in garters)

10   over-lusty at legs, then he wears wooden nether-
     stocks.
    Lear. What's he that hath so much thy place mistook
     To set thee here?
    Kent.   It is both he and she,
     Your son and daughter.
15 *Lear.* No.
    Kent. Yes.
    Lear. No, I say.
    Kent. I say yea.
    Lear. No, no, they would not.
20 *Kent.* Yes, they have.
    Lear. By Jupiter, I swear no!
    Kent. By Juno, I swear ay!
    Lear.   They durst not do't;
     They could not, would not do't. 'Tis worse than
       murder
     To do upon respect such violent outrage.
25   Resolve me with all modest haste which way
     Thou mightst deserve or they impose this usage,
     Coming from us.
    Kent.   My lord, when at their home
     I did commend your Highness' letters to them,
     Ere I was risen from the place that showed
30   My duty kneeling, came there a reeking post,
     Stewed in his haste, half breathless, panting forth
     From Goneril his mistress salutations;
     Delivered letters, spite of intermission,
     Which presently they read; on whose contents
     They summoned up their meiny, straight took
35   horse,
     Commanded me to follow and attend
     The leisure of their answer, gave me cold looks;

---

10 *over-lusty at legs* i.e. too much on the go, or too much given to
kicking 10–11 *nether-stocks* stockings (as distinct from "upper-
stocks" or breeches) 24 *To . . . outrage* i.e. to show such out-
rageous disrespect 24 *Resolve* enlighten *modest* seemly 28 *commend* entrust 31 *Stewed* steaming 33 *spite of intermission* in disregard of its being an interruption 34 *presently* immediately *on*
on the strength of 35 *meiny* attendants

And meeting here the other messenger,
Whose welcome I perceived had poisoned mine,
Being the very fellow which of late   40
Displayed so saucily against your Highness,
Having more man than wit about me, drew;
He raised the house with loud and coward cries.
Your son and daughter found this trespass worth
The shame which here it suffers.   45

Fool. Winter's not gone yet, if the wild geese fly that
way.

    Fathers that wear rags
     Do make their children blind,
    But fathers that bear bags   50
     Shall see their children kind.
    Fortune, that arrant whore,
    Ne'er turns the key to th' poor.

But for all this, thou shalt have as many dolors for
thy daughters as thou canst tell in a year.

Lear. O, how this mother swells up toward my heart!
Hysterica passio, down, thou climbing sorrow;
Thy element's below. Where is this daughter?
Kent. With the Earl, sir, here within.
Lear.   Follow me not;
Stay here.   *Exit.*
Gentleman. Made you no more offense but what you
speak of?
Kent. None.
How chance the King comes with so small a num-
ber?
Fool. An thou hadst been set i' th' stocks for that
question, thou'dst well deserved it.
Kent. Why, fool?

41 *Displayed* showed off 42 *man* manhood *wit* sense 43 *raised* aroused 46-47 *Winter's . . . way* i.e. the ill season continues according to these signs (with Cornwall and Regan equated with "wild geese," proverbially evasive) 49 *blind* (to their father's needs) 50 *bags* (of gold) 52 *Fortune . . . whore* (because so fickle and callous) 53 *turns the key* i.e. opens the door 54 *dolors* sorrows (with pun on "dollars," continental coins) 55 *tell* count 56, 57 *mother, Hysterica passio* hysteria (the popular and the medical terms) 58 *element* proper place

Fool. We'll set thee to school to an ant, to teach thee
70   there's no laboring i' th' winter. All that follow
their noses are led by their eyes but blind men,
and there's not a nose among twenty but can smell
him that's stinking. Let go thy hold when a great
wheel runs down a hill, lest it break thy neck with
75   following. But the great one that goes upward, let
him draw thee after. When a wise man gives thee
better counsel, give me mine again. I would have
none but knaves follow it since a fool gives it.

> That sir which serves and seeks for gain,
80   And follows but for form,
> Will pack when it begins to rain
>   And leave thee in the storm.
> But I will tarry; the fool will stay,
>   And let the wise man fly.
85   The knave turns fool that runs away;
>   The fool no knave, perdy.

Kent. Where learned you this, fool?

Fool. Not i' th' stocks, fool.

Enter Lear and Gloucester.

Lear. Deny to speak with me? They are sick, they are
    weary,
9   They have travelled all the night? Mere fetches,
The images of revolt and flying off!
Fetch me a better answer.

Gloucester.   My dear lord,
   You know the fiery quality of the Duke,

---

70 *no laboring . . . winter* Lear, accompanied by "so small a number," is equated with winter bereft of workers, such as ants. 70–73
All . . . stinking i.e. almost anyone can smell out a person decayed
in fortune 78 *none but knaves* Here and in what follows the Fool
repudiates his advice to abandon Lear. 80 *form* show 81 *pack* be
off 85 *The knave . . . away* i.e. faithlessness is the true folly 86
perdy I swear (from *par dieu*) 88 *fool* persiflage, but also a term
of honor 90 *fetches* counterfeit reasons, false likenesses of truth 91
images true likenesses *flying off* revolt

How unremovable and fixed he is
In his own course.

Lear.   Vengeance, plague, death, confusion!   95
Fiery? What quality? Why, Gloucester, Gloucester,
I'd speak with the Duke of Cornwall and his wife.

Gloucester. Well, my good lord, I have informed them
so.

Lear. Informed them? Dost thou understand me,
man?

Gloucester. Ay, my good lord.   100

Lear. The King would speak with Cornwall. The dear
father
Would with his daughter speak, commands —
tends — service.
Are they informed of this? My breath and blood!
Fiery? The fiery Duke, tell the hot Duke that —
No, but not yet. May be he is not well.   105
Infirmity doth still neglect all office
Whereto our health is bound. We are not ourselves
When nature, being oppressed, commands the mind
To suffer with the body. I'll forbear;
And am fallen out with my more headier will   110
To take the indisposed and sickly fit
For the sound man. — Death on my state! Where-
fore
Should he sit here? This act persuades me
That this remotion of the Duke and her
Is practice only. Give me my servant forth.   115
Go tell the Duke and's wife I'd speak with them!
Now, presently! Bid them come forth and hear me,
Or at their chamber door I'll beat the drum
Till it cry sleep to death.

Gloucester. I would have all well betwixt you.   *Exit.* 120

94 *quality* disposition 102 *tends* attends, awaits, or tenders, offers
106 *all office* duties 107 *Whereto . . . bound* to which, in health,
we are bound 110 *headier* headstrong 113 *he* i.e. Kent 114 *remotion* remaining remote, inaccessible 115 *practice* trickery 117 *presently* immediately 119 *cry* pursue with noise (like a pack or "cry"
of hounds)

Lear. O me, my heart, my rising heart! But down!

Fool. Cry to it, nuncle, as the cockney did to the eels
　　when she put 'em i' th' paste alive. She knapped
　　'em o' th' coxcombs with a stick and cried, "Down,
125　　wantons, down!" 'Twas her brother that, in pure
　　kindness to his horse, buttered his hay.

Enter Cornwall, Regan, Gloucester, Servants.

Lear. Good morrow to you both.

Cornwall.　　　　　　　　　　　Hail to your Grace.
　　　　　　　　　　　　Kent here set at liberty.

Regan. I am glad to see your Highness.

Lear. Regan, I think you are. I know what reason
130　　I have to think so. If thou shouldst not be glad,
　　I would divorce me from thy mother's tomb,
　　Sepulchring an adultress. (*to Kent*) O, are you free?
　　Some other time for that. — Beloved Regan,
　　Thy sister 's naught. O Regan, she hath tied
135　　Sharp-toothed unkindness, like a vulture, here.
　　I can scarce speak to thee. Thou'lt not believe
　　With how depraved a quality —O Regan!

Regan. I pray you, sir, take patience. I have hope
　　You less know how to value her desert
　　Than she to scant her duty.

140 *Lear.*　　　　　　　　　Say? how is that?

Regan. I cannot think my sister in the least
　　Would fail her obligation. If, sir, perchance
　　She have restrained the riots of your followers,
　　'Tis on such ground, and to such wholesome end,
145　　As clears her from all blame.

122 *cockney* city-dweller　123 *paste* pastry pie　*knapped* rapped　125
wantons i.e. frisky things　126 *buttered his hay* another example of
rustic humor at the expense of cockney inexperience　131–32 *divorce
. . . adultress* i.e. refuse to be buried with your mother since such a
child as you must have been conceived in adultery　137 *how . . .
quality* i.e. what innate depravity　138 *have hope* i.e. suspect　140
scant (in effect, a double negative; "do" would be more logical
though less emphatic)

Lear. My curses on her!

Regan.   O, sir, you are old;
Nature in you stands on the very verge
Of his confine. You should be ruled, and led
By some discretion that discerns your state
Better than you yourself. Therefore I pray you   150
That to our sister you do make return;
Say you have wronged her.

Lear.   Ask her forgiveness?
Do you but mark how this becomes the house:
"Dear daughter, I confess that I am old.   *Kneels.*
Age is unnecessary. On my knees I beg   155
That you'll vouchsafe me raiment, bed, and food."

Regan. Good sir, no more. These are unsightly tricks.
Return you to my sister.

Lear.   (*rises*) Never, Regan.
She hath abated me of half my train,
Looked black upon me, struck me with her tongue   160
Most serpentlike upon the very heart.
All the stored vengeances of heaven fall
On her ingrateful top! Strike her young bones,
You taking airs, with lameness.

Cornwall.   Fie, sir, fie!

Lear. You nimble lightnings, dart your blinding
    flames   165
Into her scornful eyes! Infect her beauty,
You fen-sucked fogs drawn by the pow'rful sun
To fall and blister.

Regan.   O the blest gods!
So will you wish on me when the rash mood is on.

Lear. No, Regan, thou shalt never have my curse.   170
Thy tender-hefted nature shall not give

147–48 *Nature . . . confine* i.e. your life nears the limit of its tenure
149 *some discretion . . . state* someone discerning enough to recognize your condition 153 *the house* household or family decorum
159 *abated* curtailed 163 *ingrateful top* ungrateful head 164 *taking*
infectious 167 *fen-sucked* drawn up from swamps 168 *fall and
blister* strike and raise blisters (such as those of smallpox) 171 *tender-
hefted* swayed by tenderness, gently disposed

Thee o'er to harshness. Her eyes are fierce, but
  thine

Do comfort, and not burn. 'Tis not in thee

To grudge my pleasures, to cut off my train,

175 To bandy hasty words, to scant my sizes,

And, in conclusion, to oppose the bolt

Against my coming in. Thou better know'st

The offices of nature, bond of childhood,

Effects of courtesy, dues of gratitude.

180 Thy half o' th' kingdom hast thou not forgot,

Wherein I thee endowed.

Regan.   Good sir, to th' purpose.

                                      Tucket within.

Lear. Who put my man i' th' stocks?

Cornwall.   What trumpet's that?

Regan. I know't — my sister's. This approves her
  letter,

That she would soon be here.

                    Enter Steward (Oswald).

                                      Is your lady come?

185 *Lear.* This is a slave, whose easy-borrowèd pride

Dwells in the fickle grace of her he follows.

Out, varlet, from my sight.

Cornwall.   What means your Grace?

Lear. Who stocked my servant? Regan, I have good
  hope

Thou didst not know on't.

                       Enter Goneril.

                           Who comes here? O heavens!

190 If you do love old men, if your sweet sway

Allow obedience, if you yourselves are old,

Make it your cause. Send down, and take my part.

---

175 *bandy* volley *sizes* allowances 176 *oppose the bolt* i.e. bar the
door 178 *offices of nature* natural duties 179 *Effects* actions 181
purpose point 183 *approves* confirms 185 *easy-borrowed* acquired
on small security 186 *grace* favor 187 *varlet* low fellow 191 *Allow*
approve 192 *Make . . . cause* i.e. make my cause yours

(to Goneril) Art not ashamed to look upon this
  beard?
O Regan, will you take her by the hand?

Goneril. Why not by th' hand, sir? How have I of-   195
  fended?
All's not offense that indiscretion finds
And dotage terms so.

Lear.   O sides, you are too tough!
Will you yet hold? How came my man i' th' stocks?

Cornwall. I set him there, sir; but his own disorders
Deserved much less advancement.

Lear.   You? Did you?   200

Regan. I pray you, father, being weak, seem so.
If till the expiration of your month
You will return and sojourn with my sister,
Dismissing half your train, come then to me.
I am now from home, and out of that provision   205
Which shall be needful for your entertainment.

Lear. Return to her, and fifty men dismissed?
No, rather I abjure all roofs, and choose
To wage against the enmity o' th' air,
To be a comrade with the wolf and owl,   210
Necessity's sharp pinch. Return with her?
Why, the hot-blooded France, that dowerless took
Our youngest born, I could as well be brought
To knee his throne, and, squirelike, pension beg
To keep base life afoot. Return with her?   215
Persuade me rather to be slave and sumpter
To this detested groom.

Goneril.   At your choice, sir.

Lear. I prithee, daughter, do not make me mad.
I will not trouble thee, my child; farewell.
We'll no more meet, no more see one another.   220

196 *indiscretion finds* ill judgment detects as such   197 *sides* breast
(which should burst with grief)   200 *less advancement* i.e. more
abasement   201 *seem so* i.e. act the part   206 *entertainment* lodging
209 *wage* fight   211 *Necessity's sharp pinch* (a summing up of the
hardships previously listed)   212 *hotblooded* choleric   214 *knee*
kneel at   *squirelike* like an attendant   216 *sumpter* packhorse   217
groom i.e. Oswald

But yet thou art my flesh, my blood, my daughter;
Or rather a disease that's in my flesh,
Which I must needs call mine. Thou art a boil,
A plague-sore, or embossèd carbuncle
225   In my corrupted blood. But I'll not chide thee.
Let shame come when it will, I do not call it.
I do not bid the thunder-bearer shoot,
Nor tell tales of thee to high-judging Jove.
Mend when thou canst, be better at thy leisure;
230   I can be patient, I can stay with Regan,
I and my hundred knights.

Regan.   Not altogether so.
I looked not for you yet, nor am provided
For your fit welcome. Give ear, sir, to my sister;
For those that mingle reason with your passion
235   Must be content to think you old, and so —
But she knows what she does.

Lear.   Is this well spoken?

Regan. I dare avouch it, sir. What, fifty followers?
Is it not well? What should you need of more?
Yea, or so many, sith that both charge and danger
240   Speak 'gainst so great a number? How in one house
Should many people, under two commands,
Hold amity? 'Tis hard, almost impossible.

Goneril. Why might not you, my lord, receive attendance
From those that she calls servants, or from mine?

Regan. Why not, my lord? If then they chanced to
245   slack ye,
We could control them. If you will come to me
(For now I spy a danger), I entreat you
To bring but five-and-twenty. To no more
Will I give place or notice.

Lear. I gave you all.

---

224 *embossèd* risen to a head   227 *thunder-bearer* i.e. Jupiter   228
high-judging judging from on high   234 *mingle . . . passion* interpret
your passion in the light of reason   237 *avouch* swear by   239 *sith
that* since   *charge* expense   245 *slack* neglect   249 *notice* recognition

Regan.   And in good time you gave it.   250

Lear. Made you my guardians, my depositaries,
   But kept a reservation to be followèd
   With such a number. What, must I come to you
   With five-and-twenty? Regan, said you so?

Regan. And speak't again, my lord. No more with me.   255

Lear. Those wicked creatures yet do look well-favored
   When others are more wicked; not being the worst
   Stands in some rank of praise. (*to Goneril*) I'll go
     with thee.
   Thy fifty yet doth double five-and-twenty,
   And thou art twice her love.

Goneril.   Hear me, my lord.   260
   What need you five-and-twenty? ten? or five?
   To follow in a house where twice so many
   Have a command to tend you?

Regan.   What need one?

Lear. O reason not the need! Our basest beggars
   Are in the poorest thing superfluous.   265
   Allow not nature more than nature needs,
   Man's life is cheap as beast's. Thou art a lady:
   If only to go warm were gorgeous,
   Why, nature needs not what thou gorgeous wear'st,
   Which scarcely keeps thee warm. But, for true
     need —   270
   You heavens, give me that patience, patience I
     need.
   You see me here, you gods, a poor old man,
   As full of grief as age, wretched in both.
   If it be you that stirs these daughters' hearts
   Against their father, fool me not so much   275
   To bear it tamely; touch me with noble anger,

---

251 *depositaries* trustees 252 *kept . . . to be* stipulated that I be
256 *well-favored* comely 258 *Stands . . . praise* i.e. is at least rela-
tively praiseworthy 260 *her love* i.e. as loving as she 264 *reason*
analyze 265 *Are . . . superfluous* i.e. have some poor possession
not utterly indispensable 266 *than nature needs* i.e. than life needs
for mere survival 268–70 *If . . . warm* i.e. if to be dressed warmly
(i.e. for need) were considered sufficiently gorgeous, you would not
need your present attire, which is gorgeous rather than warm 275
fool play with, humiliate

And let not women's weapons, water drops,
Stain my man's cheeks. No, you unnatural hags!
I will have such revenges on you both

280 That all the world shall — I will do such things —
What they are, yet I know not; but they shall be
The terrors of the earth. You think I'll weep.
No, I'll not weep.   *Storm and tempest.*
I have full cause of weeping, but this heart

285 Shall break into a hundred thousand flaws
Or ere I'll weep. O fool, I shall go mad!
                    Exit Lear, Fool, Kent, and Gloucester.

Cornwall. Let us withdraw; 'twill be a storm.
Regan. This house is little; the old man and 's people
        Cannot be well bestowed.
Goneril. 'Tis his own blame; hath put himself from

290   rest
        And must needs taste his folly.
Regan. For his particular, I'll receive him gladly,
        But not one follower.
Goneril.   So am I purposed.
        Where is my Lord of Gloucester?
Cornwall. Followèd the old man forth.

                    Enter Gloucester.

                                            He is returned.
295 *Gloucester.* The King is in high rage.
Cornwall.   Whither is he going?
Gloucester. He calls to horse, but will I know not
        whither.
Cornwall. 'Tis best to give him way; he leads himself.
Goneril. My lord, entreat him by no means to stay.
Gloucester. Alack, the night comes on, and the high

300   winds

285 *flaws* fragments 286 *Or ere* before 290 *hath . . . rest* i.e. he
himself is responsible for leaving his resting place with her, or, he is
self-afflicted 292 *particular* own person 293 *purposed* determined

    Do sorely ruffle. For many miles about
    There's scarce a bush.
Regan.   O, sir, to willful men
    The injuries that they themselves procure
    Must be their schoolmasters. Shut up your doors.
    He is attended with a desperate train,   305
    And what they may incense him to, being apt
    To have his ear abused, wisdom bids fear.
Cornwall. Shut up your doors, my lord; 'tis a wild
    night.
    My Regan counsels well. Come out o' th' storm.
                          Exit all.

301 *ruffle* rage 306-7 *apt . . . abused* i.e. predisposed to listen to
ill counsel

ACT III, SCENE I

Storm still. Enter Kent and a Gentleman severally.

Kent. Who's there besides foul weather?

Gentleman. One minded like the weather, most unquietly.

Kent. I know you. Where's the King?

Gentleman. Contending with the fretful elements;

5   Bids the wind blow the earth into the sea,
Or swell the curlèd waters 'bove the main,
That things might change or cease; tears his white hair,
Which the impetuous blasts, with eyeless rage,
Catch in their fury and make nothing of;

10 Strives in his little world of man to outscorn
The to-and-fro-conflicting wind and rain.
This night, wherein the cub-drawn bear would couch,
The lion and the belly-pinchèd wolf
Keep their fur dry, unbonneted he runs,
And bids what will take all.

III, i, 2 *minded . . . unquietly* i.e. in disturbed mood   4 *Contending* quarrelling   6 *main* mainland   7 *change* revert to chaos or improve   8 *eyeless* (1) blind (2) invisible   10 *little world* the "microcosm," which is disturbed like the great world or "macrocosm"   12 *cub-drawn* cub-sucked (and hence ravenous)   13 *belly-pinchèd* famished

Kent.   But who is with him?   15
Gentleman. None but the fool, who labors to outjest
  His heart-struck injuries.
Kent.   Sir, I do know you,
  And dare upon the warrant of my note
  Commend a dear thing to you. There is division,
  Although as yet the face of it is covered   20
  With mutual cunning, 'twixt Albany and Cornwall;
  Who have — as who have not, that their great stars
  Throned and set high? — servants, who seem no
      less,
  Which are to France the spies and speculations
  Intelligent of our state. What hath been seen,   25
  Either in snuffs and packings of the Dukes,
  Or the hard rein which both of them have borne
  Against the old kind King, or something deeper,
  Whereof, perchance, these are but furnishings —
  But, true it is, from France there comes a power   30
  Into this scatteréd kingdom, who already,
  Wise in our negligence, have secret feet
  In some of our best ports and are at point
  To show their open banner. Now to you:
  If on my credit you dare build so far   35
  To make your speed to Dover, you shall find
  Some that will thank you, making just report
  Of how unnatural and bemadding sorrow
  The King hath cause to plain.
  I am a gentleman of blood and breeding,   40
  And from some knowledge and assurance offer
  This office to you.

15 *take all* the cry of the desperate gambler in staking his last
18 *warrant . . . note* assurance of my knowledge 19 *Commend . . .
thing* entrust a precious matter 22 *that* whom *stars* destinies 23
Throned have throned *no less* i.e. truly so 24 *speculations* spies
25 *Intelligent* supplying intelligence 26 *snuffs* quarrels *packings* in-
trigues 27 *hard rein . . . borne* i.e. harsh curbs . . . exercised 29
furnishings pretexts 30 *power* army 31 *scatteréd* divided 35 *my
credit* trust in me *build* take constructive action 38 *bemadding
sorrow* maddening grievances 39 *plain* lament 42 *office* service

Gentleman. I will talk further with you.

Kent.   No, do not.

For confirmation that I am much more

45   Than my out-wall, open this purse and take

What it contains. If you shall see Cordelia,

As fear not but you shall, show her this ring,

And she will tell you who that fellow is

That yet you do not know. Fie on this storm!

50   I will go seek the King.

Gentleman. Give me your hand. Have you no more to say?

Kent. Few words, but, to effect, more than all yet:

That when we have found the King — in which your pain

That way, I'll this — he that first lights on him

55   Holla the other.   *Exit severally.*

❧

ACT III, SCENE II

Storm still. Enter Lear and Fool.

Lear. Blow, winds, and crack your cheeks. Rage, blow.

You cataracts and hurricanoes, spout

Till you have drenched our steeples, drowned the cocks.

You sulph'rous and thought-executing fires,

5   Vaunt-couriers to oak-cleaving thunderbolts,

Singe my white head. And thou, all-shaking thunder,

---

45 *out-wall* surface appearance   52 *to effect* in their import   53 *pain* pains, care   III, ii, 2 *hurricanoes* waterspouts   3 *cocks* weathercocks 4 *thought-executing fires* i.e. flashes of lightning swift as thought, or, dazing, benumbing the mind   5 *Vaunt-couriers* heralds

Strike flat the thick rotundity o' th' world,
Crack Nature's moulds, all germains spill at once,
That makes ingrateful man.

Fool. O nuncle, court holy-water in a dry house is   10
better than this rain water out o' door. Good nuncle, in; ask thy daughters blessing. Here's a night
pities neither wise men nor fools.

Lear. Rumble thy bellyful. Spit, fire. Spout, rain.
Nor rain, wind, thunder, fire are my daughters.   15
I tax not you, you elements, with unkindness.
I never gave you kingdom, called you children;
You owe me no subscription. Then let fall
Your horrible pleasure. Here I stand your slave,
A poor, infirm, weak, and despised old man.   20
But yet I call you servile ministers,
That will with two pernicious daughters join
Your high-engendered battles 'gainst a head
So old and white as this. O, ho! 'tis foul.

Fool. He that has a house to put's head in has a good   25
head-piece.

       The codpiece that will house
         Before the head has any,
       The head and he shall louse:
         So beggars marry many.   30
       The man that makes his toe
         What he his heart should make
       Shall of a corn cry woe,
         And turn his sleep to wake.

For there was never yet fair woman but she made   35
mouths in a glass.

8 *moulds* (in which Nature's creations are formed)   *germains* seeds
10 *court holy-water* flattery (slang)   16 *tax* charge   18 *subscription*
deference   19 *pleasure* will   21 *ministers* agents   23 *high-engendered*
battles heavenly battalions   27–30 *The codpiece . . . many* The moral of the rime is that improvident cohabitation spells penury.   27
codpiece padded gusset at the crotch of the trunks   29 *he* it   30
many (head-lice and body-lice, accompanying poverty)   31–34 *The*
man . . . wake a parallel instance of misery deriving from reckless
impulse: to transpose the tender and precious heart and the tough
and base toe is to invite injury; with "heart" also suggesting Cordelia
35–36 *made . . . glass* i.e. posed before a mirror (irrelevant, except
as vanity is a form of folly, the Fool's general theme)

Enter Kent.

Lear. No, I will be the pattern of all patience;
    I will say nothing.
Kent. Who's there?
40 *Fool.* Marry, here's grace and a codpiece; that's a wise
    man and a fool.
Kent. Alas, sir, are you here? Things that love night
    Love not such nights as these. The wrathful skies
    Gallow the very wanderers of the dark
45   And make them keep their caves. Since I was man,
    Such sheets of fire, such bursts of horrid thunder,
    Such groans of roaring wind and rain, I never
    Remember to have heard. Man's nature cannot
      carry
    Th' affliction nor the fear.
Lear.   Let the great gods
50 That keep this dreadful pudder o'er our heads
    Find out their enemies now. Tremble, thou wretch,
    That hast within thee undivulgèd crimes
    Unwhipped of justice. Hide thee, thou bloody hand,
    Thou perjured, and thou simular of virtue
55 That art incestuous. Caitiff, to pieces shake,
    That under covert and convenient seeming
    Has practiced on man's life. Close pent-up guilts,
    Rive your concealing continents and cry
    These dreadful summoners grace. I am a man
    More sinned against than sinning.
60 *Kent.*   Alack, bareheaded?
    Gracious my lord, hard by here is a hovel;
    Some friendship will it lend you 'gainst the tem-
      pest.
    Repose you there, while I to this hard house

44 *Gallow* frighten 45 *keep their caves* i.e. keep under cover 46
horrid horrible 48 *carry* bear 50 *pudder* turmoil 51 *Find . . .
enemies* i.e. discover sinners (by their show of fear) 54 *simular*
counterfeit 56 *seeming* hypocrisy 57 *practiced on* plotted against
Close secret 58 *Rive* split, break through *continents* containers,
covers 59 *summoners* arresting officers of ecclesiastical courts *grace*
mercy 61 *Gracious my lord* my gracious lord 63 *house* household
(both building and occupants)

(More harder than the stones whereof 'tis raised,
Which even but now, demanding after you,   65
Denied me to come in) return, and force
Their scanted courtesy.

Lear.   My wits begin to turn.
Come on, my boy. How dost, my boy? Art cold?
I am cold myself. Where is this straw, my fellow?
The art of our necessities is strange,   70
And can make vile things precious. Come, your
  hovel.
Poor fool and knave, I have one part in my heart
That's sorry yet for thee.

Fool. (*sings*)
    He that has and a little tiny wit,
      With, heigh-ho, the wind and the rain,   75
    Must make content with his fortunes fit
      Though the rain it raineth every day.

Lear. True, boy. Come, bring us to this hovel.
                 Exit Lear with Kent.

Fool. This is a brave night to cool a courtesan. I'll
speak a prophecy ere I go: 80
    When priests are more in word than matter;
    When brewers mar their malt with water;
    When nobles are their tailors' tutors,
    No heretics burned, but wenches' suitors;
    When every case in law is right,   85
    No squire in debt nor no poor knight;
    When slanders do not live in tongues,
    Nor cutpurses come not to throngs;
    When usurers tell their gold i' th' field,
    And bawds and whores do churches build —   90

---

65 *demanding after* inquiring for   67 *scanted* stinted   70 *art* magic
skill (as in alchemy)   76 *make . . . fit* i.e. reconcile himself to his
fortunes   79 *brave* fine   81 *are . . . matter* i.e. can outshine the
gospel message (At present their ability to speak is quite unworthy
of their theme.)   82 *mar* i.e. dilute (At present they dilute water
with malt, producing very small beer.)   83 *are . . . tutors* i.e. no
longer subservient to fashion (Each subsequent line also reverses the
present state of affairs.)   84 *wenches' suitors* i.e. libertines   89 *tell*
count *i' th' field* (instead of in secret places)

Then shall the realm of Albion
Come to great confusion.
Then comes the time, who lives to see't,
That going shall be used with feet.
95   This prophecy Merlin shall make, for I live before
his time.   *Exit.*

ACT III, SCENE III

Enter Gloucester and Edmund.

Gloucester. Alack, alack, Edmund, I like not this unnatural dealing. When I desired their leave that I
might pity him, they took from me the use of mine
own house, charged me on pain of perpetual dis-
5   pleasure neither to speak of him, entreat for him,
or any way sustain him.

Edmund. Most savage and unnatural.

Gloucester. Go to; say you nothing. There is division
between the Dukes, and a worse matter than that.
10   I have received a letter this night — 'tis dangerous
to be spoken — I have locked the letter in my
closet. These injuries the King now bears will be
revenged home; there is part of a power already
footed; we must incline to the King. I will look him
15   and privily relieve him. Go you and maintain talk
with the Duke, that my charity be not of him per-

91 *Albion* England   92 *confusion* ruin (ironic: an edifice of abuses
is "ruined" by reform)   94 *going . . . feet* walking will be done
with feet (the humor of anticlimax, but suggesting a return to nor-
mality)   95 *Merlin* a legendary magician associated with King Arthur,
who reigned later than King Lear, an example of a typical Shakespearean anachronism   III, iii, 3 *pity* have mercy upon   5 *entreat*
plead   8 *division* contention   9 *worse* more serious   12 *closet* chamber   13 *home* thoroughly   *power* army   14 *footed* landed   *incline to*
side with   *look* search for   15 *privily* secretly

ceived. If he ask for me, I am ill and gone to bed.
If I die for it, as no less is threatened me, the King
my old master must be relieved. There is strange
things toward, Edmund; pray you be careful.   20
Edmund. This courtesy forbid thee shall the Duke
Instantly know, and of that letter too.
This seems a fair deserving, and must draw me
That which my father loses — no less than all.
The younger rises when the old doth fall.   *Exit.*   25

꧁

ACT III, SCENE IV

Enter Lear, Kent, and Fool.

Kent. Here is the place, my lord. Good my lord, enter.
The tyranny of the open night's too rough
For nature to endure.   *Storm still.*
Lear.   Let me alone.
Kent. Good my lord, enter here.
Lear.   Wilt break my heart?
Kent. I had rather break mine own. Good my lord,
enter.   5
Lear. Thou think'st 'tis much that this contentious
storm
Invades us to the skin. So 'tis to thee,
But where the greater malady is fixed
The lesser is scarce felt. Thou'dst shun a bear;
But if thy flight lay toward the roaring sea,   10

20 *toward* imminent 21 *courtesy* kind attention (to Lear) 23 *fair
deserving* i.e. action that should win favor III, iv, 1 *Good my lord*
my good lord 4 *break my heart* i.e. by removing the distraction of
mere physical distress 8 *fixed* lodged

Thou'dst meet the bear i' th' mouth. When the
    mind's free,
The body's delicate. The tempest in my mind
Doth from my senses take all feeling else
Save what beats there. Filial ingratitude,
15 Is it not as this mouth should tear this hand
For lifting food to't? But I will punish home.
No, I will weep no more. In such a night
To shut me out! Pour on; I will endure.
In such a night as this! O Regan, Goneril,
20 Your old kind father, whose frank heart gave all —
O, that way madness lies; let me shun that.
No more of that.

Kent.   Good my lord, enter here.

Lear. Prithee go in thyself; seek thine own ease.
This tempest will not give me leave to ponder
25 On things would hurt me more, but I'll go in.
    (*to the Fool*) In, boy; go first. You houseless pov-
      erty —
Nay, get thee in. I'll pray, and then I'll sleep.

                              Exit Fool.

Poor naked wretches, wheresoe'er you are,
That bide the pelting of this pitiless storm,
30 How shall your houseless heads and unfed sides,
Your looped and windowed raggedness, defend you
From seasons such as these? O, I have ta'en
Too little care of this! Take physic, pomp;
Expose thyself to feel what wretches feel,
35 That thou mayst shake the superflux to them
And show the heavens more just.

Edgar. (*within*) Fathom and half, fathom and half!
Poor Tom!

---

11 *i' th' mouth* i.e. in the teeth *free* free of care 16 *home* i.e. to
the hilt 20 *frank* liberal 26 *houseless* unsheltered 31 *looped* loop-
holed 33 *Take physic, pomp* i.e. cure yourself, you vainglorious
ones 35 *superflux* superfluities 37 *Fathom and half* nautical cry
in taking soundings, perhaps suggested by the deluge

Enter fool.

Fool. Come not in here, nuncle; here's a spirit. Help
me, help me!

Kent. Give me thy hand. Who's there?

Fool. A spirit, a spirit. He says his name's poor Tom. 40

Kent. What art thou that dost grumble there i' th'
straw? Come forth.

Enter Edgar (as Tom o' Bedlam).

Edgar. Away! The foul fiend follows me. Through the
sharp hawthorn blow the winds. Humh! go to thy
bed, and warm thee.   45

Lear. Didst thou give all to thy daughters? And art
thou come to this?

Edgar. Who gives anything to poor Tom? Whom the
foul fiend hath led through fire and through flame,
through ford and whirlpool, o'er bog and quagmire;   50
that hath laid knives under his pillow and halters in
his pew, set ratsbane by his porridge, made him
proud of heart, to ride on a bay trotting horse over
four-inched bridges, to course his own shadow for
a traitor. Bless thy five wits, Tom's acold. O, do, de, 55
do, de, do, de. Bless thee from whirlwinds, star-
blasting, and taking. Do poor Tom some charity,
whom the foul fiend vexes. There could I have
him now — and there — and there again — and
there —   *Storm still.* 60

Lear. Has his daughters brought him to this pass?
Couldst thou save nothing? Wouldst thou give 'em
all?

Fool. Nay, he reserved a blanket, else we had been all
shamed.

43–44 *Through . . . winds* a line from a ballad 44–45 *go . . . thee*
(evidently a popular retort) 51–52 *knives, halters, ratsbane* tempta-
tions to suicide 52 *pew* a gallery or balcony 53–54 *ride . . . bridges*
i.e. take mad risks 54–55 *course . . . traitor* chase his own shadow
as an enemy 56–57 *star-blasting* i.e. becoming the victim of malig-
nant stars *taking* pestilence 61 *pass* evil condition 63 *blanket* (to
cover his nakedness)

65 *Lear.* Now all the plagues that in the pendulous air
        Hang fated o'er men's faults light on thy daughters!
    Kent. He hath no daughters, sir.
    Lear. Death, traitor; nothing could have subdued
        nature
        To such a lowness but his unkind daughters.
70   Is it the fashion that discarded fathers
        Should have thus little mercy on their flesh?
        Judicious punishment — 'twas this flesh begot
        Those pelican daughters.
    Edgar. Pillicock sat on Pillicock Hill. Alow, alow,
        loo, loo!
    Fool. This cold night will turn us all to fools and mad-
75   men.
    Edgar. Take heed o' th' foul fiend; obey thy parents;
        keep thy words' justice; swear not; commit not
        with man's sworn spouse; set not thy sweet heart
        on proud array. Tom's acold.
80 *Lear.* What hast thou been?
    Edgar. A servingman, proud in heart and mind; that
        curled my hair, wore gloves in my cap; served the
        lust of my mistress' heart, and did the act of dark-
        ness with her; swore as many oaths as I spake words,
85   and broke them in the sweet face of heaven. One
        that slept in the contriving of lust, and waked to
        do it. Wine loved I deeply, dice dearly; and in
        woman out-paramoured the Turk. False of heart,
        light of ear, bloody of hand; hog in sloth, fox in
90   stealth, wolf in greediness, dog in madness, lion in
        prey. Let not the creaking of shoes nor the rustling
        of silks betray thy poor heart to woman. Keep thy

65 *pendulous* ominously suspended 66 *Hang . . . faults* i.e. destined
to chastise sins 71 *have . . . flesh* i.e. torture themselves 73 *pelican*
i.e. feeding upon the parent's blood (a supposed habit of this species
of bird) 74 *Pillicock . . . Hill* (probably from a nursery rime;
"Pillicock" is a pet-name for a child) *Alow . . . loo* hunting cry
77 *justice* i.e. dependability *commit not* i.e. adultery 82 *gloves
. . . cap* a fashion with Elizabethan gallants 88 *out-paramoured
the Turk* outdid the Sultan in mistress-keeping 89 *light of ear* i.e.
attentive to flattery and slander 91 *creaking, rustling* both considered seductively fashionable sounds

foot out of brothels, thy hand out of plackets, thy
pen from lenders' books, and defy the foul fiend.
Still through the hawthorn blows the cold wind;   95
says suum, mun, nonny. Dolphin my boy, boy,
sessa! let him trot by.   *Storm still.*

Lear. Thou wert better in a grave than to answer with
thy uncovered body this extremity of the skies. Is
man no more than this? Consider him well. Thou   100
ow'st the worm no silk, the beast no hide, the sheep
no wool, the cat no perfume. Ha! here's three on's
are sophisticated. Thou art the thing itself; unaccommodated man is no more but such a poor, bare,
forked animal as thou art. Off, off, you lendings!   105
Come, unbutton here.   *Begins to disrobe.*

Fool. Prithee, nuncle, be contented; 'tis a naughty
night to swim in. Now a little fire in a wild field
were like an old lecher's heart — a small spark, all
the rest on's body cold. Look, here comes a walking   110
fire.

Enter Gloucester with a torch.

Edgar. This is the foul Flibbertigibbet. He begins at
curfew, and walks till the first cock. He gives the
web and the pin, squints the eye, and makes the
harelip; mildews the white wheat, and hurts the   115
poor creature of earth.
    Swithold footed thrice the 'old;
    He met the nightmare, and her nine fold;

---

93 *plackets* slits in skirts 94 *pen . . . books* in signing for loans
96 *suum . . . nonny* the refrain of the wind 96-97 *Dolphin . . .
trot by* variously explained as cant phrases or ballad refrain, equivalent to "Let it go" 98 *answer* bear the brunt of 101 *ow'st* have
borrowed from 102 *cat* civet cat 103 *sophisticated* altered by artifice
103-4 *unaccommodated* unpampered 105 *forked* two-legged *lendings* borrowed coverings 107 *naughty* evil 108 *wild* barren 112
Flibbertigibbet a light-minded, silly, or restless person *curfew* (9
p.m.) 113 *first cock* midnight *web . . . pin* cataract of the eye
114 *squints* crosses 115 *white* ripening 117 *Swithold* St. Withold
(Anglo-Saxon exorcist) *footed* walked over *'old* wold, uplands
118 *nightmare* demon *fold* offspring

    Bid her alight
120   And her troth plight,
    And aroint thee, witch, aroint thee!

Kent. How fares your Grace?

Lear. What's he?

Kent. Who's there? What is't you seek?

125 *Gloucester.* What are you there? Your names?

Edgar. Poor Tom, that eats the swimming frog, the
  toad, the todpole, the wall-newt and the water; that
  in the fury of his heart, when the foul fiend rages,
  eats cow-dung for sallets, swallows the old rat and
130 the ditch-dog, drinks the green mantle of the standing pool; who is whipped from tithing to tithing,
  and stock-punished and imprisoned; who hath had
  three suits to his back, six shirts to his body,
    Horse to ride, and weapon to wear,
135   But mice and rats, and such small deer,
    Have been Tom's food for seven long year.
  Beware my follower! Peace, Smulkin, peace, thou
  fiend!

Gloucester. What, hath your Grace no better company?

140 *Edgar.* The prince of darkness is a gentleman.
  Modo he's called, and Mahu.

Gloucester. Our flesh and blood, my lord, is grown so
  vile
  That it doth hate what gets it.

Edgar. Poor Tom's acold.

145 *Gloucester.* Go in with me. My duty cannot suffer
  T' obey in all your daughters' hard commands.
  Though their injunction be to bar my doors
  And let this tyrannous night take hold upon you,

---

119 *alight* i.e. from the horse she was afflicting 120 *her troth plight*
plight her troth, pledge her good intentions 12 *aroint thee* be gone
(a direct command, concluding the charm) 127 *todpole* tadpole
water water-newt 129 *sallets* salads 130 *ditch-dog* carcass *mantle*
scum 130–31 *standing* stagnant 131 *tithing* a ten-family district
within a parish 132 *stock-punished* placed in the stocks 135 *deer*
game 137, 141 *Smulkin, Modo, Mahu* devils 143 *gets* begets (a
reference to Edgar, Goneril, and Regan) 145 *suffer* permit

Yet have I ventured to come seek you out
And bring you where both fire and food is ready.   150

Lear. First let me talk with this philosopher.
    What is the cause of thunder?

Kent. Good my lord, take his offer; go into th' house.

Lear. I'll talk a word with this same learnèd Theban.
    What is your study?   155

Edgar. How to prevent the fiend, and to kill vermin.

Lear. Let me ask you one word in private.

Kent. Importune him once more to go, my lord.
    His wits begin t' unsettle.

Gloucester.   Canst thou blame him?
                      Storm still.

His daughters seek his death. Ah, that good Kent,   160
He said it would be thus, poor banished man!
Thou say'st the King grows mad — I'll tell thee,
    friend,
I am almost mad myself. I had a son,
Now outlawed from my blood; he sought my life
But lately, very late. I loved him, friend,   165
No father his son dearer. True to tell thee,
The grief hath crazed my wits. What a night 's this!
I do beseech your Grace —

Lear.   O, cry you mercy, sir.
    Noble philosopher, your company.

Edgar. Tom's acold.   170

Gloucester. In, fellow, there, into th' hovel; keep thee
    warm.

Lear. Come, let's in all.

Kent.   This way, my lord.

Lear.   With him!
    I will keep still with my philosopher.

Kent. Good my lord, soothe him; let him take the   175
    fellow.

---

154 *Theban* an unexplained association of Thebes with philosophy,
i.e. science 155 *study* i.e. scientific specialty 156 *prevent* thwart
164 *outlawed . . . blood* proscribed as no child of mine 168 *cry
you mercy* I beg your pardon 175 *soothe* humor

Gloucester. Take him you on.

Kent. Sirrah, come on; go along with us.

Lear. Come, good Athenian.

180 *Gloucester.* No words, no words! Hush.

Edgar.   Child Rowland to the dark tower came;
        His word was still, "Fie, foh, and fum,
        I smell the blood of a British man." *Exit all.*

※

ACT III, SCENE V

Enter Cornwall and Edmund.

Cornwall. I will have my revenge ere I depart his house.

Edmund. How, my lord, I may be censured, that nature thus gives way to loyalty, something fears
5 me to think of.

Cornwall. I now perceive it was not altogether your brother's evil disposition made him seek his death; but a provoking merit, set awork by a reproveable badness in himself.

10 *Edmund.* How malicious is my fortune that I must repent to be just! This is the letter which he spoke of, which approves him an intelligent party to the advantages of France. O heavens, that this treason were not! or not I the detector!

15 *Cornwall.* Go with me to the Duchess.

177 *you on* along with you 179 *Athenian* i.e. philosopher 181 *Child Rowland* Roland of the Charlemagne legends (the line perhaps from a lost ballad) 182 *His word was still* i.e. his repeated word, his motto, was always 182–83 *Fie . . . man* (absurdly heroic) III, v, 3 *censured* judged 4–5 *something fears me* frightens me somewhat 8–9 *a provoking . . . himself* i.e. evil justice incited by evil (a case of poison driving out poison) 12 *approves* proves 12–13 *intelligent . . . advantages* spying partisan on behalf of

Edmund. If the matter of this paper be certain, you
    have mighty business in hand.

Cornwall. True, or false, it hath made thee Earl of
    Gloucester. Seek out where thy father is, that he
    may be ready for our apprehension.   20

Edmund. (*aside*) If I find him comforting the King, it
    will stuff his suspicion more fully. — I will persever
    in my course of loyalty, though the conflict be sore
    between that and my blood.

Cornwall. I will lay trust upon thee, and thou shalt   25
    find a dearer father in my love.   *Exit both.*

⤵

ACT III, SCENE VI

Enter Kent and Gloucester.

Gloucester. Here is better than the open air; take it
    thankfully. I will piece out the comfort with what
    addition I can. I will not be long from you.

Kent. All the power of his wits have given way to his
    impatience. The gods reward your kindness.   5
                            Exit Gloucester.

Enter Lear, Edgar, and Fool.

Edgar. Frateretto calls me, and tells me Nero is an
    angler in the lake of darkness. Pray, innocent, and
    beware the foul fiend.

Fool. Prithee, nuncle, tell me whether a madman be
    a gentleman or a yeoman.   10

---

21 *comforting* aiding 22 *persever* persevere 24 *blood* natural feelings 25 *lay . . . thee* trust you, or reward you with a place of trust
III, vi, 5 *impatience* rage 6 *Frateretto* a devil 7 *innocent* hapless
victim, plaything 10 *yeoman* a property owner, next in rank to a
gentleman The allusion is to self-penalizing indulgence of one's
children.)

Lear. A king, a king.

Fool. No, he's a yeoman that has a gentleman to his
son; for he's a mad yeoman that sees his son a gentleman before him.

15 *Lear.* To have a thousand with red burning spits
Come hizzing in upon 'em —

Edgar. The foul fiend bites my back.

Fool. He's mad that trusts in the tameness of a wolf, a
horse's health, a boy's love, or a whore's oath.

20 *Lear.* It shall be done; I will arraign them straight.
   (*to Edgar*) Come, sit thou here, most learned justice.
   (*to the Fool*) Thou, sapient sir, sit here. Now, you
   she-foxes —

Edgar. Look, where he stands and glares. Want'st thou
eyes at trial, madam?

25   Come o'er the bourn, Bessy, to me.

Fool.   Her boat hath a leak,
            And she must not speak
         Why she dares not come over to thee.

Edgar. The foul fiend haunts poor Tom in the voice
30   of a nightingale. Hoppedance cries in Tom's belly
   for two white herring. Croak not, black angel; I
   have no food for thee.

Kent. How do you, sir? Stand you not so amazed.
   Will you lie down and rest upon the cushions?

35 *Lear.* I'll see their trial first. Bring in their evidence.
   (*to Edgar*) Thou, robèd man of justice, take thy
   place.
   (*to the Fool*) And thou, his yokefellow of equity,
   Bench by his side. (*to Kent*) You are o' th' commission;
   Sit you too.

---

13 *sees* i.e. sees to it 16 *hizzing* hissing (Lear is musing on vicious
military retaliation.) 20 *arraign* bring to trial 23 *he* Lear, or one
of Edgar's "devils" 24 *eyes* such eyes, or spectators 25 *bourn* brook
(Edgar's line is from a popular song; the Fool's are a ribald impro-
visation.) 30 *nightingale* i.e. the fool *Hoppedance* a devil 31 *white*
unsmoked (in contrast with "black angel," i.e. smoked devil) 33
amazed bewildered 38 *commission* those commissioned as King's jus-
tices

Edgar. Let us deal justly.   40

      Sleepest or wakest thou, jolly shepherd?
         Thy sheep be in the corn;
      And for one blast of thy minikin mouth
         Thy sheep shall take no harm.

  Purr, the cat is gray.   45

Lear. Arraign her first. 'Tis Goneril, I here take my
  oath before this honorable assembly, kicked the
  poor King her father.

Fool. Come hither, mistress. Is your name Goneril?

Lear. She cannot deny it.   50

Fool. Cry you mercy, I took you for a joint-stool.

Lear. And here's another, whose warped looks pro-
  claim
  What store her heart is made on. Stop her there!
  Arms, arms, sword, fire! Corruption in the place!
  False justicer, why hast thou let her 'scape?   55

Edgar. Bless thy five wits!

Kent. O pity! Sir, where is the patience now
  That you so oft have boasted to retain?

Edgar. (*aside*) My tears begin to take his part so much
  They mar my counterfeiting.   60

Lear. The little dogs and all,
  Tray, Blanch, and Sweetheart — see, they bark at
  me.

Edgar. Tom will throw his head at them. Avaunt, you
  curs.

      Be thy mouth or black or white,   65
      Tooth that poisons if it bite;
      Mastiff, greyhound, mongrel grim,
      Hound or spaniel, brach or lym,
      Or bobtail tike, or trundle-tail —

42 *corn* wheatfield 43 *one . . . mouth* one strain on your delicate
shepherd's pipe 45 *gray* Gray cats were among the forms supposedly
assumed by devils. 51 *Cry . . . joint-stool* a cant expression for
"Pardon me for failing to notice you," but two joint-stools were
probably the actual stage objects arraigned as Goneril and Regan
54 *Corruption . . . place* i.e. bribery in the court 59 *take his part*
i.e. fall on his behalf 60 *counterfeiting* i.e. simulating madness 68
brach hound bitch *lym* bloodhound 69 *Bobtail . . . trundle-tail*
short-tailed or long-tailed cur

70   Tom will make him weep and wail;
            For, with throwing thus my head,
               Dogs leaped the hatch, and all are fled.
       Do, de, de, de. Sessa! Come, march to wakes and
       fairs and market towns. Poor Tom, thy horn is dry.

75   *Lear.* Then let them anatomize Regan. See what
       breeds about her heart. Is there any cause in nature
       that makes these hard hearts? (*to Edgar*) You, sir,
       I entertain for one of my hundred; only I do not
       like the fashion of your garments. You will say they
80   are Persian; but let them be changed.

       Kent. Now, good my lord, lie here and rest awhile.

       Lear. Make no noise, make no noise; draw the curtains.
       So, so. We'll go to supper i' th' morning.

       Fool. And I'll go to bed at noon.

                          Enter Gloucester.

       Gloucester. Come hither, friend. Where is the King
85   my master?

       Kent. Here, sir, but trouble him not; his wits are gone.

       Gloucester. Good friend, I prithee take him in thy
          arms.
       I have o'erheard a plot of death upon him.
       There is a litter ready; lay him in't
       And drive toward Dover, friend, where thou shalt
90   meet
       Both welcome and protection. Take up thy master.
       If thou shouldst dally half an hour, his life,
       With thine and all that offer to defend him,
       Stand in assurèd loss. Take up, take up,
95   And follow me, that will to some provision
       Give thee quick conduct.

       ---

72 *hatch* lower half of a Dutch door   73 *Sessa* interjection, equivalent to "Away!"   *wakes* parish feasts   74 *Poor . . . dry* Edgar
expresses his exhaustion in his rôle, by an allusion to the horns prof-
fered by Tom o' Bedlams in begging drink.   80 *Persian* Persian cos-
tume was reputedly gorgeous. Ironically, or in actual delusion, Lear
refers thus to Edgar's rags   95 *provision* supplies

Kent.   Oppressèd nature sleeps.
  This rest might yet have balmed thy broken sinews,
  Which, if convenience will not allow,
  Stand in hard cure. (*to the Fool*) Come, help to
    bear thy master.
  Thou must not stay behind.

Gloucester.   Come, come, away!   100
                   Exit all but Edgar.

Edgar. When we our betters see bearing our woes,
  We scarcely think our miseries our foes.
  Who alone suffers suffers most i' th' mind,
  Leaving free things and happy shows behind;
  But then the mind much sufferance doth o'erskip   105
  When grief hath mates, and bearing fellowship.
  How light and portable my pain seems now,
  When that which makes me bend makes the King
    bow.
  He childed as I fathered. Tom, away.
  Mark the high noises, and thyself bewray   110
  When false opinion, whose wrong thoughts defile
    thee,
  In thy just proof repeals and reconciles thee.
  What will hap more tonight, safe 'scape the King!
  Lurk, lurk.   *Exit.*

---

96 *conduct* guidance 97 *balmed* healed *sinews* nerves 98 *convenience* propitious circumstances 99 *Stand . . . cure* will be hard to cure 101 *our woes* woes like ours 101 *our foes* i.e. our peculiar foes (They seem rather a part of universal misery.) 104 *free* carefree *shows* scenes 105 *sufferance* suffering 106 *bearing fellowship* enduring his company 107 *portable* bearable 110 *Mark . . . noises* i.e. heed the rumors concerning those in power *bewray* reveal 111 *wrong thoughts* misconceptions 112 *In . . . reconciles thee* i.e. upon your vindication recalls you and makes peace with you 113 *What . . . more* whatever more happens 114 *Lurk* i.e. keep covered

۶ٯۥ

ACT III, SCENE VII

*Enter Cornwall, Regan, Goneril, Bastard
(Edmund), and Servants.*

Cornwall. (*to Goneril*) Post speedily to my lord your
husband; show him this letter. The army of France is
landed. (*to Servants*) Seek out the traitor Gloucester.   *Exit some Servants.*

Regan. Hang him instantly.

5 *Goneril.* Pluck out his eyes.

Cornwall. Leave him to my displeasure. Edmund,
keep you our sister company. The revenges we are
bound to take upon your traitorous father are not
fit for your beholding. Advise the Duke where you
10 are going, to a most festinate preparation. We are
bound to the like. Our posts shall be swift and intelligent betwixt us. Farewell, dear sister; farewell,
my Lord of Gloucester.

Enter Steward (Oswald).

How now? Where's the King?

Oswald. My Lord of Gloucester hath conveyed him
15   hence.
Some five or six and thirty of his knights,
Hot questrists after him, met him at gate;
Who, with some other of the lord's dependants,
Are gone with him toward Dover, where they boast
To have well-armèd friends.

III, vii, 8 *bound* required   10 *festinate* speedy   11–12 *intelligent* in-
formative   13 *Lord of Gloucester* (as now endowed with his father's
title and estates)   17 *questrists* seekers

Cornwall.   Get horses for your mistress.   **20**
                                        Exit Oswald.

Goneril. Farewell, sweet lord, and sister.
Cornwall. Edmund, farewell.
                              Exit Goneril and Edmund.
                    Go seek the traitor Gloucester,
Pinion him like a thief, bring him before us.
                                        Exit other Servants.
Though well we may not pass upon his life
Without the form of justice, yet our power   **25**
Shall do a court'sy to our wrath, which men
May blame, but not control.

                Enter Gloucester and Servants.

                              Who's there, the traitor?
Regan. Ingrateful fox, 'tis he.
Cornwall. Bind fast his corky arms.
Gloucester. What means your Graces? Good my   **30**
    friends, consider.
    You are my guests. Do me no foul play, friends.
Cornwall. Bind him, I say.   *Servants bind him.*
Regan.   Hard, hard! O filthy traitor.
Gloucester. Unmerciful lady as you are, I'm none.
Cornwall. To this chair bind him. Villain, thou shalt
    find —   *Regan plucks his beard.*   **35**
Gloucester. By the kind gods, 'tis most ignobly done
    To pluck me by the beard.
Regan. So white, and such a traitor?
Gloucester.   Naughty lady,
    These hairs which thou dost ravish from my chin
    Will quicken and accuse thee. I am your host.   **40**
    With robber's hands my hospitable favors
    You should not ruffle thus. What will you do?

24 *pass upon* issue a sentence against 26 *do a court'sy to* i.e. defer
to, act in conformity with 29 *corky* (because aged) 38 *Naughty*
evil 40 *quicken* come to life 41 *favors* features 42 *ruffle* tear at

Cornwall. Come, sir, what letters had you late from
    France?

45 *Regan.* Be simple-answered, for we know the truth.

    Cornwall. And what confederacy have you with the
    traitors
    Late footed in the kingdom?

    Regan. To whose hands you have sent the lunatic
    King. Speak.

50 *Gloucester.* I have a letter guessingly set down,
    Which came from one that's of a neutral heart,
    And not from one opposed.

    Cornwall.   Cunning.

    Regan.   And false.

    Cornwall. Where hast thou sent the king?

    Gloucester. To Dover.

    Regan. Wherefore to Dover? Wast thou not charged
55   at peril —

    Cornwall. Wherefore to Dover? Let him answer that.

    Gloucester. I am tied to th' stake, and I must stand
    the course.

    Regan. Wherefore to Dover?

60 *Gloucester.* Because I would not see thy cruel nails
    Pluck out his poor old eyes; nor thy fierce sister
    In his anointed flesh stick boarish fangs.
    The sea, with such a storm as his bare head
    In hell-black night endured, would have buoyed up
65   And quenched the stellèd fires.
    Yet, poor old heart, he holp the heavens to rain.
    If wolves had at thy gate howled that stern time,
    Thou shouldst have said, "Good porter, turn the
    key."
70   All cruels else subscribe. But I shall see
    The wingèd vengeance overtake such children.

---

43 *late* of late 45 *Be simple-answered* i.e. give plain answers 47
footed landed 50 *guessingly* i.e. tentatively, not statéd as an assured
fact 54–55 *charged at peril* ordered on peril of your life 58 *course*
coursing (as by a string of dogs baiting a bear or bull tied in the
pit) 62 *anointed* (as king) 64 *buoyed* surged 65 *stelled* starry
66 *holp* helped 68–69 *turn the key* i.e. let them come in to shelter
70 *All . . . subscribe* i.e. at such times all other cruel creatures give
way, agree to renounce their cruelty 71 *winged* heavenly, or swift

Cornwall. See't shalt thou never. Fellows, hold the
    chair. Upon these eyes of thine I'll set my foot.

Gloucester. He that will think to live till he be old,
    Give me some help. — O cruel! O ye gods!   75

Regan. One side will mock another. Th' other too.

Cornwall. If you see vengeance —

1. Servant.   Hold your hand, my lord!
    I have served you ever since I was a child;
    But better service have I never done you
    Than now to bid you hold.

Regan.   How now, you dog?   80

1. Servant. If you did wear a beard upon your chin,
    I'ld shake it on this quarrel. What do you mean!

Cornwall. My villain!   *Draw and fight.*

1. Servant. Nay, then, come on, and take the chance
    of anger.

Regan. Give me thy sword. A peasant stand up thus?   85

She takes a sword and runs at him behind, kills him.

1. Servant. O, I am slain! My lord, you have one eye
    left
    To see some mischief on him. O!

Cornwall. Lest it see more, prevent it. Out, vile jelly.
    Where is thy lustre now?

Gloucester. All dark and comfortless. Where's my son
    Edmund?   90
    Edmund, enkindle all the sparks of nature
    To quit this horrid act.

Regan.   Out, treacherous villain;
    Thou call'st on him that hates thee. It was he
    That made the overture of thy treasons to us;
    Who is too good to pity thee.   95

---

74 *will think* hopes, expects   76 *mock* i.e. subject to ridicule (because
of the contrast)   82 *shake it* (as Regan has done with Gloucester's
— an act of extreme defiance)   *on this quarrel* in this cause   *What
... mean* i.e. how dare you (The words are given to Regan by
most editors, but they are no more "unservantlike" than those that
precede them.)   83 *My villain* i.e. my serf (with play on its more
modern meaning   87 *mischief* injury   91 *nature* natural feeling   92
quit requite, avenge   *horrid* horrible   94 *overture* disclosure

Gloucester. O my follies! Then Edgar was abused.
   Kind gods, forgive me that, and prosper him.
Regan. Go thrust him out at gates, and let him smell
   His way to Dover.   *Exit one with Gloucester.*
            How is't, my lord? How look you?
100 *Cornwall.* I have received a hurt. Follow me, lady.
   Turn out that eyeless villain. Throw this slave
   Upon the dunghill. Regan, I bleed apace
   Untimely comes this hurt. Give me your arm.
                Exit Cornwall and Regan.
2. Servant. I'll never care what wickedness I do,
   If this man come to good.
105 *3. Servant.*   If she live long,
   And in the end meet the old course of death,
   Women will all turn monsters.
2. Servant. Let's follow the old Earl, and get the bedlam
   To lead him where he would. His roguish madness
110 Allows itself to anything.   *Exit.*
3. Servant. Go thou. I'll fetch some flax and whites of
   eggs
   To apply to his bleeding face. Now heaven help
   him.   *Exit.*

---

96 *abused* wronged 99 *How look you* i.e. how looks it with you, what
is your condition 106 *meet . . . death* i.e. die a natural death 109–
10 *his roguish . . . anything* i.e. his being an irresponsible wanderer
allows him to do anything

ACT IV, SCENE I

Enter Edgar.

Edgar. Yet better thus, and known to be contemned,
    Than still contemned and flattered. To be worst,
    The lowest and most dejected thing of fortune,
    Stands still in esperance, lives not in fear.
    The lamentable change is from the best;   5
    The worst returns to laughter. Welcome then,
    Thou unsubstantial air that I embrace:
    The wretch that thou hast blown unto the worst
    Owes nothing to thy blasts.

Enter Gloucester and an Old Man.

                                But who comes here?
    My father, poorly led? World, world, O world!   10
    But that thy strange mutations make us hate thee,
    Life would not yield to age.
Old Man.   O my good lord,
    I have been your tenant, and your father's tenant,
    These fourscore years.

IV, i, 1 *contemned* despised 3 *dejected* cast down, abased 4 *esperance* hope 6 *The worst . . . laughter* i.e. the worst extreme is the point of return to happiness 9 *nothing* i.e. nothing good (and hence he is free of debt) 10 *poorly* poorlike, i.e. like a blind beggar 11–12 *But . . . age* i.e. were it not for your hateful mutability, we would never be reconciled to old age and death

Gloucester. Away, get thee away. Good friend, be
15   gone.

    Thy comforts can do me no good at all;

    Thee they may hurt.

Old Man.   You cannot see your way.

Gloucester. I have no way, and therefore want no eyes;

    I stumbled when I saw. Full oft 'tis seen

20   Our means secure us, and our mere defects

    Prove our commodities. O dear son Edgar,

    The food of thy abusèd father's wrath,

    Might I but live to see thee in my touch

    I'ld say I had eyes again!

Old Man.   .How now? Who's there?

Edgar. (*aside*) O gods! Who is't can say "I am at
25   the worst?"

    I am worse than e'er I was.

Old Man.   'Tis poor mad Tom.

Edgar. (*aside*) And worse I may be yet. The worst is
    not

    So long as we can say "This is the worst."

Old Man. Fellow, where goest?

Gloucester.   Is it a beggarman?
30 *Old Man.* Madman and beggar too.

Gloucester. He has some reason, else he could not
    beg.

    I' th' last night's storm I such a fellow saw,

    Which made me think a man a worm. My son

    Came then into my mind, and yet my mind

    Was then scarce friends with him. I have heard
35   more since.

    As flies to wanton boys are we to th' gods;

    They kill us for their sport.

---

16 *comforts* ministrations 17 *hurt* do injury (since they are forbidden) 18 *want* need 20–21 *Our means . . . commodities* i.e. prosperity makes us rash, and sheer affliction proves a boon 22 *food*
i.e. the object fed upon *abusèd* deceived 23 *in* i.e. by means of
27–28 *The worst . . . worst* because at the very worst there will be
no such comforting thought 31 *reason* powers of reason 33–34 *My
son . . . mind* because it was actually he — a natural touch 36
wanton irresponsibly playful

Edgar.   (*aside*) How should this be?
  Bad is the trade that must play fool to sorrow,
  Ang'ring itself and others. — Bless thee, master.
Gloucester. Is that the naked fellow?
Old Man.   Ay, my lord.   40
Gloucester. Get thee away. If for my sake
  Thou wilt o'ertake us hence a mile or twain
  I' th' way toward Dover, do it for ancient love;
  And bring some covering for this naked soul,
  Which I'll entreat to lead me.
Old Man.   Alack, sir, he is mad.   45
Gloucester. 'Tis the time's plague when madmen lead
      the blind.
  Do as I bid thee, or rather do thy pleasure.
  Above the rest, be gone.
Old Man. I'll bring him the best 'parel that I have,
  Come on't what will.   *Exit.*   50
Gloucester. Sirrah naked fellow —
Edgar. Poor Tom's acold. (*aside*) I cannot daub it
      further.
Gloucester. Come hither, fellow.
Edgar. (*aside*) And yet I must. — Bless thy sweet eyes,
      they bleed.
Gloucester. Know'st thou the way to Dover?   55
Edgar. Both stile and gate, horseway and footpath.
  Poor Tom hath been scared out of his good wits.
  Bless thee, good man's son, from the foul fiend.
  Five fiends have been in poor Tom at once: of lust,
  as Obidicut; Hobbididence, prince of dumbness;   60
  Mahu, of stealing; Modo, of murder; Flibbertigib
  bet, of mopping and mowing, who since possesses
  chambermaids and waiting women. So, bless thee,
  master.

---

39 *Ang'ring* offending 43 *ancient love* i.e. such love as formerly
bound master and man (nostalgic) 46 *time's plague* i.e. malady
characteristic of these times 47 *thy pleasure* as you please 49 *'parel*
apparel 52 *daub it* lay it on, act the part 60 *Obidicut* Hoberdicut
(a devil, as are the four following) *dumbness* muteness (Shakespeare identifies each devil with some form of possession.) 62 *mopping and mowing* grimaces, affected facial expressions.

Gloucester. Here, take this purse, thou whom the
65   heavens' plagues
      Have humbled to all strokes. That I am wretched
      Makes thee the happier. Heavens, deal so still!
      Let the superfluous and lust-dieted man,
      That slaves your ordinance, that will not see
70   Because he does not feel, feel your pow'r quickly;
      So distribution should undo excess,
      And each man have enough. Dost thou know Dover?

Edgar. Ay, master.

Gloucester. There is a cliff, whose high and bending
      head
75   Looks fearfully in the confinèd deep.
      Bring me but to the very brim of it,
      And I'll repair the misery thou dost bear
      With something rich about me. From that place
      I shall no leading need.

Edgar.   Give me thy arm.
80   Poor Tom shall lead thee.   *Exit both.*

ACT IV, SCENE II

Enter Goneril, Bastard (Edmund),
and Steward (Oswald).

Goneril. Welcome, my lord. I marvel our mild hus-
      band
      Not met us on the way. *(to Oswald)* Now, where's
      your master?

66 *humbled to* reduced to bearing humbly 67 *happier* i.e. less
wretched 68 *superfluous* possessed of superfluities *lust-dieted* i.e.
whose desires are feasted 69 *slaves your ordinance* subordinates your
injunction (to share) 74 *bending* overhanging 75 *in . . . deep* i.e.
to the sea hemmed in below IV, ii, 2 *Not met* has not met

Oswald. Madam, within, but never man so changed.
   I told him of the army that was landed:
   He smiled at it. I told him you were coming: 5
   His answer was, "The worse." Of Gloucester's
      treachery
   And of the loyal service of his son
   When I informed him, then he called me sot
   And told me I had turned the wrong side out.
   What most he should dislike seems pleasant to him;   10
   What like, offensive.
Goneril. (to Edmund) Then shall you go no further.
   It is the cowish terror of his spirit,
   That dares not undertake. He'll not feel wrongs
   Which tie him to an answer. Our wishes on the way
   May prove effects. Back, Edmund, to my brother.   15
   Hasten his musters and conduct his pow'rs.
   I must change names at home, and give the distaff
   Into my husband's hands. This trusty servant
   Shall pass between us. Ere long you are like to hear
   (If you dare venture in your own behalf)   20
   A mistress's command. Wear this. Spare speech.
                                   Gives a favor.
   Decline your head. This kiss, if it durst speak,
   Would stretch thy spirits up into the air.
   Conceive, and fare thee well.
Edmund. Yours in the ranks of death.   *Exit.*
Goneril.   My most dear Gloucester.   25
   O, the difference of man and man:
   To thee a woman's services are due;
   My fool usurps my body.
Oswald.   Madam, here comes my lord. *Exit.*

8 *sot* fool   11 *What like* what he should like   12 *cowish* cowardly
13 *undertake* engage   14 *an answer* retaliation   14–15 *Our wishes
. . . effects* i.e. our wishes, that you might supplant Albany, may
materialize   16 *musters* enlistments   *conduct his pow'rs* lead his
army   17 *change names* i.e. exchange the name of "mistress" for
"master"   *distaff* spinning-staff (symbol of the housewife)   21 *mistress's* (At present she plays the rôle of master, but, mated with
Edmund, she would again "change names.")   24 *Conceive* understand   28 *usurps* wrongfully occupies

Enter Albany.

Goneril. I have been worth the whistle.

Albany.   O Goneril,

30   You are not worth the dust which the rude wind
      Blows in your face. I fear your disposition:
      That nature which contemns its origin
      Cannot be borderèd certain in itself.
      She that herself will sliver and disbranch

35   From her material sap, perforce must wither
      And come to deadly use.

Goneril. No more; the text is foolish.

Albany. Wisdom and goodness to the vile seem vile
      Filths savor but themselves. What have you done?

40   Tigers not daughters, what have you performed?
      A father, and a gracious agèd man,
      Whose reverence even the head-lugged bear would
          lick,
      Most barbarous, most degenerate, have you madded.
      Could my good brother suffer you to do it?

45   A man, a prince, by him so benefited!
      If that the heavens do not their visible spirits
      Send quickly down to tame these vile offenses,
      It will come,
      Humanity must perforce prey on itself,
      Like monsters of the deep.

50 *Goneril.*   Milk-livered man,
      That bear'st a cheek for blows, a head for wrongs;
      Who hast not in thy brows an eye discerning
      Thine honor from thy suffering; that not know'st
      Fools do those villains pity who are punished

---

29 *worth the whistle* i.e. valued enough to be welcomed home ("not
worth the whistle" applying proverbially to a "poor dog")   31 *fear
your disposition* distrust your nature   33 *borderèd certain* safely con-
tained (It will be unpredictably licentious.)   34 *sliver, disbranch* cut
off   35 *material sap* sustaining stock, nourishing trunk   39 *savor*
relish   42 *head-lugged* dragged with a head-chain (hence, surly)   *lick*
i.e. treat with affection   43 *degenerate* unnatural   *madded* maddened
46 *visible* made visible, material   48 *It* i.e. chaos   50 *Milk-livered*
i.e. spiritless   52–53 *discerning . . . suffering* distinguishing between
dishonor and tolerance   54 *Fools* i.e. only fools

Ere they have done their mischief. Where's thy
   drum?   55
France spreads his banners in our noiseless land,
With plumèd helm thy state begins to threat,
Whilst thou, a moral fool, sits still and cries
"Alack, why does he so?"

Albany.   See thyself, devil:
Proper deformity seems not in the fiend   60
So horrid as in woman.

Goneril.   O vain fool!

Albany. Thou changèd and self-covered thing, for
   shame
Bemonster not thy feature. Were't my fitness
To let these hands obey my blood,
They are apt enough to dislocate and tear   65
Thy flesh and bones. Howe'er thou art a fiend,
A woman's shape doth shield thee.

Goneril. Marry, your manhood — mew!

Enter a Messenger.

Albany. What news?

Messenger. O, my good lord, the Duke of Cornwall's
   dead,   70
   Slain by his servant, going to put out
   The other eye of Gloucester.

Albany.   Gloucester's eyes?

Messenger. A servant that he bred, thrilled with remorse,

---

55 *drum* i.e. military preparation   56 *noiseless* i.e. unaroused   57
helm war-helmet   58 *moral* moralizing   60 *Proper* i.e. fair-surfaced
62 *changèd* transformed (diabolically, as in witchcraft)   *self-covered*
i.e. your natural self overwhelmed by evil, or, devil disguised as
woman   63 *Bemonster . . . feature* i.e. do not exchange your human
features for a monster's   *my fitness* fit for me   64 *blood* passion
68 *Marry* oath, derived from "By Mary"   *your manhood — mew*
i.e. "What a man!" followed by a contemptuous interjection, or mew
up (contain) this display of manliness   71 *going to* about to   73
bred reared   *thrilled with remorse* in the throes of pity

Opposed against the act, bending his sword
75 To his great master; who, thereat enraged,
Flew on him, and amongst them felled him dead;
But not without that harmful stroke which since
Hath plucked him after.

Albany   This shows you are above,
You justicers, that these our nether crimes
80 So speedily can venge. But, O poor Gloucester,
Lost he his other eye?

Messenger.   Both, both, my lord.
This letter, madam, craves a speedy answer.
'Tis from your sister.

Goneril.   (aside) One way I like this well;
But being widow, and my Gloucester with her,
85 May all the building in my fancy pluck
Upon my hateful life. Another way
The news is not so tart. — I'll read, and answer.
                                                    Exit.

Albany. Where was his son when they did take his
eyes?

Messenger. Come with my lady hither.

Albany.   He is not here.
90 Messenger. No, my good lord; I met him back again.

Albany. Knows he the wickedness?

Messenger. Ay, my good lord. 'Twas he informed
against him,
And quit the house on purpose, that their punishment
Might have the freer course.

Albany.   Gloucester, I live
95 To thank thee for the love thou showed'st the King,
And to revenge thine eyes. Come hither, friend.
Tell me what more thou know'st.   Exit all.

76 *amongst them* i.e. aided by the others 78 *plucked him after*
drawn him along (to death) 79 *justicers* dispensers of justice *nether
crimes* sins committed here below 80 *venge* avenge 82 *craves* requires 85–86 *May . . . life* i.e. may make my life hateful by destroying my dream castles 86 *Another way* the other way (probably
the removal of Cornwall as an obstacle to sole reign with Edmund)
87 *tart* distasteful 90 *back* going back

※

ACT IV, SCENE III

Enter Kent and a Gentleman.

Kent. Why the King of France is so suddenly gone
    back know you no reason?
Gentleman. Something he left imperfect in the state,
    which since his coming forth is thought of, which
    imports to the kingdom so much fear and danger   **5**
    that his personal return was most required and
    necessary.
Kent. Who hath he left behind him general?
Gentleman. The Marshal of France, Monsieur La Far.
Kent. Did your letters pierce the Queen to any dem-   **10**
    onstration of grief?
Gentleman. Ay, sir. She took them, read them in my
       presence,
    And now and then an ample tear trilled down
    Her delicate cheek. It seemed she was a queen
    Over her passion, who, most rebel-like,   **15**
    Sought to be king o'er her.
Kent.   O, then it movèd her?
Gentleman. Not to a rage. Patience and sorrow strove
    Who should express her goodliest. You have seen
    Sunshine and rain at once — her smiles and tears
    Were like, a better way: those happy smilets   **20**
    That played on her ripe lip seem not to know
    What guests were in her eyes, which parted thence
    As pearls from diamonds dropped. In brief,
    Sorrow would be a rarity most belovèd,
    If all could so become it

IV, iii, 3 *imperfect . . . state* i.e. rift in affairs of state 5 *imports*
means *fear* uneasiness 6 *most* most urgently 10 *pierce* goad 13
trilled trickled 15 *who* which 18 *goodliest* i.e. most becomingly
20 *Were . . . way* i.e. improved upon that spectacle 24 *rarity* gem

25 *Kent.*   Made she no verbal question?
    Gentleman. Faith, once or twice she heaved the name
        of father
        Pantingly forth, as if it pressed her heart;
        Cried "Sisters, sisters, shame of ladies, sisters!
        Kent, father, sisters? What, i' th' storm i' th' night?
30   Let pity not be believed!" There she shook
        The holy water from her heavenly eyes,
        And clamor moistened; then away she started
        To deal with grief alone.
    Kent.   It is the stars,
        The stars above us govern our conditions;
35   Else one self mate and make could not beget
        Such different issues. You spoke not with her since?
    Gentleman. No.
    Kent. Was this before the King returned?
    Gentleman.   No, since.
    Kent. Well, sir, the poor distressèd Lear's i' th' town;
40   Who sometime, in his better tune, remembers
        What we are come about, and by no means
        Will yield to see his daughter.
    Gentleman.   Why, good sir?
    Kent. A sovereign shame so elbows him; his own un-
        kindness,
        That stripped her from his benediction, turned her
45   To foreign casualties, gave her dear rights
        To his dog-hearted daughters — these things sting
        His mind so venomously that burning shame
        Detains him from Cordelia.
    Gentleman.   Alack, poor gentleman.
    Kent. Of Albany's and Cornwall's powers you heard
        not?
50 *Gentleman.* 'Tis so; they are afoot.

26–27 *heaved . . . forth* uttered . . . chokingly 30 *Let pity* let it
for pity 32 *clamor moistened* i.e. mixed, and thus muted, lamentation with tears 34 *govern our conditions* determine our characters
35 *Else . . . make* otherwise the same husband and wife 36 *issues*
children 40 *better tune* i.e. more rational state, less jangled 43
sovereign overruling *elbows* jogs 44 *stripped* cut off *benediction*
blessing 45 *casualties* chances 50 *'Tis so* i.e. I have to this extent

Kent. Well, sir, I'll bring you to our master Lear
　　And leave you to attend him. Some dear cause
　　Will in concealment wrap me up awhile.
　　When I am known aright, you shall not grieve
　　Lending me this acquaintance. I pray you go　　　　　　55
　　Along with me.　　　　　　　　　　　*Exit both.*

✄

ACT IV, SCENE IV

*Enter, with Drum and Colors, Cordelia, Gentle-
man (Doctor), and Soldiers.*

Cordelia. Alack, 'tis he! Why, he was met even now
　　As mad as the vexed sea, singing aloud,
　　Crowned with rank fumiter and furrow weeds,
　　With hardocks, hemlock, nettles, cuckoo flow'rs,
　　Darnel, and all the idle weeds that grow　　　　　　5
　　In our sustaining corn. A century send forth!
　　Search every acre in the high-grown field
　　And bring him to our eye. (*Exit an Officer.*) What
　　　　can man's wisdom
　　In the restoring his bereavèd sense?
　　He that helps him take all my outward worth.　　　10
Doctor. There is means, madam.
　　Our foster nurse of nature is repose,
　　The which he lacks. That to provoke in him
　　Are many simples operative, whose power
　　Will close the eye of anguish.

---

52 *dear cause* important purpose IV, iv, 3 *fumiter* fumitory *furrow
weeds* those that appear after ploughing 4 *hardocks* variously iden-
tified as burdock, "hoar dock," "harlock," etc. 5 *Darnel* tares *idle*
useless 6 *sustaining corn* life-giving wheat *century* troop of a hundred men 8 *can* i.e. can accomplish 9 *bereavèd* bereft 10 *outward
worth* material possessions 12 *foster* fostering 13 *provoke* induce
14 *simples operative* medicinal herbs, sedatives

15 *Cordelia.*   All blest secrets,
   All you unpublished virtues of the earth,
   Spring with my tears; be aidant and remediate
   In the good man's distress. Seek, seek for him,
   Lest his ungoverned rage dissolve the life
   That wants the means to lead it.

Enter Messenger.

20 *Messenger.*   News, madam.
   The British pow'rs are marching hitherward.
   Cordelia. 'Tis known before. Our preparation stands
   In expectation of them. O dear father,
   It is thy business that I go about.
25 Therefore great France
   My mourning, and importuned tears hath pitied.
   No blown ambition doth our arms incite,
   But love, dear love, and our aged father's right.
   Soon may I hear and see him!   *Exit all*

ACT IV, SCENE V

Enter Regan and Steward (Oswald).

Regan. But are my brother's pow'rs set forth?
Oswald.   Ay, madam
Regan. Himself in person there?
Oswald.   Madam, with much ado
   Your sister is the better soldier.

---

16 *unpublished virtues* i.e. little-known benign herbs 17 *Spring* grow
remediate remedial 20 *means* i.e. power of reason *lead it* govern it
(the rage) 25 *Therefore* therefor, because of that 26 *importuned*
importunate 27 *blown* swollen IV, v, 2 *much ado* great bother

Regan. Lord Edmund spake not with your lord at
   home?   5

Oswald. No, madam.

Regan. What might import my sister's letter to him?

Oswald. I know not, lady.

Regan. Faith, he is posted hence on serious matter.
   It was great ignorance, Gloucester's eyes being out,   10
   To let him live. Where he arrives he moves
   All hearts against us. Edmund, I think, is gone,
   In pity of his misery, to dispatch
   His nighted life; moreover, to descry
   The strength o' th' enemy.   15

Oswald. I must needs after him, madam, with my
   letter.

Regan. Our troops set forth tomorrow. Stay with us.
   The ways are dangerous.

Oswald.   I may not, madam.
   My lady charged my duty in this business.

Regan. Why should she write to Edmund? Might not
   you   20
   Transport her purposes by word? Belike,
   Some things — I know not what. I'll love thee
   much,
   Let me unseal the letter.

Oswald.   Madam, I had rather —

Regan. I know your lady does not love her husband,
   I am sure of that; and at her late being here   25
   She gave strange eliads and most speaking looks
   To noble Edmund. I know you are of her bosom.

Oswald. I, madam?

Regan. I speak in understanding — y'are, I know't —
   Therefore I do advise you and take this note: 30
   My lord is dead; Edmund and I have talked,

---

7 *import* bear as its message 9 *is posted* has sped 10 *ignorance*
error 14 *nighted* benighted, blinded 19 *charged* strictly ordered 21
Transport her purposes convey her intentions *Belike* probably 25
late recently 26 *eliads* amorous glances 27 *of her bosom* in her
confidence 30 *take this note* note this

And more convenient is he for my hand
Than for your lady's. You may gather more.
If you do find him, pray you give him this;
35   And when your mistress hears thus much from you,
I pray desire her call her wisdom to her.
So fare you well.
If you do chance to hear of that blind traitor,
Preferment falls on him that cuts him off.

Oswald. Would I could meet him, madam! I should
40   show
What party I do follow.

Regan.   Fare thee well. *Exit both.*

❧

ACT IV, SCENE VI

Enter Gloucester and Edgar.

Gloucester. When shall I come to th' top of that same
hill?
Edgar. You do climb up it now. Look how we labor.
Gloucester. Methinks the ground is even.
Edgar.   Horrible steep.
Hark, do you hear the sea?
Gloucester.   No, truly.
5   *Edgar.* Why, then your other senses grow imperfect
By your eyes' anguish.
Gloucester.   So may it. be indeed.
Methinks thy voice is altered, and thou speak'st

---

32 *convenient* appropriate   33 *gather more* i.e. draw your own conclusions   34 *this* this word, this reminder   36 *call* recall   39 *Preferment* advancement   IV. vi, 6 *anguish* affliction

In better phrase and matter than thou didst.

Edgar. Y'are much deceived. In nothing am I changed
But in my garments.

Gloucester.   Methinks y'are better spoken.   10

Edgar. Come on, sir; here's the place. Stand still.
How fearful
And dizzy 'tis to cast one's eyes so low!
The crows and choughs that wing the midway air
Show scarce so gross as beetles. Halfway down
Hangs one that gathers sampire — dreadful trade;   15
Methinks he seems no bigger than his head.
The fishermen that walk upon the beach
Appear like mice; and yond tall anchoring bark,
Diminished to her cock; her cock, a buoy
Almost too small for sight. The murmuring surge   20
That on th' unnumb'red idle pebble chafes
Cannot be heard so high. I'll look no more,
Lest my brain turn, and the deficient sight
Topple down headlong.

Gloucester.   Set me where you stand.

Edgar. Give me your hand. You are now within a foot   25
Of th' extreme verge. For all beneath the moon
Would I not leap upright.

Gloucester.   Let go my hand.
Here, friend, 's another purse; in it a jewel
Well worth a poor man's taking. Fairies and gods
Prosper it with thee. Go thou further off;   30
Bid me farewell, and let me hear thee going.

Edgar. Now fare ye well, good sir.

Gloucester.   With all my heart.

Edgar. (*aside*) Why I do trifle thus with his despair
Is done to cure it.

---

13 *choughs* jackdaws *midway* i.e. halfway down 14 *gross* large
15 *sampire* samphire (aromatic herb used in relishes) 18 *anchoring*
anchored 19 *Diminished . . . cock* reduced to the size of her cock-
boat 21 *unnumb'red idle pebble* i.e. barren reach of countless pebbles 23 *the deficient sight* i.e. my dizziness 24 *Topple* topple me
27 *upright* i.e. even upright, let alone forward 29 *Fairies* the usual
wardens of treasure 33 *Why . . . trifle* i.e. the reason I toy with
("done" in l. 34 being redundant)

Gloucester.   O you mighty gods!

                                                    He kneels.

35   This world I do renounce, and in your sights
        Shake patiently my great affliction off.
        If I could bear it longer and not fall
        To quarrel with your great opposeless wills,
        My snuff and loathèd part of nature should
40   Burn itself out. If Edgar live, O bless him!
        Now, fellow, fare thee well.

                                        He falls forward and swoons.

Edgar.   Gone, sir — farewell.
        And yet I know not how conceit may rob
        The treasury of life when life itself
        Yields to the theft. Had he been where he thought,
45   By this had thought been past. Alive or dead?
        Ho you, sir! Friend! Hear you, sir? Speak!
        Thus might he pass indeed. Yet he revives.
        What are you, sir?

Gloucester.   Away, and let me die.

Edgar. Hadst thou been aught but gossamer, feathers,
        air,
50   So many fathom down precipitating,
        Thou'dst shivered like an egg; but thou dost
        breathe,
        Hast heavy substance, bleed'st not, speak'st, art
        sound.
        Ten masts at each make not the altitude
        Which thou hast perpendicularly fell.
55   Thy life's a miracle. Speak yet again.

Gloucester. But have I fall'n, or no?

Edgar. From the dread summit of this chalky bourn.
        Look up a-height. The shrill-gorged lark so far
        Cannot be seen or heard. Do but look up.

37–38 *fall . . . with* i.e. rebel against (irreligiously) 38 *opposeless*
not to be opposed 39 *My snuff . . . nature* i.e. the guttering and
hateful tag end of my life 42 *conceit* imagination 44 *Yields to* i.e.
welcomes 50 *precipitating* falling 53 *at each* end to end 55 *life*
survival 57 *bourn* boundary, headland 58 *a-height* on high *gorged*
throated

Gloucester. Alack, I have no eyes.   60
  Is wretchedness deprived that benefit
  To end itself by death? 'Twas yet some comfort
  When misery could beguile the tyrant's rage
  And frustrate his proud will.
Edgar.   Give me your arm.
  Up — so. How is't? Feel you your legs? You stand.   65
Gloucester. Too well, too well.
Edgar.   This is above all strangeness.
  Upon the crown o' th' cliff what thing was that
  Which parted from you?
Gloucester.   A poor unfortunate beggar.
Edgar. As I stood here below, methought his eyes
  Were two full moons; he had a thousand noses,   70
  Horns whelked and waved like the enridgèd sea.
  It was some fiend. Therefore, thou happy father,
  Think that the clearest gods, who make them honors
  Of men's impossibilities, have preservèd thee.
Gloucester. I do remember now. Henceforth I'll bear   75
  Affliction till it do cry out itself
  "Enough, enough, and die." That thing you speak
    of,
  I took it for a man. Often 'twould say
  "The fiend, the fiend" — he led me to that place.
Edgar. Bear free and patient thoughts.

Enter Lear mad, bedecked with weeds.

                              But who comes here?   80
  The safer sense will ne'er accommodate
  His master thus.
Lear. No, they cannot touch me for coining;
  I am the King himself.

63 *beguile* outwit 65 *Feel* test 71 *whelked* corrugated *enridgèd*
blown into ridges 72 *happy father* lucky old man 73 *clearest* purest
73–74 *who . . . impossibilities* i.e. whose glory it is to do for man
what he cannot do for himself 80 *free* (of despair) 81 *safer* saner
accommodate accoutre 82 *His* its 83 *touch* i.e. interfere with *coining* minting coins (a royal prerogative)

85 *Edgar.* O thou side-piercing sight!

Lear. Nature's above art in that respect. There's your
press money. That fellow handles his bow like a
crow-keeper. Draw me a clothier's yard. Look, look,
a mouse! Peace, peace; this piece of toasted cheese
90 will do't. There's my gauntlet; I'll prove it on a
giant. Bring up the brown bills. O, well flown,
bird. I' th' clout, i' th' clout — hewgh! Give the
word.

Edgar. Sweet marjoram.

95 *Lear.* Pass.

Gloucester. I know that voice.

Lear. Ha! Goneril with a white beard? They flattered
me like a dog, and told me I had the white hairs in
my beard ere the black ones were there. To say
100 "ay" and "no" to everything that I said! "Ay" and
"no" too was no good divinity. When the rain
came to wet me once, and the wind to make me
chatter; when the thunder would not peace at my
bidding; there I found 'em, there I smelt 'em out.
105 Go to, they are not men o' their words. They told
me I was everything. 'Tis a lie — I am not ague-
proof.

Gloucester. The trick of that voice I do well remember.
Is't not the King?

Lear.   Ay, every inch a king.

---

86 *Nature . . . respect* i.e. a born king is above a made king in
legal immunity (cf. the coeval debate on the relative merits of poets
of nature, i.e. born, and poets of art, i.e. made by self-effort) 87
press money i.e. the "king's shilling" (token payment on military
impressment or enlistment) 88 *crow-keeper* i.e. farmhand warding
off crows *clothier's yard* i.e. arrow (normally a yard long) 90
gauntlet armored glove (hurled as challenge) *prove it on* maintain
it against 91 *well flown* hawking cry 92 *clout* bull's eye, archery
term 93 *word* password 94 *Sweet marjoram* herb, associated with
treating madness 98 *like a dog* i.e. fawningly *I . . . beard* i.e.
was wise 99–100 *To say . . . "no"* i.e. to agree 101 *no good divinity* i.e. bad theology (For "good divinity" cf. 2 Corinthians 1:18:
"But as God is true, our word to you was not yea and nay"; also
Matthew 5:36–37, James 5:12). 106–7 *ague-proof* proof against
chills and fever 108 *trick* peculiarity

When I do stare, see how the subject quakes.   110
I pardon that man's life. What was thy cause?
Adultery?
Thou shalt not die. Die for adultery? No.
The wren goes to't, and the small gilded fly
Does lecher in my sight.   115
Let copulation thrive; for Gloucester's bastard son
Was kinder to his father than my daughters
Got 'tween the lawful sheets.
To't, luxury, pell-mell, for I lack soldiers.
Behold yond simp'ring dame,   120
Whose face between her forks presages snow,
That minces virtue, and does shake the head
To hear of pleasure's name.
The fitchew nor the soilèd horse goes to't
With a more riotous appetite.   125
Down from the waist they are Centaurs,
Though women all above.
But to the girdle do the gods inherit,
Beneath is all the fiend's.
There's hell, there's darkness, there is the sulphur-   130
ous pit; burning, scalding, stench, consumption.
Fie, fie, fie! pah, pah! Give me an ounce of civet;
good apothecary, sweeten my imagination! There's
money for thee.

Gloucester. O, let me kiss that hand.   135

Lear. Let me wipe it first; it smells of mortality.

Gloucester. O ruined piece of nature; this great world
    Shall so wear out to naught. Dost thou know me?

---

111 *cause* case 118 *Got* begotten 119 *luxury* lechery *for . . . soldiers* (and therefore a higher birth rate) 121 *whose . . . snow* i.e.
who presents the signs of being sexually cold 122 *minces* mincingly
affects 124 *fitchew* polecat, prostitute *soilèd* pastured 126 *Centaurs*
(lustful creatures of mythology, half-human and half-beast) 128
girdle waist *inherit* possess 132 *civet* musk perfume 136 *mortality*
death 137–138 *this . . . naught* i.e. the universe (macrocosm) will
decay like this man (microcosm)

Lear. I remember thine eyes well enough. Dost thou
140 squiny at me? No, do thy worst, blind Cupid; I'll
not love. Read thou this challenge; mark but the
penning of it.

Gloucester. Were all thy letters suns, I could not see.

Edgar. (*aside*) I would not take this from report — it
is,
145 And my heart breaks at it.

Lear. Read.

Gloucester. What, with the case of eyes?

Lear. O, ho, are you there with me? No eyes in your
head, nor no money in your purse? Your eyes are in
150 a heavy case, your purse in a light; yet you see how
this world goes.

Gloucester. I see it feelingly.

Lear. What, art mad? A man may see how this world
goes with no eyes. Look with thine ears. See how
155 yond justice rails upon yond simple thief. Hark in
thine ear. Change places and, handy-dandy, which
is the justice, which is the thief? Thou hast seen a
farmer's dog bark at a beggar?

Gloucester. Ay, sir.

160 *Lear.* And the creature run from the cur. There thou
mightst behold the great image of authority — a
dog's obeyed in office.

Thou rascal beadle, hold thy bloody hand!

Why dost thou lash that whore? Strip thy own back.
165 Thou hotly lusts to use her in that kind

For which thou whip'st her. The usurer hangs the
cozener.

144 *take* accept   147 *case* sockets   148 *are . . . me* is that the situation   150 *case* plight (pun)   152 *feelingly* (1) only by touch (2) by feeling pain   155 *simple* mere   156 *handy-dandy* old formula used in the child's game of choosing which hand   161 *great image* universal symbol   161–62 *a dog's . . . office* i.e. man bows to authority regardless of who exercises it   163 *beadle* parish constable   165 *lusts wish* *kind* i.e. same act   166 *The usurer . . . cozener* i.e. the great cheat, some money-lending judge, sentences to death the little cheat

Through tattered clothes small vices do appear;
Robes and furred gowns hide all. Plate sin with
  gold,
And the strong lance of justice hurtless breaks;
Arm it in rags, a pygmy's straw does pierce it.   170
None does offend, none — I say none! I'll able 'em.
Take that of me, my friend, who have the power
To seal th' accuser's lips. Get thee glass eyes
And, like a scurvy politician, seem
To see the things thou dost not. Now, now, now,
  now!   175
Pull off my boots. Harder, harder! So.

Edgar. O, matter and impertinency mixed;
  Reason in madness.

Lear. If thou wilt weep my fortunes, take my eyes.
  I know thee well enough; thy name is Gloucester.   180
  Thou must be patient. We came crying hither;
  Thou know'st, the first time that we smell the air
  We wawl and cry. I will preach to thee. Mark.

Gloucester. Alack, alack the day.

Lear. When we are born, we cry that we are come   185
  To this great stage of fools. — This' a good block.
  It were a delicate stratagem to shoe
  A troop of horse with felt. I'll put't in proof,
  And when I have stol'n upon these son-in-laws,
  Then kill, kill, kill, kill, kill, kill!   190

Enter a Gentleman with Attendants.

Gentleman. O, here he is! Lay hand upon him. — Sir,
  Your most dear daughter —

Lear. No rescue? What, a prisoner? I am even
  The natural fool of fortune. Use me well;

---

167 *appear* show plainly 169 *hurtless* without hurting 170 *Arm
. . . rags* i.e. armored only in rags 171 *able* authorize 172 *that*
(i.e. the assurance of immunity) 174 *scurvy politician* vile oppor-
tunist 177 *matter and impertinency* sense and nonsense 186 *block*
felt hat 187 *delicate* subtle 188 *in proof* to the test 194 *natural
fool* born plaything

195   You shall have ransom. Let me have surgeons;
    I am cut to th' brains.

Gentleman.   You shall have anything.

Lear. No seconds? All myself?
    Why, this would make a man a man of salt,
    To use his eyes for garden waterpots,
200   Ay, and laying autumn's dust. I will die bravely,
    Like a smug bridegroom. What, I will be jovial!
    Come, come, I am a king; masters, know you that?

Gentleman. You are a royal one, and we obey you.

Lear. Then there's life in't. Come, an you get it, you
205   shall get it by running. Sa, sa, sa, sa!

                  Exit running, followed by Attendants.

Gentleman. A sight most pitiful in the meanest
    wretch,
    Past speaking of in a king. Thou hast one daughter
    Who redeems nature from the general curse
    Which twain have brought her to.

Edgar. Hail, gentle sir.

210 *Gentleman.*   Sir, speed you. What's your will?

Edgar. Do you hear aught, sir, of a battle toward?

Gentleman. Most sure and vulgar. Every one hears that
    Which can distinguish sound.

Edgar.   But, by your favor,
    How near's the other army?

215 *Gentleman.* Near and on speedy foot. The main descry
    Stands on the hourly thought.

Edgar.   I thank you, sir. That's all.

Gentleman. Though that the Queen on special cause
    is here,
    Her army is moved on.

---

196 *cut* wounded   198 *salt* i.e. all tears   201 *smug bridegroom* spruce bridegroom (the image suggested by the secondary meaning of "bravely," i.e. handsomely, and the sexual suggestion of "will die") 204 *life* (and therefore "hope")   205 *Sa . . . sa* hunting and rallying cry   208 *general curse* universal condemnation   209 *twain* i.e. the other two   210 *speed* God speed   211 *toward* impending   212 *sure and vulgar* commonly known certainty   215 *on speedy foot* rapidly marching   215–16 *main . . . thought* sight of the main body is expected hourly

Edgar.   I thank you, sir.
                                    Exit Gentleman.

Gloucester. You ever-gentle gods, take my breath
   from me;
  Let not my worser spirit tempt me again   220
  To die before you please.

Edgar.   Well pray you, father.

Gloucester. Now, good sir, what are you?

Edgar. A most poor man, made tame to fortune's
   blows,
  Who, by the art of known and feeling sorrows,
  Am pregnant to good pity. Give me your hand;   225
  I'll lead you to some biding.

Gloucester.   Hearty thanks.
  The bounty and the benison of heaven
  To boot, and boot.

Enter Steward (Oswald).

Oswald.   A proclaimed prize! Most happy;
  That eyeless head of thine was first framed flesh
  To raise my fortunes. Thou old unhappy traitor,   230
  Briefly thyself remember. The sword is out
  That must destroy thee.

Gloucester.   Now let thy friendly hand
  Put strength enough to't.   *Edgar interposes.*

Oswald.   Wherefore, bold peasant,
  Dar'st thou support a published traitor? Hence,
  Lest that th' infection of his fortune take   235
  Like hold on thee. Let go his arm.

Edgar. Chill not let go, zir, without vurther 'casion.

Oswald. Let go, slave, or thou diest.

Edgar. Good gentleman, go your gait, and let poor
  voke pass. An chud ha' bin zwaggered out of my life,   240

220 *worser spirit* i.e. bad angel 223 *tame* submissive 224 *art . . .
sorrows* i.e. lesson of sorrows painfully experienced 225 *pregnant*
prone 226 *biding* biding place 228 *proclaimed prize* i.e. one with
a price on his head *happy* lucky 229 *framed flesh* born, created
231 *thyself remember* i.e., pray, think of your soul 232 *friendly* i.e.
unconsciously befriending 234 *published* proclaimed 237 *Chill* I'll
(rustic dialect) *vurther 'casion* further occasion 239 *gait* way 240
voke folk

'twould not ha' bin zo long as 'tis by a vortnight.
Nay, come not near th' old man. Keep out, che
vore ye, or Ise try whether your costard or my ballow be the harder. Chill be plain with you.

245 Oswald. Out, dunghill!   *They fight.*

Edgar. Chill pick your teeth, zir. Come, No matter
vor your foins.   *Oswald falls.*

Oswald. Slave, thou hast slain me. Villain, take my
purse.
If ever thou wilt thrive, bury my body,
250 And give the letters which thou find'st about me
To Edmund Earl of Gloucester. Seek him out
Upon the English party. O, untimely death!
Death!   *He dies.*

Edgar. I know thee well. A serviceable villain,
255 As duteous to the vices of thy mistress
As badness would desire.

Gloucester.   What, is he dead?

Edgar. Sit you down, father; rest you.
Let's see these pockets; the letters that he speaks of
May be my friends. He's dead; I am only sorry
260 He had no other deathsman. Let us see.
Leave, gentle wax; and, manners, blame us not
To know our enemies' minds. We rip their hearts;
Their papers is more lawful.   *(reads the letter)*
"Let our reciprocal vows be remembered. You have
265 many opportunities to cut him off. If your will
want not, time and place will be fruitfully offered.
There is nothing done, if he return the conqueror.
Then am I the prisoner, and his bed my gaol; from
the loathed warmth whereof deliver me, and supply
270 the place for .your labor.

243 *An chud* if I could *zwaggered* swaggered, bluffed 242–43 *che
vore* I warrant, assure 243 *Ise* I shall *costard* head 243–44 *ballow*
cudgel 246 *Chill pick* i.e. I'll knock out 247 *foins* thrusts 248
Villain serf 250 *letters* letter *about* upon 252 *party* side 254 *serviceable* usable 255 *duteous* dutiful 260 *deathsman* executioner 261 *Leave, gentle wax* by your leave, kind seal (formula
used in opening sealed documents) 262 *To know* i.e. for growing
intimate with 267 *Their papers* i.e. to rip their papers 266 *want not*
is not lacking 268 *gaol* jail

"Your (wife, so I would say) affectionate servant,
                                              "GONERIL."

O indistinguished space of woman's will —
A plot upon her virtuous husband's life,
And the exchange my brother! Here in the sands   275
Thee I'll rake up, the post unsanctified
Of murderous lechers; and in the mature time
With this ungracious paper strike the sight
Of the death-practiced Duke. For him 'tis well
That of thy death and business I can tell.   28c

Gloucester. The King is mad. How stiff is my vile
    sense,
That I stand up, and have ingenious feeling
Of my huge sorrows! Better I were distract;
So should my thoughts be severed from my griefs,
And woes by wrong imaginations lose   23'
The knowledge of themselves.   *Drum afar off.*
Edgar.   Give me your hand.
Far off methinks I hear the beaten drum.
Come, father, I'll bestow you with a friend.
                                         Exit both.

ACT IV, SCENE VII

Enter Cordelia, Kent, Doctor, and Gentleman.

Cordelia. O thou good Kent, how shall I live and
    work
To match thy goodness? My life will be too short
And every measure fail me.
Kent. To be acknowledged, madam, is o'erpaid.

271 *would* wish to   273 *indistinguished* unlimited   *will* desire   275 *exchange* substitute   276 *rake up* cover, bury   277 *in the mature* at the ripe   278 *strike* blast   279 *death-practiced* whose death is plotted   281 *stiff* obstinate   *vile sense* i.e. hateful consciousness   282 *ingenious feeling* i.e. awareness   283 *distract* distracted   285 *wrong imaginations* i.e. delusions   288 *bestow* lodge

5   All my reports go with the modest truth;
   Nor more nor clipped, but so.

Cordelia.   Be better suited.
   These weeds are memories of those worser hours.
   I prithee put them off.

Kent.   Pardon, dear madam.
   Yet to be known shortens my made intent.

10   My boon I make it that you know me not
   Till time and I think meet.

Cordelia. Then be't so, my good lord. (*to the Doctor*)
   How does the King?

Doctor. Madam, sleeps still.

Cordelia. O you kind gods,

15   Cure this great breach in his abusèd nature!
   Th' untuned and jarring senses, O, wind up
   Of this child-changèd father!

Doctor.   So please your Majesty
   That we may wake the King? He hath slept long.

Cordelia. Be governed by your knowledge, and proceed

20   I' th' sway of your own will. Is he arrayed?

       Enter Lear in a chair carried by Servants.

Gentleman. Ay, madam. In the heaviness of sleep
   We put fresh garments on him.

Doctor. Be by, good madam, when we do awake him.
   I doubt not of his temperance.

Cordelia.   Very well.   *Music.*

25 *Doctor.* Please you draw near. Louder the music there.

Cordelia. O my dear father, restoration hang
   Thy medicine on my lips, and let this kiss
   Repair those violent harms that my two sisters
   Have in thy reverence made.

IV, vii, 5 *go* conform 6 *clipped* i.e. less (curtailed) *suited* attired
7 *weeds* clothes *memories* reminders. 9 *Yet . . . intent* i.e. to
reveal myself just yet would mar my plan 10 *My boon . . . it* the
reward I ask is 11 *meet* proper 15 *abused* confused, disturbed 16
jarring discordant *wind up* tune 17 *child-changèd* (1) changed to
a child (2) changed by his children (suggesting "changeling," wherein
mental defect is associated with the malignance of witches) 20 *I' th'
sway of* according to 28 *harms* wounds 29 *reverence* reverend
person

Kent.   Kind and dear princess.

Cordelia. Had you not been their father, these white
    flakes   30
  Did challenge pity of them. Was this a face
  To be opposed against the jarring winds?
  To stand against the deep dread-bolted thunder?
  In the most terrible and nimble stroke
  Of quick cross lightning to watch, poor perdu,   35
  With this thin helm? Mine enemy's dog,
  Though he had bit me, should have stood that
    night
  Against my fire; and wast thou fain, poor father,
  To hovel thee with swine and rogues forlorn
  In short and musty straw? Alack, alack,   40
  'Tis wonder that thy life and wits at once
  Had not concluded all. —He wakes. Speak to him.

Doctor. Madam, do you; 'tis fittest.

Cordelia. How does my royal lord? How fares your
    Majesty?

Lear. You do me wrong to take me out o' th' grave.   45
  Thou art a soul in bliss; but I am bound
  Upon a wheel of fire, that mine own tears
  Do scald like molten lead.

Cordelia.   Sir, do you know me?

Lear. You are a spirit, I know. Where did you die?

Cordelia. Still, still, far wide!   50

Doctor. He's scarce awake. Let him alone awhile.

Lear. Where have I been? Where am I? Fair daylight?
  I am mightily abused. I should e'en die with pity
  To see another thus. I know not what to say.
  I will not swear these are my hands. Let's see —   55
  I feel this pin prick. Would I were assured
  Of my condition.

Cordelia.   O look upon me, sir,

30 *flakes* strands of hair   31 *challenge* demand   33 *deep dread-bolted*
deep-voiced and full of dreadful bolts   35 *perdu* (1) expendable out-
post (military term) (2) lost one   36 *helm* military helmet; here.
thin hair   38 *fain* glad   40 *short* scanty, tramped to fragments   47
wheel of fire (implement combining the tortures of breaking and burning, figuring in medieval visions of hell)   50 *wide* off the mark   53
abused confused

And hold your hand in benediction o'er me.
You must not kneel.

Lear.   Pray, do not mock me.
60   I am a very foolish fond old man,
Fourscore and upward, not an hour more nor less;
And, to deal plainly,
I fear I am not in my perfect mind.
Methinks I should know you, and know this man;
65   Yet I am doubtful, for I am mainly ignorant
What place this is; and all the skill I have
Remembers not these garments; nor I know not
Where I did lodge last night. Do not laugh at me;
For, as I am a man, I think this lady
To be my child Cordelia.
70   *Cordelia.*   And so I am! I am!
Lear. Be your tears wet? Yes, faith. I pray weep not.
If you have poison for me, I will drink it.
I know you do not love me; for your sisters
Have, as I do remember, done me wrong.
75   You have some cause, they have not.
Cordelia.   No cause, no cause.
Lear. Am I in France?
Kent.   In your own kingdom, sir.
Lear. Do not abuse me.
Doctor. Be comforted, good madam. The great rage
You see is killed in him; and yet it is danger
80   To make him even o'er the time he has lost.
Desire him to go in. Trouble him no more
Till further settling.
Cordelia. Will't please your Highness walk?
Lear.   You must bear with me.
Pray you now, forget and forgive. I am old and fool-
ish.   *Exit all but Kent and Gentleman.*
Gentleman. Holds it true, sir, that the Duke of Corn-
85   wall was so slain?
Kent. Most certain, sir.

77 *abuse* deceive   80 *even o'er* fill in   82 *settling* calming

Gentleman. Who is conductor of his people?

Kent. As 'tis said, the bastard son of Gloucester.

Gentleman. They say Edgar, his banished son, is with
the Earl of Kent in Germany.   90

Kent. Report is changeable. 'Tis time to look about;
the powers of the kingdom approach apace.

Gentleman. The arbitrement is like to be bloody. Fare
you well, sir.   *Exit.*

Kent. My point and period will be throughly wrought,   9.
Or well or ill, as this day's battle's fought.   *Exit.*

ACT V, SCENE I

Enter, with Drum and Colors, Edmund, Regan,
Gentleman, and Soldiers.

Edmund. Know of the Duke if his last purpose hold,
Or whether since he is advised by aught
To change the course. He's full of alteration
And self-reproving. Bring his constant pleasure.

Exit an Officer.

5 **Regan.** Our sister's man is certainly miscarried.
Edmund. 'Tis to be doubted, madam.
Regan.   Now, sweet lord,
You know the goodness I intend upon you.
Tell me, but truly — but then speak the truth —
Do you not love my sister?
Edmund.   In honored love.
10 **Regan.** But have you never found my brother's way
To the forfended place?
Edmund.   That thought abuses you.
Regan. I am doubtful that you have been conjunct
And bosomed with her, as far as we call hers.

V, i, s.d. *Drum and Colors* drummer and standard-bearers 1 *Know*
learn *last purpose hold* most recent intention (i.e. to fight) holds
good 2 *advised* induced 4 *constant pleasure* firm decision 5 *miscarried* met with mishap 6 *doubted* feared 7 *goodness I intend*
boon I plan to confer 9 *honored* honorable 11 *forfended* forbidden
abuses deceives 12–13 *doubtful . . . hers* i.e. fearful you have been
intimately linked with her both in mind and body

Edmund. No, by mine honor, madam.

Regan. I never shall endure her. Dear my lord,   15
  Be not familiar with her.

Edmund.   Fear me not.
  She and the Duke her husband!

> *Enter, with Drum and Colors, Albany,*
> *Goneril, Soldiers.*

Goneril. (aside) I had rather lose the battle than that
    sister
  Should loosen him and me.

Albany. Our very loving sister, well bemet.   20
  Sir, this I heard: the King is come to his daughter,
  With others whom the rigor of our state
  Forced to cry out. Where I could not be honest,
  I never yet was valiant. For this business,
  It touches us as France invades our land,   25
  Not bolds the King with others, whom I fear
  Most just and heavy causes make oppose.

Edmund. Sir, you speak nobly.

Regan.   Why is this reasoned?

Goneril. Combine together 'gainst the enemy;
  For these domestic and particular broils   30
  Are not the question here.

Albany.   Let's then determine
  With th' ancient of war on our proceeding.

Edmund. I shall attend you presently at your tent.

Regan. Sister, you'll go with us?

Goneril. No.   35

Regan. 'Tis most convenient. Pray go with us.

Goneril. O ho, I know the riddle. — I will go.

> *Exit both the Armies.*

---

19 *loosen* separate 20 *bemet* met 22 *rigor* tyranny 23 *honest* honorable 25 *touches us as* concerns me because 26–27 *Not bolds . . . oppose* i.e. but not because he supports the King and others whose truly great grievances arouse them to arms 28 *reasoned* argued 30 *particular broils* private quarrels 31 *question* issue 32 *th' ancient of war* i.e. seasoned officers 33 *presently* immediately 36 *convenient* fitting *with us* (i.e. with her rather than Edmund as each leads an "army" from the stage) 37 *riddle* (i.e. the reason for Regan's strange demand)

Enter Edgar.

Edgar. (to Albany) If e'er your Grace had speech with
    man so poor,
  Hear me one word.
Albany.   (to those departing) I'll overtake you.
40   (to Edgar) Speak.
Edgar. Before you fight the battle, ope this letter.
  If you have victory, let the trumpet sound
  For him that brought it. Wretched though I seem,
  I can produce a champion that will prove
45 What is avouchèd there. If you miscarry,
  Your business of the world hath so an end,
  And machination ceases. Fortune love you.
Albany. Stay till I have read the letter.
Edgar.   I was forbid it.
  When time shall serve, let but the herald cry,
50 And I'll appear again.
Albany. Why, fare thee well. I will o'erlook thy paper.
                         Exit Edgar.

Enter Edmund.

Edmund. The enemy's in view; draw up your powers.
  Here is the guess of their true strength and forces
  By diligent discovery; but your haste
  Is now urged on you.
55 Albany.   We will greet the time.
                                      Exit.
Edmund. To both these sisters have I sworn my love;
  Each jealous of the other, as the stung
  Are of the adder. Which of them shall I take?
  Both? One? Or neither? Neither can be enjoyed,

38 *had speech* i.e. has condescended to speak 42 *sound* sound a
summons 44 *prove* (in trial by combat) 45 *avouchèd* charged 47
machination i.e. all plots and counterplots 51 *o'erlook* look over 52
powers troops 53 *guess* estimate 54 *discovery* reconnoitering 55
greet i.e. meet the demands of 57 *jealous* suspicious

If both remain alive. To take the widow   60
Exasperates, makes mad her sister Goneril;
And hardly shall I carry out my side,
Her husband being alive. Now then, we'll use
His countenance for the battle, which being done,
Let her who would be rid of him devise   65
His speedy taking off. As for the mercy
Which he intends to Lear and to Cordelia —
The battle done, and they within our power,
Shall never see his pardon; for my state
Stands on me to defend, not to debate.   *Exit.*   70

❧

ACT V, SCENE II

Alarum within. Enter, with Drum and Colors,
Lear held by the hand by Cordelia; and Soldiers
of France, over the stage and exit.

Enter Edgar and Gloucester.

Edgar. Here, father, take the shadow of this tree
For your good host. Pray that the right may thrive.
If ever I return to you again,
I'll bring you comfort.
Gloucester.   Grace go with you, sir.
                              Exit Edgar.

Alarum and retreat within. Enter Edgar.

62 *hardly . . . side* with difficulty shall I play my part (as Goneril's
lover, or as a great power in England)   64 *countenance* backing
69–70 *my state . . . debate* i.e. my status depends upon my strength,
not my arguments   V. ii. 4 s.p. *Alarum and retreat* (trumpet sounds,
signalling the beginning and the ending of a battle)

5   *Edgar.* Away, old man! Give me thy hand. Away!
       King Lear hath lost, he and his daughter ta'en.
       Give me thy hand. Come on.
    Gloucester. No further, sir. A man may rot even here.
    Edgar. What, in ill thoughts again? Men must endure
10   Their going hence, even as their coming hither;
       Ripeness is all. Come on.
    Gloucester.   And that's true too.

                                Exit both.

ACT V, SCENE III

*Enter, in conquest, with Drum and Colors,
Edmund; Lear and Cordelia as prisoners;
Soldiers, Captain.*

  Edmund. Some officers take them away. Good guard
    Until their greater pleasures first be known
    That are to censure them.
  Cordelia.   We are not the first
    Who with best meaning have incurred the worst.
5   For thee, oppressèd king, I am cast down;
    Myself could else outfrown false Fortune's frown.
    Shall we not see these daughters and these sisters?
  Lear. No, no, no, no! Come, let's away to prison.
    We two alone will sing like birds i' th' cage.
10   When thou dost ask me blessing, I'll kneel down
    And ask of thee forgiveness. So we'll live,
    And pray, and sing, and tell old tales, and laugh
    At gilded butterflies, and hear poor rogues
    Talk of court news; and we'll talk with them too —

6 *ta'en* captured 8 *rot* i.e. die 9 *ill* i.e. suicidal *endure* put up
with, suffer through 11 *Ripeness* i.e. the time decreed by the gods
for the fruit to fall from the branch V, iii, 2 *greater pleasures* i.e.
the desires of those in higher command 3 *censure* judge 4 *meaning*
intentions 12–14 *laugh* . . . *news* view with amusement bright ephem-
era, such as gallants preoccupied with court gossip

Who loses and who wins; who's in, who's out —   15
And take upon 's the mystery of things
As if we were God's spies; and we'll wear out,
In a walled prison, packs and sects of great ones
That ebb and flow by th' moon.

Edmund   Take them away.

Lear. Upon such sacrifices, my Cordelia,   20
The gods themselves throw incense. Have I caught
   thee?
He that parts us shall bring a brand from heaven
And fire us hence like foxes. Wipe thine eyes.
The goodyears shall devour them, flesh and fell,
Ere they shall make us weep! We'll see 'em starved   25
   first.
Come.   *Exit Lear and Cordelia, guarded.*

Edmund.   Come hither, captain; hark.
Take thou this note. (*gives a paper.*) Go follow
   them to prison.
One step I have advanced thee. If thou dost
As this instructs thee, thou dost make thy way   30
To noble fortunes. Know thou this, that men
Are as the time is. To be tender-minded
Does not become a sword. Thy great employment
Will not bear question. Either say thou'lt do't,
Or thrive by other means.

Captain.   I'll do't, my lord.   35

Edmund. About it; and write happy when th' hast
   done.
Mark, I say instantly, and carry it so
As I have set it down.

Captain. I cannot draw a cart, nor eat dried oats —
If it be man's work, I'll do't.   *Exit.* 40

16–17 *take . . . spies* i.e. contemplate the wonder of existence as if
with divine insight, seek eternal rather than temporal truths   17 *wear
out* outlast   18–19 *packs . . . moon* i.e. partisan and intriguing clus-
ters of "great ones" who gain and lose power monthly   20–21 *Upon
. . . incense* i.e. the gods themselves are the celebrants at such sacrifi-
cial offerings to love as we are   22–23 *He . . . foxes* i.e. to separate
us, as foxes are smoked out and scattered, would require not a human
but a heavenly torch   24 *goodyears* undefined forces of evil   *fell* hide
32 *as the time is* (i.e. ruthless in war)   33 *become* befit   34 *bear
question* admit discussion   36 *write happy* consider yourself fortunate

Flourish. Enter Albany, Goneril, Regan, Soldiers.

Albany. Sir, you have showed today your valiant strain,
And fortune led you well. You have the captives
Who were the opposites of this day's strife.
I do require them of you, so to use them
45 As we shall find their merits and our safety
May equally determine.

Edmund.   Sir, I thought it fit
To send the old and miserable King
To some retention and appointed guard;
Whose age had charms in it, whose title more,
50 To pluck the common bosom on his side
And turn our impressed lances in our eyes
Which do command them. With him I sent the
        Queen,
My reason all the same; and they are ready
Tomorrow, or at further space, t' appear
55 Where you shall hold your session. At this time
We sweat and bleed, the friend hath lost his friend,
And the best quarrels, in the heat, are cursed
By those that feel their sharpness.
The question of Cordelia and her father
Requires a fitter place.
60 *Albany.*   Sir, by your patience,
I hold you but a subject of this war,
Not as a brother.

Regan.   That's as we list to grace him.
Methinks our pleasure might have been demanded
Ere you had spoke so far. He led our powers,
65 Bore the commission of my place and person,
The which immediacy may well stand up
And call itself your brother.

---

43 *opposites of* enemies in 45 *merits* deserts 48 *some . . . guard*
detention under duly appointed guards 50 *pluck . . . bosom* draw
popular sympathy 51 *turn . . . eyes* i.e. make our conscripted lanc-
ers turn on us 54 *space* interval 55 *session* trials 57 *best quarrels*
worthiest causes 58 *sharpness* i.e. painful effects 61 *subject of*
subordinate in 62 *list to grace* please to honor 66 *immediacy* i.e.
present status (as my deputy)

Goneril.   Not so hot!
In his own grace he doth exalt himself
More than in your addition.

Regan.   In my rights
By me invested, he compeers the best.   70

Albany. That were the most if he should husband you.

Regan. Jesters do oft prove prophets.

Goneril.   Holla, holla!
That eye that told you so looked but asquint.

Regan. Lady, I am not well; else I should answer
From a full-flowing stomach. General,   75
Take thou my soldiers, prisoners, patrimony;
Dispose of them, of me; the walls is thine.
Witness the world that I create thee here
My lord and master.

Goneril.   Mean you to enjoy him?

Albany. The let-alone lies not in your good will.   80

Edmund. Nor in thine, lord.

Albany.   Half-blooded fellow, yes.

Regan. (*to Edmund*) Let the drum strike, and prove
    my title thine.

Albany. Stay yet; hear reason. Edmund, I arrest thee
On capital treason; and, in thy attaint,
This gilded serpent. (*points to Goneril*) For your
    claim, fair sister,   85
I bar it in the interest of my wife.
'Tis she is subcontracted to this lord,
And I, her husband, contradict your banes.
If you will marry, make your loves to me;
My lady is bespoke.

69 *your addition* honors conferred by you   70 *compeers* equals   71
most i.e. most complete investiture in your rights   *husband* wed   73
asquint cross-eyed, crookedly   75 *stomach* anger   76 *patrimony* inheritance   77 *walls is thine* i.e. you have stormed the citadel (myself)
80 *let-alone* permission   81 *Half-blooded* i.e. by birth only half noble
82 *Let . . . thine* i.e. fight and win for yourself my rights in the
kingdom   84 *in thy attaint* i.e. as party to your corruption (cf. the
"serpent" of Eden)   87 *subcontracted* i.e. engaged, though previously
married (sarcastic play on "precontracted," a legal term applied to
one facing an impediment to marriage because previously engaged
to another)   88 *contradict your banes* forbid your banns, i.e. declare
an impediment   89 *loves* love-suits

90 *Goneril.*   An interlude!
Albany. Thou art armed, Gloucester. Let the trumpet
     sound.
     If none appear to prove upon thy person
     Thy heinous, manifest, and many treasons,
     There is my pledge. (*throws down a glove*) I'll
        make it on thy heart,
95   Ere I taste bread, thou art in nothing less
     Than I have here proclaimed thee.
Regan.   Sick, O, sick!
Goneril. (*aside*) If not, I'll ne'er trust medicine.
Edmund. There's my exchange. (*throws down a glove*)
     What in the world he is
100 That names me traitor, villainlike he lies.
     Call by the trumpet. He that dares approach,
     On him, on you, who not? I will maintain
     My truth and honor firmly.
Albany. A herald, ho!
Edmund.   A herald, ho, a herald!
105 *Albany.* Trust to thy single virtue; for thy soldiers,
     All levied in my name, have in my name
     Took their discharge.
Regan.   My sickness grows upon me.
Albany. She is not well. Convey her to my tent.
                              Exit Regan, attended.

                      Enter a Herald.

     Come hither, herald. Let the trumpet sound,
110 And read out this.
Captain. Sound, trumpet!   *A trumpet sounds.*
Herald. (*reads*) "If any man of quality or degree within
     the lists of the army will maintain upon Edmund,
     supposed Earl of Gloucester, that he is a manifold

---

90 *An interlude* a quaint playlet (equivalent to saying "How dramatic!" or "How comical!") 94 *make* prove 95 *nothing less* i.e.
no respect less guilty 97 *medicine* i.e. poison 101 *trumpet* trumpeter
105 *single virtue* unaided prowess 112 *degree* rank 113 *lists* muster

traitor, let him appear by the third sound of the ¹¹⁵
trumpet. He is bold in his defense."

Edmund. Sound!   **First trumpet.**
Herald. Again!   **Second trumpet.**
  Again!   **Third trumpet.**
                                          Trumpet answers within.

Enter Edgar, armed, at the third sound,
a Trumpet before him.

Albany. Ask him his purposes, why he appears   ¹²⁰
  Upon this call o' th' trumpet.
Herald.   What are you?
  Your name, your quality, and why you answer
  This present summons?
Edgar.   Know my name is lost,
  By treason's tooth bare-gnawn and canker-bit;
  Yet am I noble as the adversary   ¹²⁵
  I come to cope.
Albany.   Which is that adversary?
Edgar. What's he that speaks for Edmund Earl of
  Gloucester?
Edmund. Himself. What say'st thou to him?
Edgar.   Draw thy sword.
  That, if my speech offend a noble heart,
  Thy arm may do thee justice. Here is mine.   ¹³⁰
  Behold it is my privilege,
  The privilege of mine honors,
  My oath, and my profession. I protest —
  Maugre thy strength, place, youth, and eminence,
  Despite thy victor sword and fire-new fortune,   ¹³⁵
  Thy valor and thy heart — thou art a traitor,
  False to thy gods, thy brother, and thy father,
  Conspirant 'gainst this high illustrious prince,
  And from th' extremest upward of thy head

---

124 *canker-bit* eaten, as by the rose-caterpillar   131–33 *it . . . pro-*
fession i.e. wielding this sword is the privilege of my knightly honor,
oath, and function   134 *Maugre* in spite of   135 *fire-new* brand-new
136 *heart* courage   138 *Conspirant* in conspiracy   139 *extremist up-*
ward uppermost extreme

140   To the descent and dust below thy foot
        A most toad-spotted traitor. Say thou "no,"
        This sword, this arm, and my best spirits are bent
        To prove upon thy heart, whereto I speak,
        Thou liest.

Edmund.   In wisdom I should ask thy name,
145   But since thy outside looks so fair and warlike,
        And that thy tongue some say of breeding breathes,
        What safe and nicely I might well delay
        By rule of knighthood I disdain and spurn.
        Back do I toss these treasons to thy head,
150   With the hell-hated lie o'erwhelm thy heart,
        Which — for they yet glance by and scarcely
          bruise —
        This sword of mine shall give them instant way
        Where they shall rest for ever. Trumpets, speak!

                      Alarums. Fight. Edmund falls.

Albany. Save him, save him.

Goneril.   This is practice, Gloucester.
155   By th' law of war thou wast not bound to answer
        An unknown opposite. Thou art not vanquished,
        But cozened and beguiled.

Albany.   Shut your mouth, dame,
        Or with this paper shall I stop it. — Hold, sir. —
        (to Goneril) Thou worse than any name, read thine
          own evil.
160   No tearing, lady! I perceive you know it.

Goneril. Say if I do — the laws are mine, not thine.
        Who can arraign me for't?

Albany.   Most monstrous! O,
        Know'st thou this paper?

140 *descent and dust* i.e. all that intervenes from the head to the dust
141 *toad-spotted* i.e. exuding venom like a toad   142 *bent* directed
144 *wisdom* prudence   146 *some say* some assay, i.e. proof or, one
might say   147 *safe and nicely* cautiously and punctiliously   149
treasons accusations   150 *hell-hated* hateful as hell   151-53 *Which
. . . ever* i.e. the accusations of treason, now flying about harmlessly,
will be routed into you with my sword-thrust and lodge there perma-
nently   154 *Save him* spare him   *practice* trickery   157 *cozened*
cheated   158 *Hold* wait. If addressed to Edmund, this suggests a motive for the "Save him" of l. 152: i.e. Albany hopes to obtain a confession.   161 *mine* (i.e. as ruler)

Goneril.   Ask me not what I know.

Exit.

Albany. Go after her. She's desperate; govern her.

Exit an Officer.

Edmund. What you have charged me with, that have
    I done,   165
  And more, much more. The time will bring it out.
  'Tis past, and so am I. — But what art thou
  That hast this fortune on me? If thou'rt noble,
  I do forgive thee.

Edgar.   Let's exchange charity.
  I am no less in blood than thou art, Edmund;   170
  If more, the more th' hast wronged me.
  My name is Edgar and thy father's son.
  The gods are just, and of our pleasant vices
  Make instruments to plague us.
  The dark and vicious place where thee he got   175
  Cost him his eyes.

Edmund.   Th' hast spoken right; 'tis true.
  The wheel is come full circle; I am here.

Albany. Methought thy very gait did prophesy
  A royal nobleness. I must embrace thee.
  Let sorrow split my heart if ever I   180
  Did hate thee, or thy father.

Edgar.   Worthy prince, I know't.

Albany. Where have you hid yourself?
  How have you known the miseries of your father?

Edgar. By nursing them, my lord. List a brief tale;
  And when 'tis told, O that my heart would burst!   185
  The bloody proclamation to escape
  That followed me so near (O, our lives' sweetness!
  That we the pain of death would hourly die
  Rather than die at once) taught me to shift
  Into a madman's rags, t' assume a semblance   190

---

164 *govern* control   168 *fortune on* i.e. victory over   169 *charity* forgiveness and love   171 *If more* if greater (since legitimate)   173 *of
our pleasant* out of our pleasurable   175 *got* begot   177 *wheel* of fortune   *here* at its bottom   178 *prophesy* promise   187–89 *O . . . die*
i.e. how sweet is life that we would prefer to suffer death-pangs hourly

That very dogs disdained; and in this habit
Met I my father with his bleeding rings,
Their precious stones new lost; became his guide,
Led him, begged for him, saved him from despair;
195 Never — O fault! — revealed myself unto him
Until some half hour past, when I was armed,
Not sure, though hoping of this good success,
I asked his blessing, and from first to last
Told him our pilgrimage. But his flawed heart —
200 Alack, too weak the conflict to support —
'Twixt two extremes of passion, joy and grief,
Burst smilingly.

Edmund.   This speech of yours hath moved me,
And shall perchance do good; but speak you on —
You look as you had something more to say.

205 *Albany.* If there be more, more woeful, hold it in,
For I am almost ready to dissolve,
Hearing of this.

Edgar.   This would have seemed a period
To such as love not sorrow; but another,
To amplify too much, would make much more,
210 And top extremity.
Whilst I was big in clamor, came there in a man,
Who, having seen me in my worst estate,
Shunned my abhorred society; but then, finding
Who 'twas that so endured, with his strong arms
215 He fastenèd on my neck, and bellowèd out
As he'd burst heaven, threw him on my father,
Told the most piteous tale of Lear and him
That ever ear received; which in recounting
His grief grew puissant, and the strings of life
220 Began to crack. Twice then the trumpets sounded,
And there I left him tranced.

Albany.   But who was this?

191 *habit* attire 192 *rings* sockets 196 *armed* in armor 199 *our*
pilgrimage of our journey *flawed* cracked 206 *dissolve* melt into
tears 207 *a period* the limit 208–10 *another . . . extremity* i.e. another sorrow, too fully described, would exceed the limit 211 *big in*
clamor loud in lamentation 212 *estate* state 219 *puissant* powerful
221 *tranced* insensible

Edgar. Kent, sir, the banishèd Kent; who in disguise
　Followèd his enemy king and did him service
　Improper for a slave.

Enter a Gentleman with a bloody knife.

Gentleman. Help, help! O, help!
Edgar.　　　　　　　　　　What kind of help?
Albany.　　　　　　　　　　　　Speak, man. 225
Edgar. What means this bloody knife?
Gentleman.　　　　　　　　　'Tis hot, it smokes.
　It came even from the heart of — O, she's dead.
Albany. Who dead? Speak, man.
Gentleman. Your lady, sir, your lady; and her sister
　By her is poisonèd; she confesses it.　　　　　　230
Edmund. I was contracted to them both. All three
　Now marry in an instant.
Edgar.　　　　　　　　Here comes Kent.

Enter Kent.

Albany. Produce the bodies, be they alive or dead.
　　　　　　　　　　　　　　Exit Gentleman.
　This judgment of the heavens, that makes us trem-
　　ble,
　Touches us not with pity. —O, is this he?　　　235
　The time will not allow the compliment
　Which very manners urges.
Kent.　　　　　　　　I am come
　To bid my king and master aye good night.
　Is he not here?
Albany.　　　　Great thing of us forgot!
　Speak, Edmund, where's the King? and where's
　　Cordelia?　　　　　　　　　　　　　　240

223 *enemy* inimical　226 *smokes* steams　231 *contracted* engaged　232
marry i.e. in death　236 *compliment* ceremony　237 *very manners*
i.e. sheer decency　239 *thing* matter　*of* by

Goneril and Regan's bodies brought out.

Seest thou this object, Kent?

Kent. Alack, why thus?

Edmund.   Yet Edmund was beloved.
The one the other poisoned for my sake,
And after slew herself.

245 **Albany.** Even so. Cover their faces.

Edmund. I pant for life. Some good I mean to do,
Despite of mine own nature. Quickly send —
Be brief in it — to the castle, for my writ
Is on the life of Lear and on Cordelia.
Nay, send in time.

250 **Albany.**   Run, run, O, run!

Edgar. To who, my lord? Who has the office? Send
Thy token of reprieve.

Edmund. Well thought on. Take my sword;
Give it the captain.

Edgar.   Haste thee for thy life.

Exit Officer.

255 **Edmund.** He hath commission from thy wife and me
To hang Cordelia in the prison and
To lay the blame upon her own despair
That she fordid herself.

Albany. The gods defend her! Bear him hence awhile.

Edmund is borne off.

*Enter Lear, with Cordelia in his arms, Gentle-
man, and others following.*

260 **Lear.** Howl, howl, howl! Oh, you are men of stones.
Had I your tongues and eyes, I'd use them so
That heaven's vault should crack. She's gone for
ever.
I know when one is dead, and when one lives.

---

241 *object* sight   242 *Yet* despite all   246 *pant for life* i.e. gasp for
life's breath   248 *writ* i.e. order of execution   251 *office* commission
258 *forbid* destroyed

She's dead as earth. Lend me a looking glass.
If that her breath will mist or stain the stone, 265
Why then she lives.

Kent. Is this the promised end?

Edgar. Or image of that horror?

Albany. Fall and cease.

Lear. This feather stirs; she lives! If it be so,
It is a chance which does redeem all sorrows
That ever I have felt.

Kent. O my good master. 270

Lear. Prithee away.

Edgar. 'Tis noble Kent, your friend.

Lear. A plague upon you murderers, traitors all;
I might have saved her; now she's gone for ever.
Cordelia, Cordelia, stay a little. Ha,
What is't thou say'st? Her voice was ever soft, 275
Gentle, and low — an excellent thing in woman.
I killed the slave that was a-hanging thee.

Gentleman. 'Tis true, my lords, he did.

Lear. Did I not, fellow?
I have seen the day, with my good biting falchion
I would have made them skip. I am old now, 280
And these same crosses spoil me. Who are you?
Mine eyes are not o' th' best. I'll tell you straight.

Kent. If fortune brag of two she loved and hated,
One of them we behold.

Lear. This is a dull sight. Are you not Kent?

Kent. The same: 285
Your servant Kent; where is your servant Caius?

Lear. He's a good fellow, I can tell you that.
He'll strike, and quickly too. He's dead and rotten.

265 *stone* i.e. glass 266 *promised end* i.e. doomsday 267 *image* duplicate *Fall and cease* i.e. strike once and for all, make an end of things 269 *redeem* atone for 279 *falchion* small sword slightly hooked 281 *crosses* adversities *spoil me* i.e. sap my strength 282 *tell you straight* i.e. recognize you in a moment 283 *two* i.e. Lear, and a hypothetical second extreme example of Fortune's cruelty with whom he may be equated *loved and hated* i.e. favored, then victimized 285 *sight* eyesight (Instinctively Lear shuns the admission that he is dazed and weeping.) 286 *Caius* Kent's alias

Kent. No, my good lord; I am the very man.

290 *Lear.* I'll see that straight.

Kent. That from your first of difference and decay
    Have followed your sad steps.

Lear.   You are welcome hither.

Kent. Nor no man else. All's cheerless, dark, and
    deadly.
    Your eldest daughters have fordone themselves,
    And desperately are dead.

295 *Lear.*   Ay, so I think.

Albany. He knows not what he says; and vain is it
    That we present us to him.

Edgar.   Very bootless.

Enter a Messenger.

Messenger. Edmund is dead, my lord.

Albany.   That's but a trifle here.
    You lords and noble friends, know our intent.

300   What comfort to this great decay may come
    Shall be applied. For us, we will resign,
    During the life of this old Majesty,
    To him our absolute power; *(to Edgar and Kent)*
        you to your rights,
    With boot and such addition as your honors

305   Have more than merited. All friends shall taste
    The wages of their virtue, and all foes
    The cup of their deservings. — O, see, see!

Lear. And my poor fool is hanged: no, no, no life?
    Why should a dog, a horse, a rat, have life,

310   And thou no breath at all? Thou'lt come no more,
    Never, never, never, never, never.
    Pray you undo this button. Thank you, sir.

290 *see that straight* understand that in a moment   291 *difference and decay* change and decline in fortune   293 *Nor no man else* i.e. no, nor anyone else   294 *fordone* destroyed   295 *desperately* in a state of despair   297 *bootless* useless   300 *What . . . come* i.e. whatever means of aiding this ruined great one presents itself   304 *boot* good measure   *addition* titles, advancement in rank   308 *fool* i.e. Cordelia ("Fool" was often a term of affection, and sometimes, as elsewhere in Shakespeare, of praise — as ironic commentary upon self-seeking "worldly wisdom.")

Do you see this? Look on her! Look her lips,
Look there, look there —   *He dies.*

Edgar.   He faints. My lord, my lord —

Kent. Break, heart, I prithee break!

Edgar.   Look up, my lord.   315

Kent. Vex not his ghost. O, let him pass! He hates
     him
   That would upon the rack of this tough world
   Stretch him out longer.

Edgar.   He is gone indeed.

Kent. The wonder is, he hath endured so long.
   He but usurped his life.   320

Albany. Bear them from hence. Our present business
   Is general woe. (*to Kent and Edgar*) Friends of my
      soul, you twain
   Rule in this realm, and the gored state sustain.   325

Kent. I have a journey, sir, shortly to go.

Edgar. The weight of this sad time we must obey,
   Speak what we feel, not what we ought to say.
   The oldest hath borne most; we that are young
   Shall never see so much, nor live so long.

                         Exit all with a dead march.

316 *Vex . . . ghost* do not trouble his departing spirit   317 *rack* instrument of torture   320 *usurped* possessed contrary to (natural) law
326 *obey* i.e. accept